Charles E

Selected Letters Volume 1
1958–1965

Other books by Charles Bukowski available from Virgin Books:

Post Office
Factotum
Women
Pulp
New Poems Book 1
New Poems Book 2
New Poems Book 3

Charles Bukowski

Selected Letters Volume 1
1958–1965

First published in 2004 by
Virgin Books Ltd
Thames Wharf Studios
Rainville Road
London
W6 9HA

Previously published in the USA by Black Sparrow Press in *Screams from the Balcony* and *Living on Luck*

A catalogue record for this book is available from the British Library.

ISBN 0 7535 0901 6

Typeset by Phoenix Photosetting, Chatham, Kent
Printed and bound in Great Britain by Clays Ltd, St Ives PLC

EDITOR'S NOTE

The last thing this book needs is an academic introduction – so the few comments I have to offer will *be* the last thing, relegated to an Afterword.

All that's required here is an explanation of how the letters have been edited. Working from photocopies of letters in private and public collections available to me, I have transcribed and selected roughly 50% of their contents. My only criterion was vividness and interest of the contents, while trying to minimize repetition. Except for three or four word changes, there has been no censorship or expurgation. Letters from the seventies and later will appear in a subsequent volume, where earlier letters found too late for printing here may also be included. Headnote comments about his correspondents are quoted from notes Charles Bukowski made at my request.

A few reproductions of letters (not all of them transcribed for inclusion) will let readers glimpse what this book cannot render: the total visual effect of many Bukowski letters, often decorated with drawings, painting, or collages. Not only are such visual components regrettably sacrificed, but making a readable text has also meant imposing some regularity on Bukowski's spacing, spelling, and the like. There is no way these things could be fully preserved in setting type, in any case. And after a few instances (some of which I've preserved), typos grow distracting. But to give the flavor, I have presented a couple of representative letters verbatim and uncorrected.

Other editorial changes are regularizing of dates and the omission of most salutations and signoffs. For emphasis and for titles in his letters, Bukowski often typed in ALL CAPS. In a book these are hard on the eye. Here, when they are for emphasis, we print them as SMALL CAPS; when they name titles, we print them in regular title format: italics for books, quotes for separate poems or stories. I have indicated editorial omissions by asterisks in square brackets. A few editorial additions are similarly bracketed. A minimum of explanatory material has been included preceding some letters. References to *Hank* are to the biography of Bukowski by

Neeli Cherkovski. 'Dorbin' refers to Sanford Dorbin's *A Bibliography of Charles Bukowski* (Black Sparrow, 1969).

The title for this volume was supplied by Charles Bukowski.

Acknowledgments

The editor and publisher are grateful to the owners, institutional and private, of the letters here printed. These include:

The University of California, Santa Barbara, Special Collections
Boston University Libraries
State University of New York at Buffalo, Poetry/Rare Books
    Collection
Mr. Louis Delpino
Mr. Joseph Erdelac
Mr. Arthur Feldman
Mr. Carl Weissner

Some letters are reprinted from their appearance in the following books and magazines:

Magazine, 3 (1966), ed. Kirby Congdon
Down Here, 1 (1966), ed. Tom McNamara
Wormwood Review, 14 (1964), ed. Marvin Malone
All's Normal Here: A Charles Bukowski Primer, ed. Loss Pequeño
    Glazier (Fremont: Ruddy Duck Press, 1985).

· 1958 ·

In mid-1958, the time of the earliest letters available, Bukowski had recently begun working in the post office in a permanent position as a mail sorter, after an earlier spell of three years as a mail carrier. Not long before, he had resumed writing after a ten-year interval, and by now had a handful of little magazine publications. E. V. Griffith, editor of Hearse *magazine, had agreed to do a chapbook. But the delay in publication was to test Bukowski's patience to the limit. He finally received his author's copies in October, 1960.*

Until May 1, 1964, Bukowski's letters are dated from 1623 N. Mariposa Avenue, Los Angeles 27, California.

(The following letter is printed in full.)

[To E.V. Griffith]

June 6, 1958

Dear E.V. Griffith:

Here are some more. Thanks for returning others. No title ideas yet. Post office pen no damn good. Trying to say – no title ideas yet.

Fire, Fist and Bestial Wail? No. Thought about using title of one of my short stories – 'Confessions of a Coward and Man Hater.' No.

'The Mourning, Morning Sunrise.' No.

I don't know, E.V.

I don't know.

Anyhow, I'm thinking about it.

Sincerely,
Charles Bukowski

Gil Orlovitz (1918–1973) frequently published pamphlets of verse.

[To E.V. Griffith]
July 9, 1958

I still think *Flower, Fist and Bestial Wail* just about covers the nature of my work. If you object to this title I'll send along some others.

I'm quite pleased with your selections. 'The Birds,' which I had just written, I like personally but I found others would not like this type of thing because of its philosophical oddity. Poem, by the way, is factual and not fictional. All of my stuff you have is, except '59 and drinks' & '[Some Notes of Dr.] Klarstein.'

Thanks for sending *Arrows of Longing*.

As to Orlovitz, I find him at his best, very good. Certainly his delivery seems original.

Do you have my short stories about anywhere?

I suppose I mentioned I unloaded one at *Coastlines* and a couple at *Views* (Univ. of Louisville), but I think what you picked is pretty much my best stuff, and I have been honored to have been singled out by you and gathered up this way.

· 1959 ·

Griffith published Carl Larsen's Arrows of Longing *as Hearse Chapbook no. 1 in 1958. He was also the editor of* Gallows, *in the first issue of which Bukowski had two poems printed.*

[To E.V. Griffith]
August 10, 1959

Verification of existence substantiated.

I am alive and drinking beer. As to the literary aspect, I have appeared recently in *Nomad* #1, *Coastlines* (spring '59), *Quicksilver* (summer '59) and *Epos* (summer '59). I haven't submitted further to you because I have sensed that you are overstocked.

There are 10 or 12 other magazines that have accepted my stuff but as you know there is an immense lag in some cases between acceptance and publication. Much of this type of thing makes one feel as if he were writing into a void. But that's the literary life, and we're stuck with it.

I am looking forward, of course, to the eventual chapbook, and I hope it moves better for you than the Larsen thing. Of course, I don't consider Carl Larsen a very good writer and am always surprised when anyone does. But to hell with Larsen, now where was I? Oh yes, I have never received a copy of *Gallows* and since you say I have a couple in it, I would like a copy. Could you send one down?

Well, there really isn't much more to say . . . the horses are running poorly, the women are f/ruffing me up, the rent's due, but as I said, I'm still alive and drinking beer. Glad to get your card. Don't forget to send me to the *Gallows*. Thanx.

[To E.V. Griffith]
October 3, 1959

Dashing this off before going to the track with a couple of grifters. I hate these Saturdays – all the amateurs are out there with the greed glittering in their eyes, half-drunk on beer, pinching the women, stealing seats, screaming over nothing. [★ ★ ★]

Thanks for card and news of *Hearse* fame in *Nation* and *Poetry* (Ch.). Can't seem to find the correct issue of *Nation* for this but am still trying. Success is wonderful if we can achieve it without whoring our concepts. Keep publishing the good live poets as in the past.

[To E.V. Griffith]
early December, 59

Are you still alive?

Everything that's happening to me is banal or venal, and perhaps later a more flowery and poesy versification – right now drab and bare as the old-lady-in-the-shoe's panties.

I don't know, there's one hell of a lot of frustration and fakery in this poetry business, the forming of groups, soul-handshaking, I'll print you if you print me, and wouldn't you care to read before a small select group of homosexuals?

I pick up a poetry magazine, flip the pages, count the stars, moon, and frustrations, yawn, piss out my beer and pick up the want-ads.

I am sitting in a cheap Hollywood apartment pretending to be a poet but sick and dull and the clouds are coming over the fake paper mountains and I peck away at these stupid keys, it's 12 degrees in Moscow and it's snowing; a boil is forming between my eyes and somewhere between Pedro and Palo Alto I lost the will to fight: the liquor store man knows me like a cousin: he cracks the paper bag and looks like a photograph of Francis Thompson.

· 1960 ·

Jory Sherman, described by Bukowski as 'an early talent,' was a poet then living in San Francisco and publishing alongside Bukowski in little magazines like Epos, *whose editor, Evelyn Thorne, suggested the two men should correspond (Hank, p. 116).*

[To Jory Sherman]
[April 1, 1960]

Tell the staunch Felicia to hang on in: you are, to my knowledge, the best young poet working in America today. And rejections are no hazard; they are better than gold. Just think what type of miserable cancer you would be today if all your works had been accepted. The beef-eaters, the half-percepted wags who give you the pages and the print have forced you deeper in to show them the sight of light and color. [★ ★ ★]

Hell, if you want to read some of my poems, go ahead. I embrace you with luck. But I am tired of them, I am tired of my stuff, and I try very hard not to write anymore. I suppose I might sound like Patchen although I have not read much of him. Jeffers, I suppose, is my god – the only man since Shakey to write the long narrative poem that does not put one to sleep. And Pound, of course. And then Conrad Aiken is so truly a *poet*, but Jeffers is stronger, darker, more exploratatively modern and mad. Of course, Eliot's gone down, Auden's gone down, and William C. Williams has completely fallen apart. Do you think it's age? And E. E. Cummings blanking out. Sherman's coming on, though, taking them in the stretch, stride by stride, clomp, clomp, clomp, Sherman's coming on toward the wire and the ugly crowd screams. Bukowski drinks a cheap beer. [★ ★ ★]

Sheri Martinelli, mentioned in this next and several subsequent letters, was an American artist for whose book Ezra Pound wrote an introduction: La Martinelli *(Milan, 1956). Bukowski notes, 'She wrote heavy letters, downgrading me. Everything was, "Ezra said . . .," "Ezra did . . ." She was said to be a looker. I never met her. Lived in San Francisco.'*

[To Jory Sherman]
[ca. April, 1960]

[★ ★ ★] Rather like Sheri M. altho when she sent back my poems she tried to relegate me with some rather standard formula and I had to take the kinks out of her wiring. [★ ★ ★] The Cantos make fine reading, the sweep and command of the langwidge (my spell) carries it even o'r the thin spots, although I have never been able to read the whole damn thing or remember what I've read, but it's going to last, I guess, just for that reason: a well of Pounding unrecognized.

[★ ★ ★] Thanks again for *Beat'd*. Anonymous poem not good because guy thinks he can compromise life. There is no compromise: if you are going to write tv rifleman crap, tv rifleman crap will show in your poems, and if he thinks he's an old timer at 34, he'd better towel behind the ears and elsewhere too, because Bukowski, who nobody's heard of will be 40 on August 16th., and Pound who everybody's heard of will be almost twice that old and has never compromised with anybody, nations or gods or gawkers and has signed his name to everything he has written, not for fame but for establishment of point and stance. Let the baker compromise, the cop and the mailman, some of us must hold the hallowed ground . . . [★ ★ ★]

'S & S' is Scimitar and Song, *whose March 1960 issue prints a Bukowski poem, with a typographical error.*

[To Jory Sherman]
[ca. April, 1960]

[★ ★ ★] Do you double space your poems? I know that one is supposed to double space stories, articles, etc. for clarity and easy reading but thot poem due to its construction (usually much space) read easy enough singled. And I think a double-spaced poem loses its backbone, it flops in the air. I don't know: the world is always sniping sniping so hard at the petty rules petty mistakes, I don't get it, what doesn't it mean? bitch, bitch, bitch. meanwhile the point going by: is the poem good or bad in your opinion? Rules are for old maids crossing the street.

Saw your poem in *S & S*. [★ ★ ★] She messed up my poem – eve instead of eye, but it was a rotter anyway. She's a very old woman and prints the same type of poesy. Wrote me a letter about how the birds were chirping outside her window, all was peace, men like me who liked to drink and gamble, oh talented but lost. I saw a bird when I was driving home from the track the other day. It was in the mouth of a cat crouched down in the asphalt street, the clouds overhead, the sunset, love and God overhead, and it saw my car and rose, cat-rose insane, stiff back like mad love depravity, and it walked toward the curbing, and I saw the bird, a large grey, flip broken winged, wings large and out, dipped, feathers spread, still alive, cat-fanged; nobody saying anything, signals changing, my motor running, and the wings the wings in my mind and the teeth, grey bird, a large grey. *Scimitar and Song*, yes indeed. Shit. [★ ★ ★]

The poem 'Death Wants More Death' was published in Harlequin *in 1957. Sherman must have proposed reading it aloud to an audience.*

[To Jory Sherman]
[Spring 1960]

[★ ★ ★] On 'D. Wants More D.,' I am afraid it would disturb an audience a bit too much. My father's garage had windows in it full of webs, flies and spiders churning blood-death in my brain, and tho I'm told nature has its meaning, I'm still infested with horror, and all the charts and graphs of the chemists and biologists and anthropologists and naturalists and sound-thinking men are nothing to the buzzing of this death.

'Crews' is Judson Crews, since 1949 a prolific author of books and pamphlets from the little presses.

[To E.V. Griffith]
April 25, 1960

No, I haven't seen any of the Crews clip-out type production, and know very little of the mechanics of this sort of thing. But does this mean that a poem must have been published elsewhere in some magazine before it can be included in the chapbook? On much of my published work I only have one magazine and I would not care to tear them up for the chapbook. And you also hold much work of mine that has never been published. I don't quite know; it is all rather puzzling. And I know that if we had to go after the missing magazines to get the clips it would take long long months, and perhaps many of them could never be acquired.

I wish you could write me a bit more on how this works, for as you can see I am mixed up. What would it cost some other way? Or do they *have* to be published pieces?

The prices seem fair enough and I could go up to the 32 pages if you have enough material to fill them. Perhaps we might add the 2 poems out of *San Francisco Review* #1, and I have some stuff coming out in the *Coastlines* and *Nomad*, due off the press any day now, I'm told. I don't know if you'll like it or not. And you've probably seen some of my other crap around. I think 'Regard Me' in *Nomad* #1 was pretty good, but it's hard for me to judge my own work and I'd rather leave that task up to you.

Right now I don't know how many pages you can fill or just whether or not this clip-out method restricts the filling. So I guess we'll have some more delay while you are kind enough to write me and fill in my ignorance.

Hoping to hear from you soon,

[To E.V. Griffith]
June 2, 1960

Good of you to write or even think chapbook while auto-torn. Like your lineup of poems ok, and should they run into more pages, please do let me know and I will money order you the difference. I would rather send you more than have you cut out a poem you want in there but are restricted on pages. I guess it's pretty hard to tell how many pages the thing will run at a loose glance like that and you will probably find out from your printer. Let me know how things work out this way on the pages. [★ ★ ★]

I just hope you can move a few copies so you won't get stung too badly on your end of the deal. I have visions of chapbooks stacked in a closet gathering dust and nobody knowing Bukowski and Griffith are alive and I begin to have horrible qualms. Maybe not. Maybe if this works out ok, sometime in the future we can go in on another half and half deal. It seems *very* reasonable since you do all the work and are promoting *another* person's work and not your own. The money end, from my side of it, seems less than nothing, but I realize that from your end with so many things going, different mags, chapbooks, it can get very very big, mountain-like. Well, hope all is ok, and you needn't write for a while, I realize you are in tough shape – unless you have some suggestions or et al. I feel pretty good that this thing is going thru, although it's hard to finally realize. [★ ★ ★]

Norman Winski was editor of the little magazine Breakthru.

[To Jory Sherman]
June 28, [1960]

[★ ★ ★] Winski, he's been phoning and I've been ducking. Jesus, I can't see any sense in it but I don't want to hurt his feelings. He pinned me down and I told him I'd be over to his place last night, but at last minute I phoned his wife and told her something had come up, I couldn't make it. She sounded pretty hurt and in about 10 minutes the phone started ringing, Winski I suppose and I just laid there slugging down the beer. I guess I'm insane, a mess-up. He told me to bring over some of my poems, wanted me to read something. Jesus, I can't do that sort of thing, Jory!

[★ ★ ★] Do, if you see Sheri, tell her I said hello. She wrote me a wonderful 3 page letter bout Pound and things, almost a poem, the whole thing. Deserves answer but I can't get untracked. [★ ★ ★]

[To Jory Sherman]
[July 9, 1960]

u in bed weigh & I am answering right off altho I do not know if I have anything to say but will let the keys roll and see what comes off. not me, I hope. No women around. One lugcow just left, sitting on couch all old out of shape red in face fat, jesus I told her I'm really going to heave a big one, one old big shitsigh when u drag it outa here. I'll have a brew and fall on the springs and begin to dream sweet dreams, only I did not say it in exactly this manner and she laughed. old women everywhere, lord. [★ ★ ★]

Spicer stupid to ask if you have read Lorca. Everybody has read Lorca. Everybody has read anything, everything. Why ask. I hate these meetings. Have u read. oh yeah. he's good, how about. o yeah. he's good too. [★ ★ ★]

Stan phoned yesterday. told him I was going to races. phone me, see me that night. I didn't hear. guess he pissed. well, what is there to see . . . me . . . old man on couch or edge of chair trying to think of something to say, and all the time everybody thinking, is *this* the guy who wrote those poems? No, it can't be!

WHAT PEOPLE FORGET IS THAT YOU *WRITE* THE POEM, YOU DON'T *TALK* IT.

to hell with everybody but Jory Sherman, S. Martinelli, Pound, Jeffers, T. Williams and the racing form. you are not a bastard and I do not like to hear yourself call urself one, and I am not a saint. let's go with the poem, straight down the stretch to the wire, first. sure.

Hearse Chapbook no. 4 was Mason Jordan Mason's A Legionere *(1960).*
Bukowski's book would be no. 5 in the series.

[To E.V. Griffith]
August 1, 1960

Again the long silence from Eureka, although I see in *Trace* 38 you are coming on with more Mason Jordan Mason as fast as Crews can write it, also a couple of more editors. Well, that's all right. What you do is yours. I hate to bitch, but is anything happening with the *Flower and the Fist etc.* I have told a couple of more magazines, and few people and I am beginning to feel foolish because as you know, this is the second time around with the same act. Let me hear something or other. Stamped self-addressed enclosed.

Marvin Bell and a couple of others seem to think my 'Death of a Roach' in *Epos*, Winter 1959, is a pretty good poem? Too late to work it in? More loot? You don't care for poem? Anyway, I'll be glad when it's all over. The thing has become more than a few pages of my poems. It has been going on so long that it has become like a disease, an obsession, purgatory, Alcatraz. . . . how long has it been? 2 years? 3? Please, E.V., be reasonable. Let's get this thing out of the way. Let Mason screw his lambs for a while. I am beginning to talk to myself in the mirror.

ps – I see where Witt crossed you up on 'Lowdermilk,' having appeared with it in *Decade* 1953. How they want their fame! over and over again! instead of writing something new. Frankly, E.V., I'm getting pretty sick of the literary world but I don't know where else to go. Yeah. I know. I can go to hell. I dropped a hundred and fifty on the ponies Saturday. Riding back on the train drunk, all the women looking at somebody else. Bukowski old and grey and shrunk. all the rivers dry. all the pockets empty. best anyhow, damn it, they haven't dropped the bomb yet.

The broadside referred to in the next letter was the first separate Bukowski publication, a poem called 'His Wife the Painter,' published by E. V. Griffith and included as an insert in the magazine Coffin, *no. 1 (1960).*

[To E.V. Griffith]
August 6, 1960

Thank you for the quick response on inquiry. Hope I have not piqued you.

Yes, this little mag game discouraging and that is why I try to keep quiet and not scratch at editors, just write the poem. When I bitch occasionally it's just the nerves reaching the throat, mine really, and I'm eating at myself rather than anybody else.

Thank you for broadsides: they are beautiful type jobs. I have at least a half dozen friends, places in mind that I'd like to see these. Tonight I am mailing out the ones you send. They are wonderfully presented, can't quite get over that. Do you have a few more sets? [★ ★ ★]

No, I don't have any particular mags in mind for review copies. I don't have any particular feuds going nor, on the other hand, any strong supporters who would swing for me. [★ ★ ★]

Nice to hear from you Griff and I promise not to cry anymore.

A little outa the way, but I rec. a note from Ann Reynolds of the *Sixties* this morn. little photo a duff and bly. I roasted Duffy and he ducked out and joined the French Foreign Legion. Who says I'm not a tough baby? [★ ★ ★]

P.S. – If this works out ok, perhaps sometime in the future – the far future – we can work out another half-and-half deal. I think right now we have both suffered too much with it . . . [★ ★ ★]

The next letter records the first contact with Outsider *magazine and its editors and publishers, Jon and Louise Webb, a connection which was to prove so beneficial to Bukowski. It also, like the preceding letter, notes his incompatibility with the kind of poetry being furthered by Robert Bly's magazine* The Sixties *(formerly* The Fifties*). Bukowski had eleven poems in* Outsider *No. 1 (Fall 1961), under the collective title 'A Charles Bukowski Album.'*

[To Jory Sherman]

August 17, 1960

[★ ★ ★] Martinelli called me down something . . . called me a 'prick,' said I built 'ass-hole palaces,' called me 'bug-job,' I can't remember all. [★ ★ ★] I can't be bothered with gash trying to realign my outlook. And Pound may have been 'lonely' and 'fell in love with a great SssPLLLANGggg' 'like a rain in a dry dusty summer,' but I am not Pound and I am not lonely. The last thing I wanna see is more gash and more people.

No, regarding Griff, broadsides not of book, but insert style thing to be slipped into pages of *Coffin* and *Hearse* loosely, later to be assembled into collection of some sort. I am broadside #1, *Hearse*. Tibbs freelance pen ink sketcher who fulfills frus[trations] by playing little mag pages with scratchy pen. Rather ordinary talent, I think, but not too much compo[sition]. Think I could do better but I am supposed to be a poet.

No, I'm not in *Sixties*. One reject they sent me, trying to place me in *Evergreen Review* class, had hangover and straightened them. Hence this bit of corres., photo etc., which I am not going to answer, my point already have b. made, and I don't care too much to leave the poem and jaw unless it is crit. article. Ann Reynolds sounds like somebody to fill Duffy-gap. [★ ★ ★]

Thanks for word on *Outsider* Finally got card from them through *Coastlines*. Asking me for contributions. Ah, well.

Bukowski's birthday is August 16th.

[To Jory Sherman]

August 17, 1960

it's all over, I'm 40, over the hill, down the other side . . . made the rounds Sunday nite . . . alone . . . sat in strip joint, watched them shake and wiggle like something going on . . . bored . . . $1.25 for beer, but drank em like water. water hell. I don't drink much water. Place after place . . . faces sitting there empty as jugs. shit. shit. oh, I got a lovely buncha coconuts! nothing. woke up with cracked toe, blood, couldn't walk. oh I got a lovely buncha, a lovely buncha coconuts!

old girlfriend sent over huge buncha flowers, all kinds, quite nicea her. like a funeral, like a beautiful funeral, buried at 40 . . .

sick today. [* * *]

Do you mind if I sign myself Charles? it is old habit. when I write or when somebody writes me I am Charles. When they talk to me in a room I am Hank. This, my solidification. A chunk of 40 stone.

[To Jory Sherman]
[August 22, 1960]

black day, they have kicked my horse-ass good. 3 rejects, *San Fran. Review*, *White Dove*, and *Oak Leaves*. [* * *]

Girlfriend said I was as drunk the other night as she'd ever seen me. I used vile lang. and yanked the mattress off her bed and then leaned back in chair and gave 2 hours lecture (while drinking) on the arts and what they meant or didn't mean, and who was what and why.

Kid, I am definitely cracking. These last 3 or 4 months have ended me. I think I'm written out. I've said it all. What the hell else? I don't care. I've still go the horses and the whores and Schlitz. Let these 19 year old editors gobble the gugga of rooster.

I'm going to try to buy a shack somewhere and give everything up. Just be dirty old man waiting to die. I'm sick of all the 8 hour faces and laughter and babble, Dodger talk and pussy-talk and zero-talk. A roof, no rent. That's my aim. Pick up enough washing dishes 3 times a week or pimping. Lord, I'm sick of it all. And poetry too. No wonder Van Gogh blasted his head off. Crows and sunlight. Idle zero. Zero eating your guts like an animal inside, letting you shit and fuck and blink your eyes, but nothing, a nothing. I couldn't die stretched in a blizzard because I'm already dead. So let Pound have it. And Keats. and Shelley. and belly. piss. the mailman with his smirking white rejectee envelopes, and all the grass growing and the cars going by as if it all doesn't matter. Christ, I'm watching a guy water his lawn now. His mind is as empty as a department store flowerbowl. Water. water. water. make the grass grow green. GREAT. G R E A T. [★ ★ ★]

[To E.V. Griffith]
[September 19, 1960]

Got you plug in *Quagga* vol. I, no. 2, just off the press: 'Charles Bukowski's new book will be off the press early next month, *Flower, Fist and Bestial Wail*. It is being published by Hearse Chapbooks in California.' So you see, I'm working at it. Pretty lively poem in *Quagga* about a riot that occurred while I was in Moyamensing Prison. Might instigate the sale of a couple of chapbooks. I feel that you have been somehow reluctant to put out the Wail, perhaps feeling it would not move, since I am an isolationist socially speaking and have only enemies, but life is sometimes odd Griff, and it might be that this thing will put some dough in your pockets. I feel I am a more lively writer than Crews, Creeley, Mason, etc., Eckman, but we'll see.

[To E.V. Griffith]
Mid September, [1960]

Got your note on chapbook progress the other day. It appears to me that you are doing too much at once, getting out too many chapbooks at once, and although mine was started long ago others seem to be coming out ahead of me. I don't know what the hell to make of it all and often wonder how another writer would have taken it. From my experiences as an editor I found they wail and bitch pretty much, and can be quite damned nasty. This thing is even beginning to get me. Now the pages have come out wrong sequenced . . . what kind of a printer is that?

Well, I hope this thing does get done . . . sometime . . . somehow. The strain is getting unbearable.

[To E.V. Griffith]

October 7, 1960

My dear E.V. Griffith:

Since you have failed to contact me since about last August – 'and I should have something in your hands by the end of the month' – and then the note about wrong sequenced pages – 'and I should have something in your hands in just a few more days,' I haven't heard and we are now sailing well into October.

It seem to me that all mistakes could have been rectified by now! My famed patience, has at last, after a 2 years wait, *had* it.

And in case you have forgotten, I finally sent you some money – between 30 and 40 bucks – to help you get this thing rolling.

You have put me out on the limb by again asking me to make announcements to the magazines that *Hearse* is to issue *Flower, Fist and Bestial Wail.* This is getting to be the joke of the literary world, but I am no longer laughing.

I am going to wait a short period longer and if no results are achieved I am going to write *Trace*, the San Francisco newspapers and the editors of other literary magazines of the whole history of this notorious and impossible chapbook nightmare. I can not see it that sloppy and amateur editorialism, a downright horror of coldness and cruelty and ineptness go unchallenged.

If you feel that I am being unfair, hasty or unreasonable, I would be most glad to get any statements from you. However, further silence or delay, would be construed to mean that you intend to continue your slipshod policies and the writer be damned.

We of the literary world, we like to feel that we are not here to wrangle or to claw, but to create. Protest is more a political and worldly thing, but even as a poet, I feel I have a right and a duty, in this case, to make public protest.

[To E.V. Griffith]
October 14, 1960

I went down to the post office this morning with card left in my box yesterday – and *yowl!* – there it was, set of *Hearse* chapbooks by one Charles Bukowski. I opened the package right in the street, sunlight coming down, and there it was: *Flower, Fist and Bestial Wail*, never a baby born in more pain, but finally brought through by the good Doctor Griffith – a beautiful baby, beautiful! The first collected poems of a man of 40, who began writing late.

Griff, this was an event! Right in the middle of the street between the post office and a new car agency.

But then the qualms came on and the fear and the shame. I remembered my last letter to you when I had finally cracked, scratching and blaming and cursing, and the sickness came.

I DON'T KNOW HOW IN THE HELL TO APOLOGIZE, E. V., BUT JESUS I ASK FOR-GIVENESS. That's all I can say.

It's a beautiful job, clean and pure, poem arrangement perfect. I'm mailing out copies to some people who think I am alive, but first off with this letter to you.

I hope I can live down any disgust I have caused you.

· 1 9 6 1 ·

[To Jory Sherman]
[1961?]

[★ ★ ★] The fact that the poets of the world are drunk is a damn good indication of its shape. Cresspoolcrews says something about the essence of poetry being in the shape of a woman's body. It must be wonderful to be so beautifully simple and uninvolved. Sex is the final trap, the closing of the steel-kissed door. Lawrence was closer in seeking muliebrity from flesh to soul, and to perstringe [*sic*] the awkward-working and the ugly. Crews simply swallows sex in great drunken drafts because he doesn't know what else to do, which, of course, is common Americana: thinking about it, simpering about it, carrying dirty pictures in the back pocket, and yet this country, for it all, is the most puritanical you can find. Women here have put the price too high and the boys go behind the barn with the cow. Which makes it tough on boys, cows, and women.

I have just read the immortal poems of the ages and come away dull. I don't know who's at fault; maybe it's the weather, but I sense a lot of pretense and poesy footwork: I am writing a poem, they seem to say, *look* at me! Poetry must be forgotten; we must get down to raw paint, splatter. I think a man should be forced to write in a roomful of skulls, bits of raw meat hanging, nibbled by fat slothy rats, the sockets musicless staring into the wet ether-sogged, love-sogged, hate-sogged brain, and forevermore the rockets and flares and chains of history winging like bats, bat-flap and smoke and skulls ringing in the beer. Yes. [★ ★ ★]

[To John William Corrington]

January 17, 1961

Hello Mr. Corrington:

Well, it helps sometimes to receive a letter such as yours. This makes two. A young man out of San Francisco wrote me that someday they would write books about me, if that would be any help. Well, I'm not looking for help, or praise either, and I'm not trying to play tough. But I had a game I used to play with myself, a game called *Desert Island* and while I was laying around in jail or art class or walking toward the ten dollar window at the track, I'd ask myself, Bukowski, if you were on a desert island by yourself, never to be found, except by the birds and the maggots, would you take a stick and scratch words in the sand? I had to say 'no,' and for a while this solved a lot of things and let me go ahead and do a lot of things I didn't want to do, and it got me away from the type-writer and it put me in the charity ward of the county hospital, the blood charging out of my ears and my mouth and my ass, and they waited for me to die but nothing happened. And when I got out I asked myself again, Bukowski, if you were on a desert island and etc.; and do you know, I guess it was because the blood had left my brain or something, I said, YES, yes, I would. I would take a stick and I would scratch words in the sand. Well, this solved a lot of things because it allowed me to go ahead and do the things, all the things I didn't want to do, and it let me have the type-writer too; and since they told me another drink would kill me, I now hold it down to 2 gallons of beer a day.

But writing, of course, like marriage or snowfall or automobile tires, does not always last. You can go to bed on Wednesday night being a writer and wake up on Thursday morning being something else altogether. Or you can go to bed on Wednesday night being a plumber and wake up on Thursday morning being a writer. This is the best kind of writer.

. . . Most of them die, of course, because they try too hard; or, on the other hand, they get famous, and everything they write is published and they don't have to try at all. Death works a lot of avenues, and although you say you like my stuff, I want to let you know that if it turns to rot, it was not because I tried too hard or too little but because I either ran out of beer or blood.[★ ★ ★]

For what it's worth, I can afford to wait: I have my stick and I have my sand.

The mention of Frost below alludes to his reciting of his poem 'The Gift Outright' ('The land was ours before we were the land's. / . . . (The deed of gift was many deeds of war). . .') at the inauguration of President John F. Kennedy on January 20, 1961.

[To John William Corrington]
[ca. February 1,] 1961

I am listening to 'Belly up to the bar, boys!' and I took the ponies for $150 today, so what the hell, Cor, I will answer, tho this letter-writing is not my meat, except to maybe gently laugh at the cliffs coming down. And it has to end sometimes, even though it has just begun. I'd rather you were the one who finally didn't answer. And I'd never kick a man out because he was drunk, although I've kicked out a few women for it, and the 'wives-to-pinch,' they are gone, mental cruelty, they say; at least the last one, the editoress of *Harlequin* said that, and I said, ok. *my* mind was cruel to *yours* . . .

I think it is perfectly ok to write short stories and think they're poems, mostly because short stories *waste* so many words. So we violate the so-called poem form with the non-false short story word and we violate the story form by saying a lot in the little time of the poem form. We may be in between by borrowing from each BUT BECAUSE WE CANNOT ANSWER A PRE-CONCEIVED FORMULA OF EITHER STORY OR POEM, does this mean we are necessarily wrong? When Picasso stuck pinches of cardboard and extensions of space upon the flat surface of his paper

> did we accuse him of
> > being a sculptor
> > or an architect?

A man's either an artist or a flat tire and what he does need not answer to anything, I'd say, except the energy of his creation.

I'd say that a lot of abstract poetry lets a man off the hook with a can of polish. Now being subtle (which might be another word for 'original') and being abstract is the difference between *knowing* and saying it in a different way and *not* knowing and saying it as if you sounded like you might *possibly* know. This is what most poetry classes are for: the teaching of the application of the polish, the rubbing out of dirty doubt between writer and reader as to any flaws between the understanding of what a poem *ought* to be.

Culture and knowledge are too often taken as things that please or do not disturb or say it in a way that sounds kindly. It's time to end this bullshit. I am thinking now of Frost slavering over his poems, blind, the old rabbit hair in his eyes, everybody smiling kindly, and Frost grateful, saying some lie, part of it: '. . . the deed of gift was the deed of many wars' . . . An abstract way of saying something kind about something that was not kind at all.

Christ, I don't call for cranks or misanthropes or people who knock knock knock because their spleen has a burr in it or because their grandmother once fucked the iceman, but let's try to use just a little bit of sense. And I don't expect too much; but when a blind blubbering poet in his white years is USED . . . I don't know by WHAT OR WHO . . . himself, they, something . . . it ills me even to drink a glass of water and I guess that makes me the greatest crank of all time. [★ ★ ★]

Robert Vaughan, whose essay in Trace *Bukowski responds to below, edited a short-lived magazine called* Element, *published in Glendora, California.*

[To John William Corrington]
February 14, 1961

[★ ★ ★] Now, Bill, since we are discussing poetry and what makes it or doesn't make it, and I think it *is* important to attempt to figure out just what we are or aren't doing, and along this line I have written a letter to James Boyar May of *Trace* regarding an article that appeared in the Jan–Mar 1961 edition. And since Mr. May probably will not publish this I would like to repeat the letter here, because, in a manner, it falls in with our discussion . . . Well, it goes like this:

Dear Mr. May:

    In regards to Robert Vaughan's 'Essay on the Recent History of Immortality,' I really don't know *where* to begin. I rather imagine Robert V. as an intellectual and serious person (I know that he edits a magazine), and that his morals are proper and his study of the poem is more complete, certainly, than mine. And it's just here where the difficulty begins. If anybody has ever been forced to attend a poetry class or made the mistake of attending a poetry party, one is made to realize what is 'proper' in poetic and artistic approach, and if I may use a discarded term . . . I don't give a SHIT about either. Mr. Vaughan and the class professors make much of the fact that PROSE IS CREEPING INTO POETRY! God damn it, here we work with our IMAGES and some guy comes along and says . . . all that matters is a red wheelbarrow in the back yard, gathering rain. These are not the exact words but I don't have time to look up my Williams. It *was* Williams, wasn't it? Oh well . . . Anyhow, the prose statement in a poem seems to bother the editors ('This is excellent, but it is *not* a poem!') and it seems to bother the Vaughans and the professors. But *I* say, why not? What the hell's *wrong* with a 6 or 7 or 37 line long prose state-ment that is broken into the readable advantage and clearness of the poem-form? As long as it says what it must and says it as well or better than the mould and sound that says THIS IS A POEM, SO LISTEN TO ME. What's wrong with a 7 line short story or a 37 line novel which is placed within the poem-form, if this form makes it read better than it would if chunked together as a regular sentence or paragraph of regular English prose? Must we always DEFINE AND CLASSIFY what is done? Can't, for God's sake, can't ART be ART without a program and numbers?

There is NOTHING 'basically immoral about a poetry that does not attempt to communicate emotions or dredge up from the reader's subconscious a prior experience.' In fact, I would be tempted to say that a poetry that DOES ATTEMPT to do this is . . . Christ, I don't like to use the word 'immoral,' just let me say that this type of poetry ('that attempts') is apt to be confused and repetitive and dull, except to the school of holy rollers who have LEARNED THE RULES and yap and holler when they see the face of their god in the mirror. I know that much poetry is a hand-holding of the lonely at heart. But hell, there are clubs for these people, dances, and bashful kisses upon the terrace. Great poetry sharpens its swords for larger game.

'If the creator does not have, for his firm foothold, a moral attitude or ethical approach – ' etc. Let me say that there are no firm footholds in creation. Ask Van Gogh who blew his brains out among the blackbirds with a borrowed shotgun beneath the hot sun that moved the hand that moved the color. Although Van believed in God there wasn't any APPROACH here except the approach of the unknown, THE PROSE PAINT OF HIS COLORS that made Gauguin and Pissaro and other post-impressionists, great as they were, laugh at him because they painted down through the learned rule, the POEM within the line – if I may stretch a point to lay bare these similarities. And when Tolstoy found God his lines went limp, and Turgenev on his deathbed grieved for him because although Tolstoy had given up his land and his coppers for God, he had also given up something else. And although Dostoevski ended up on believing in Christ, he took the long road to get there, a most interesting and perhaps unwholesome road over roulette tables, raping a small child, standing before a wall waiting for the rifles to fire, he found that 'adversity is the main-spring of self-realism,' he found his Christ, but what a most *interesting* Christ, a self-made Christ, and I bow to him.

Now I realize that in the (and within the) word 'Morals' Mr. Vaughan does not specifically mean religion, but more the religion of thinking and writing in the way that we should. Morals transferred down to 1961 mean a way of thinking and acting that is acceptable upon a fund of realistic and humane reaction to what has happened and what will probably happen. But actually, although the Robert Vaughans mean well, and I have nothing but respect for them, they clutter the way of forwardness. Give me men of *apparent* evil, for they are the forerunners of a future good – much of what was *evil* at 5 : 30 p.m. yesterday is something else today.

I think sometimes of the great symphonies that we have accepted today that were hissed at and walked out upon when first heard.

'Writing poems is difficult: sweating out the coming of the correct image, the precise phrase, the turn of a thought . . .'

Writing poems is not difficult; living them is. Let's be realistic: every time you say 'good morning' to somebody and you do not mean 'good morning,' you are that much less alive. And when you write a poem within the accepted poem-form, making it *sound* like a poem because a poem is a poem is a poem, you are saying 'good morning' in that poem, and well, your morals are straight and you have not said SHIT, but wouldn't it be wonderful if you could . . . instead of sweating out the correct image, the precise phrase, the turn of a thought . . . simply sit down and write the god damned thing, throwing on the color and sound, shaking us alive with the force, the blackbirds, the wheat fields, the ear in the hand of the whore, sun, sun, sun, SUN!; let's make poetry the way we make love; let's make poetry and leave the laws and the rules and the morals to the churches and the politicians; let's make poetry the way we tilt the head back for the good liquor; let a drunken bum make his flame, and some day, Robert, I'll think of you, pretty and difficult, measuring vowels and adverbs, making rules instead of poetry.

Well, that's the letter, more or less, Cor, although I've changed and added a few words in transposing. I thought, though, that you might want to hear it. Poetry can be such a depressing thing, such a dead thing. How they want to run the chains around us! Why? I really don't understand. It seems as if they are trying to make it . . . well, like learning to weld or be an engineer. Always this is *right* and this is *wrong*, meanwhile not getting to the core at all. [★ ★ ★]

[To John William Corrington]
February 23, 1961

This is a short one. I am on a tear, ill and shaky; no complaints, I guess it's something I must burn out of my system, and if I make it, I make it. I don't want to short-circuit you but your last letter shed more light than a powerhouse. That sentence makes me sick. You see how easy it is to roll off a log and just *say* something? I hate to do you a disservice with an ill description . . . I only repeat, I can barely see out of the front of my eyes this morning.

There was another one who wrote me for a while. But about what? New listings of magazines, about how he met an editor on the street. This guy lives with editors, sleeps with them, goes to the parties, snudges [*sic*] his nose up all the blind spots – and in a manner, for him, it pays off. He makes a lot of pages and his poems are full of words like STAR SEA NIGHT

DEATH LOVE WOUND and you name the rest. What his name is doesn't matter and you can multiply him by the hairs of grass that look so sickly up at me from my 3rd floor rented window. I had to sock him down in a poem to stop him from nibbling the eternal edge of my guts. [★ ★ ★]

Cummings, yes, sometimes. His weakness is that he has devised a form that is easy to fall into. What I mean is that he can say almost anything or nothing and run it through his form and he has a lot of people believing it. This is Cummings, they say, the way they say, this is a Van Gogh, and all critical faculties fall lax because they have been pre-sold. People are pretty hard to sell, but once they believe, they believe and you cannot make them say no with a hammer. That's not good. Cummings must be made to produce every time he sits down, and not merely sign his name. *For Whom the Bell Tolls* is one of the poorest novels ever written but nobody knows it because Hem wrote it. Nobody knows but another writer who is close enough to smell it. Nobody knows that a smaller work like *To Have and Have Not* was really art. And I don't like the word 'art.' How they sound on words and drivel on them and drive us away from them. I had a wife once who divorced me because more in essence than reality I would never say I loved her. How could I say this without dragging in Hollywood and my next door neighbor and patriotism and the barber's cough and the cat's ass?

Really, Bill, I am sick this morning. Must stop. [★ ★ ★]

[To John William Corrington]
March 1, 1961

[★ ★ ★] The problem is, Corr, that as we work toward a purer, looser, more holy warmth of expression and creation, the critics are going to have to work a little harder to find out whether it's water or piss in the holy grail, and even then they might end up wrong. You know the old comic strip joke about the painting hung upside down or etc., well, there's a lot of practical truth in this. But pure creation will always have its own answer finally, and it will neither be a set of disciplines or undisciplines, it will simply be. [★ ★ ★]

[To John William Corrington]
April 12, 1961

[★ ★ ★] There are some men who can create with a perception of what they are doing and what is happening not only to them but to those around them. I am not one of those. Sometimes the poem wans on me, everything wans on me. The sense of excitement, of explosion is gone. I have been sent a couple of free journals by editors these last few days and reading through them I am disturbed by the fact that we are all writing pretty much alike. It could well be one man's voice under 36 different names. I do not care for this at all. I had long ago given up hope of being an extraordinary poet, and most of the time I do not think of myself as a poet at all; but when I do think of it, at least I would like to think I have failed with a more or less individual voice, but it seems as if we have pared everything down to a ghastly likeness. Whether this is caused by a simplification of language, a cutting out of extremes, a sidewalk grammar I don't know. You can look at the new buildings going up and the old buildings going down. Everything is now a straight line and a square corner. Ornament is gone. It is a reaction. Falsity *can* breed in ornamentation. But falsity can also breed in the flat voice. Steiner, I believe the name is, says in this quarterly *Kenyon Review* that we are drifting toward mathematics and away from the word, and to this I must agree. By the way, I know that the *Kenyon Review* is supposed to be our enemy . . . but the articles are, in most cases, sound, and I would almost say, poetic and vibrant; the poetry, of course, remains almost unbelievably flat and lifeless. It seems that forever in the university circles we are allowed truth in the article or the discussion, but when it comes down to the old brass tracks [*sic*] of actual creation we are supposed to take it easy and look the other way. [★ ★ ★]

In the following, Bukowski defends his earlier favorable mention (in a letter not included here) of an article by Harry Hooton, an Australian poet, in a recent issue of Trace.

[To John William Corrington]
April 26, 1961

[★ ★ ★] Hooton, of course, overstates his case. Why must they be such holy-rollers about everything? Your enemy or the devil might turn out to be a pretty good guy if you could learn his language and drink beer with him and pinch his wife when he goes to the bathroom. He has Yeats 'sneering.' Hooton beats a loud drum. Yeats could have told him, 'The best lack all conviction, while the worst are full of passionate intensity.' This is most certainly a 'message' . . . but without preaching; or from the same poem:

> '. . . what rough beast, its hour come round at last,
> Slouches toward Bethlehem to be born?'

Yeats died in 1939. [★ ★ ★]

Eliot, of course, began well, then got fancy with the *Four Quartets*, took on Catholicism and Criticism, was listened to by everybody, and paled off because he sold too many things at once and was not essentially a fighter or strong enough to stand firm. And yet Eliot did leave us something, perhaps a clearer flowing diction, and if Hooton says he voted with Yeats, that should make him (T.S.) pretty strong. About Stevens, I don't know. The Kenyon school, of course. Stevens tries very hard to be bright by saying nothing in a manner that would seem to imply something if only *you* were intelligent enough to understand, but, of course, since you aren't, you should be god damned glad to god damn read the shape of the words anyhow. Tate is another dry as dust faker who has had no more than one or two toothaches of the soul . . . and although Hooton did not mention Tate, and it is getting out of bounds to do so, I get out of bounds anyhow. I would never like Tate if I drank beer with him for 40 years or I pinched his wife's autographed copy of Wallace Stevens.

To hell with Hooton.

Give me Conrad Aiken, Robinson Jeffers, Ezra Pound and Yeats. [★ ★ ★]

[To John William Corrington]
June 8, 1961

Just got out of jail, I must see judge Friday, 1 p.m. [★ ★ ★] I will be 41 in August and I don't know whether the courage is gone or what, but the sight of jails that once meant nothing to me now sickens me to the roots. I don't like people messing with me and closing doors on me and throwing me on the floor with a bunch of other silverfish. A common drunk rap, of course, calls for no shame, just, of course, as murder calls for no shame if you murder the right one, *Crime and Punishment* be damned. The worst is, this might cause me to lose my job and I have no training of any sort and the job as a job means nothing, of course, only to keep me breathing and eating in order to write a poem. My old girl friend, who was with me, has a knot on her hard Irish head that would have killed the less hardy; believe we were walking down the street and she kept falling and I kept trying to catch her when the fuzz netted us both in their wily civic net. Her land-lady finally bailed us out and I guess the reason is that I have been giving her the flirt on the side, kissing her behind the ear and filling it with idle banter. If I were the writer of *The Hostage* they would have greeted me with a brass band but since I was Charles Bukowski, they threw me in and I sat there and a fat Mexican gave me 2 cigarettes and advice. 'Don't worry,' he said, 'it doesn't matter. Since you are with the Feds you probably will be out in 4 hours.' I hadn't finished my 2nd cigarette when my name was called, I shoved some cash upon a trusty with slow typewriter fingers and the release was speeded up. Outside I met Irish and hardluck Bob who I'd seen at the track earlier that day. I gave him 7 one dollar bills, tipped the cabby a buck and we sailed across the silken 5 a.m. skies that had no bars and no locks. I gave Frenchy a 50 buck bill (bail money), a kiss behind the ear, and there went my profits from the track. But you were right when you said you somehow had the idea that I was destroying myself or trying to go goofy, but maybe my soul is tough as an Irish head or maybe my luck will hold.

Ben Tibbs, a printer, a poet and artist who published alongside Bukowski in many little magazines, lived in Kalamazoo, Michigan. He did the cover art for Flower, Fist and Bestial Wail.

[To Ben Tibbs]
June 8, 1961

Sorry I can only ship one copy but I am down to the end of mine. Other people have written me that Griffith does not respond either to money or written request. I have attempted to send copies to all those who asked for them but Griffith only sent me a limited number. What has gone wrong up in Eureka I really don't know.

Thank you for doing the Art work on *Flower, Fist*. I think you caught the spirit of the poems and the title quite well.

[To John William Corrington]
November 17, 1961

[★ ★ ★] I am soft. Deer I cannot do in. I was riding with this gal in the car and it was Sunday and I was looking for a liquor store and we saw this sign, CHICKEN, and she said, oh, let's get a chicken, we'll have a nice roast chicken, and I said sure, and I drove up to the place and they had chicken all right, only it was standing up and it had white feathers, 60 or 70 strong had white feathers and when I walked in a couple of them shit and one of them winked at me and I just stood there and the guy said, yes, a nice chicken, no? . . . and I turned around and walked out and the gal said, where's the chicken and I said, hell, they all looked scrawny, you can't tell what you're getting with all the feathers, and she said, that's easy, you just pick em up and feel em with your fingers, and check the eye, get a clear-eyed chicken. Chickens are just like people, if the eye is not clear he is malfunctioning.

How do you kill 'em? I asked.

My father used to whirl em, WHIRR, ZIP!!

Let's have a banana sandwich, I said.

I remember the slaughterhouse down where the streetcar turns, and the floors were greasy with blood, green floors, blood has a special smell that will not leave and there is nothing harder to remove than a blood stain, blood is life, and death came on minute after minute but unlike the docs and interns and nurses at the L. A. County General Hospital I could not get used to it, and I did not have a car then and I would get on the streetcar and people would smell the blood on me and look, look, and then go home and eat a porterhouse.

I am not building a case for the vegetarians who might be too soft for the formula we were conceived in and have to work out of; I will eat meat, only I don't want to see it happen, not anymore, not once more, I don't want to hear the sound. When life changes to death in that very small instant it is an explosion against the mind that can never be rebuilt.

No deershoots, kid, I might really go wacky tying roping the thing across the hood. Guys like Hem would think me queer.

Although, I don't know how we got on this. There is a funny story. It was told to me by this person who used to go to group therapy sessions to try to help himself. Played some instrument in symphony orchestra but right now, like me, not doing much, just hanging on. Well, he went to this guy's house. The guy said, come on, I'll show you something. I've got 2 chickens. You save money. You get 'em when they're young and grow 'em. I wonder how you kill em? he asked my friend. Well, this guy didn't know how to kill 'em. He got a hammer and he let them out in the yard and he tried to kill both of them at once. It was a mess. The chickens would not die. He kept hitting them with the hammer. The noise, you know, the blood, one eye hanging out on a long string, a beak all twisted back into the head and the thing going on, running, and the other one just standing there, the hammer coming down on the head and slipping off and the thing just standing there waiting. Finally, my friend, out of mercy, he did not help but he got excited and started giving instructions and finally the job was done, and then the guy took the 2 chickens and threw them in the garbage. His girl friend left him and never spoke to him again and she never spoke to the one who gave the instruction either. [★ ★ ★]

[To John William Corrington]
November 26, 1961

[★ ★ ★] Yes, killing a chicken with a hammer is imbecile, although I doubt this person was sadistic, simply not a clear thinker, the way the story was told to me. [★ ★ ★]

And don't think that when I walk into a butcher shop that I don't know. A voice always says to me, 'They have done it for you.' It costs me in several ways, but I don't think becoming a week-end huntsman would spring me clear. Old lady Hemingway said she felt or liked to feel 'chic' when she made the kill. I don't think much of old lady Hemingway, she read too many of the old man's books. No more than we have. But believed them. But as I said in one of my poems now floating around, it seems sport to knock Hemingway now, so I will lay off for a while. [★ ★ ★]

[To John William Corrington]
December [?3], 1961

the hem can be over-evaluated like anything else, and while he understood the mathematics of life and cut it fine, bravado and hardfire, there was essentially some music missing, and what he cut out in his figuring as unnecessary is what turned the shotgun in on him. He wrote well early and then got burned in the Spanish war thing. Won't these fuckers ever learn that politics is the biggest whore, the biggest hole any fine man can fall into? Hem built an image and had to write up to the image. It's all right to be tough cob but it doesn't wear well when you get into your fifties. It's better then to have some soft culture, something like the organ works of Bach, some Vivaldi, something going for you that may have a knife-edge but still a screen for softness to enter. You are still young, though a very wise young, and Hem is good to you like your $7^1/_2'$ barrel with 20% more reach n' yr 6 shots in 5 inch square at 50 to 60 feet firing rapid clip. There is beauty in this, I can see beauty in this, and I can also see that you are nobody to mess with if you get pissed. I hope I don't sound like an old man preaching. I've gone the route. You should've seen my fight with Tommy McGillan in a Philadelphia alley in 1948. They're still talking that one and they wouldn't serve me for 3 days because I busted their hero. Faulkner? Faulkner is a cutie, he left jabs, jabs, jabs, and an occasional hook. But who am I, shit, to say? I have never written a novel, don't feel like writing a novel, although if I live to be fifty I will try one. I made myself this promise once sitting in a bar. I figured then that I would never live to be fifty so it was a soft promise and I was not too worried about it. I still may not have much to worry about, ah so many parts burned out and missing, including good fat portions of the mind, but mainly there is some singing left, the gut is soft and the sun comes down.

[★ ★ ★] Of course we all fail and it doesn't take a Faulkner to say it, it would be short-peckered wisdom indeed if we thought we could pull the curtain on God and expose his kisser . . . or the small pile of bleached bones. All we can do is work against the tide as best we may. I think that's why the horses interest me: the beauty of loss, the working against the irresistible mathematics of death. You can piss on death and forget it until it finds you. Most people do this. That is why they cry at funerals. [★ ★ ★]

· 1962 ·

Carl Larsen published Bukowski's third book, Longshot Poems for Broke Players, *at his 7 Poets Press in New York early in 1962.*

[To Ben Tibbs]

[early 1962]

I had meant to ask you not to send dollar; certainly this is one hell of a price to pay to see the fine cover you did for Griffith. But instead of sending the dollar back, I am going to suffer you with a copy of *Longshot Poems for Broke Players.* Am sending the buck on to Larsen for this purpose, but am having the beers anyhow. Many thanks for your graciousness and understanding.

---

*Neeli Cherkovsky, then known as Neeli Cherry, recounts an incident of Bukowski's reacting to Cherry's writing a poem about him by throwing the MS in the fire. Cherry retrieved it, Bukowski praised it, but added 'I hope you don't devote a career to writing about me' (*Hank, p. 293). Cherry published the poem in his magazine,* Black Cat Review, *no. 1, June 1962.*

[To Neeli Cherry]

Sunday [early 1962]

without too much reverence

Thank you for the poem. Are you going to devote a career writing about me? Better chose yr subjects more carefully.

Your poetic style is good. I mean that it is loose enough to allow truth to enter or anything you want to say enter

```
            without worry about preconceptions
            or the poetic line
        which thoughts
            choke up most of them
            before they begin
        I mean, before they begin
            they have ended.
                they are done.
```

a good style is important. style is what makes you different from the run. it lets yr voice be heard. Some good men have learned this.

to wit: Shakespeare, Hem, Sherwood Anderson, D. H. Lawrence, Gertie Stein, Faulkner, Picasso, Van Gogh, Stravinsky.

Stein had more style than genius. Her style was her genius. Faulk was next. He put very little fire into a forge of style that fooled almost everybody. Hem had style and genius that went with it, for a little while, then he tottered, rotted, but was man enough, finally, and had style enough, finally. Lawrence was a cock-freak who never had nerve enough to face the world as a man and so faced the world behind a nerve-soothing soul-soothing whirl of sex proteins, but who ever and nevertheless wrote some penetrating lines. Sherwood A. was just a good old fuck who suffered without too much pretense but who was aware of style, of cutting words into paper so you could see them, like blood or paint. This is important. It is a painting. Writing is painting and the sooner people realize this the less dull crap will dull the market and I will have to get drunk that much less. Picasso does with paint what I would like to do with words, only some day may try to do with paint, only not, fuck of course like P. but like B., and style only means opening into light simply and cleanly. Van Gogh, of course, was never insane. He simply realized the world was elsewhere. And his style, the purest of styles.

A good style comes primarily from a lack of pretentiousness, and what is pretentious changes from year to year from day to day from minute to minute. We must be ever more careful. A man does not get old because he nears death; a man gets old because he can no longer see the false from the good.

Enough of speech-making. [★ ★ ★]

[To John William Corrington]
January 12, 1962

yr damned intelligent well written letters are backing me off into some back closet fulla mops and old *Esquires* but I carry on because, as I once decided, coming out of a St. Louis basement where I was getting 55 cents an hour for packing ladies' dresses into boxes for shipment and the fat little Jew smiled his yellow-face smile because I was in his cage and he had a 12 room house and a wife more beautiful than I cd even have in my dreams

> I decided that I was losing
> not the money part
> fuck that

but if I may be corny – the soul part that I was packing away in boxes with the ladies' dresses – and since I was losing this, wt could I do besides start a ladies' dress shop myself – which even if I could wd be very obnoxious – I decided

> that since I was losing
> I COULD EITHER GIVE UP AND LOSE IT ALL
> OR LOSE ALMOST EVERYTHING
> BUT SAVE
>> SAVE THE LITTLE BIT THAT WAS LEFT.

this does not sound like much; it does not seem like much, but that night walking to my room between the frozen trees of a St. Louis night, it seemed very right, it was my savior grown and walking beside me, a tiny flame. It made sense then and it still does now. You say you never care much for losers, but it's all I've known, from celling with proud swindlers to shooting crap under a swinging light in Albuquerque (or was it El Paso?) as a member of a railroad section gang. Well, I don't like winners. Winners get fat and careless and write things like *The Old Man and the Sea* which is printed in *Life* magazine for a public which was long ago gaffed by the formula, and while it is typical of little men like myself to bitch and scratch at the great dead, I will still have my say. Hemingway wanted to save man by giving him a sense of honor through action. The trouble with his action is that it was A STAND AGAINST SOMETHING: an army, a bull, a dog with horns, a country, a fish, the sea, the moon, the rich, the poor, anything that countered movement toward some *seeming* need for victory. Shit on that. That is child's play. We need knock nothing down. It's time we begin picking up. saving what is left. what is worth saving. so when we clean our shotguns we only clean our shotguns. I do not have the master's talent but I can see a lot of fool in him, which does not make me better, but sometimes in packing in the dresses the mind did say, will say, no one must fool me now because there is so very little left; but how did I get on this? does not sound too good. it is a kind of preaching. I forgot to laugh. dead in a bed I will laugh, or in a gutter I will laugh, or red on a mutual ticket in a cool Arcadia wind where my great dead uncle raped a lady he had picked up on his dandy motorcycle. ah, my family, all maniacs, and now all gone. just one. the end of a bad line. a tiny flame. [★ ★ ★]

> three niggers smiling could not reproduce
> the tumult of that kiss

I don't know why, but that's a very good line. it's a shame you have to lose it. it reminds me of a room full of electricity and heat when it's very cold outside and you sit and listen to the clock tick. of course, Jon [Webb]'s got to protect himself. for all we know, the mag's his only income. by doing the work himself, enough dollars to carry on. This is a bad time. People are frightened of doing any wrong. A formula has been set up and everything has been pushed inside of this formula. I don't know if this is the right way of doing things at all. I must agree with some that fucking wd eventually clear up the whole mess. I have 3 black mamas chasing me now. One with long black hair she winds over her ears in shell shapes n wata big can tits wowwowwow, only my bloody ass says no, and I run out to the race track with my new system (60 bucks profit today) and come back here and read your good letter. The main trouble with the black race is that they wanna be white; outside of that and hot weather, they are ok with me. but back to the poem, opening lines: 3 niggers smiling . . . the trouble with the word 'nigger' is that it is very poetic. negro is soft and round and says nothing. It is as it looks. I had the same trouble with the poem 'On a Night You Don't Sleep' (see *Flower, Fist and Bestial Wail* if you have the beast around) and I had to go with nigger because that is what he *was* when I saw him through the doorway with the salt water in my eyes and this Barbara Fry walking along mumbling nonsense by my side. I thought, if I put 'negro' then I am a coward, I am doing something because I am told to do something and not because I want to, and that's about where we stand on the racial question now. The racial question is too large for me. [★ ★ ★]

[To John William Corrington]
January 22, 1962

I am unable to write. The woman I have know for so long has been critically ill since Saturday and died 2 hours ago.

This is going to be the longest night of them all.

[To John William Corrington]
January 28, 1962

I am somewhat over the thing now, alive, that is, something gone, that is, but the language of the thing is bad, I cannot get through, writing has nothing to do with it, and it is better to leave it alone if it will leave me alone. In the week gone I have done things that are not in the classic normal mourning, but she will know that they were necessary.

A letter from Sherman. Jeffers died. Couple of nights back I thought, well, maybe I go see the kid, I feel better. It's a hundred miles round trip to San Berdo, hadn't slept or eaten for 5 or 6 days. The kid's split with the wife again. Found him out back someplace on 'I' st. He had his book of poems propped on the mantle, *So Many Rooms*. The typewriter was going when I knocked on the door. Went to liquor store where he tried to tap me when I opened my wallet but I wasn't in the mood. Went back and sat there a couple of hours while he read me his poems.

Met a high yellow negress at racetrack next day and she wound up riding me at her apartment, bobbing, bobbing, bobbing, and I said beautiful, my dear, beautiful, and grabbed her can, but it wasn't any good – I guess the old woman was watching me from heaven and she shut off my water, and the negress rolled off and I finally fell asleep.

Went over to Winski's and we made the rounds – A turkish joint upstairs next to the *Daily Racing Form*, people sitting on the floor, women dancing alone; then a dull American place, then a strip joint, and all the time Winski talking sex sex eyow sex sex sex sex – I'd like to chew on her gold panties all night etc., and there was my old woman down underneath, the grass already knitting the cuts of earth, the worms making their move, the son already half way back to Texas in his god damned Mercedes Benz after a quicky cut-rate funeral, and so passes a bad taste, and along with it the only real woman and real friend I could ever stand.

I don't think that following up one death with another one is the answer. If I am wrong I am real wrong but once the razor goes through or the other leg swings out the window it's too late daddieo . . . Any other profound statements of this nature will have to wait another letter.

Right now, a quiet beer. This quietness. And giving her the real homage. Jane Cooney Baker. deceased. but never gone.

Ann Bauman was and is a poet living in Sacramento, publishing in some of the same little magazines Bukowski appeared in. (On her marriage, she became Ann Menebroker.) Evidently their correspondence began with her note of appreciation for a poem of his which appears in Signet, *May 1962. Bukowski notes: 'Fair poet. I believe we bucked each other up for a while, perhaps she helped me more than I helped her. There was an off-hand, rather ho hum attitude from her, more toward life than toward me.'*

[To Ann Bauman]
May 10, 1962

got yr note on 'Dead Stay Alive Too Long' and etc., and it filled a hole in the mailbox where a rejected poem usually sits. Am sitting here having a beer and staring out the same window, 3 floors up, miles out into the nowhere of Hollywood. If you saw something in the poem (or poems) good. Yet a little praise is a bad thing, and a lot of it is worse. We cannot be too careful. It is better for the artist to work out of a vacuum, going from creation to creation, each a new beginning, until it is all over, until he is dead in the sense that he can no longer create or he can no longer create because he is dead (physically). The latter, of course, is preferable.

Jory is another case entirely, and it would do little good to discuss him here.

Joyce Odam wrote a poem for me about the death of a lady, for which I wrote her my thanks.

I recall seeing a large group of your work somewhere (*Signet?*). Well, keep going. But we have to, don't we?

[To John William Corrington]
May [?15], 1962

[★ ★ ★] the jon jazz bit not for me. I prefer the symphony – Shostakovitch 5th, Symphony in D by Franck, Stravinsky, the better parts of Mahler, etc., but don't care for the symphony crowd. Stiff phoney crows, all this marble hall exaltation, this church-like holiness. They ought to play this stuff in the juke-boxes of beerhalls, bars. Think of trying to hold the price-line with a whore while listening to Beethoven. This would be life out of the stems of flowers. [★ ★ ★]

[To Ann Bauman]
[May 19, 1962]

rec. yr letter but I am a bastard and usually do not bother with these correspondii? or haven't you heard? this has nothing to do with fathead or fat in the frying pan or limping dogs.

all my elements are hung up like a shirt on a hanger and there is not much I can do with them.

Yes, everything I do is 'breathlessly new' – for this same reason people continue to make love. I am not interested in history or theory – or argument. The best argument is a new poem.

It is may the 19th somebody has just told me. Fine.

what does one do at poetry festivals? surely, dear, there must be a better way.

I sent yr Friedman at SIGNET a poem but have not heard and she is pretty quick usually. I told her it was a bad poem and this might have her confused. It's called 'Keats and Marlowe.' I told her it was bad and then I rewrote it. It might still be prob. bad.

God, I am running out of beer! this is madness . . .

ah, hahah ahha ha ha ha ha!

[To Ann Bauman]
May 21, 1962

Getting this off while drinking a beer and listening to a little Sibelius before going to work. I am sorry you do not believe I do not like to argue. I believe you are bothered with too many concepts.

You should avoid these poetry festivals etc. as they are nothing but a melting pot of watered-down talents, high-class lonely heart club for those with typewriters. [★ ★ ★]

Study yr keeds. Kids. There are a lot of poems there. But don't write about yr kids. Write about the human, what's left of him, where he's going, what he dropped on the floor.

Don't tell me about insanity. I wrote a short story about a man who murdered a blanket that fell in love with him and appeared to look at him and follow him around. 'Very believable,' wrote back the first mag, 'but this man appears too bizarre.' Or this is the condensation of it. I do not believe in writing a short story unless it crawls out of the walls. I watch the walls daily but very little happens.

[To John William Corrington]
May 27, 1962

I received your letter in which you mentioned your father's cancer, and that you feel more than lowly is understood. It is our own deaths that will be easiest to take; it is the other deaths, the coming of them, that we cannot bear. I have tried, in these cases, to apply history, the history of death, the fact of death; I have tried to think of Napoleon gone, Hitler, the bird, the cat, the movie star, the hero, the murderer, names of things, of things that once were . . . but it did not help. The mind cannot overcome the instinct. The mind is only a recent development; the instinct was there long before. When love burns to the ground do not be ashamed of your grief, or even your madness or bitterness.

My mother died of cancer. I took her the most beautiful rosary I could buy on Christmas Eve but when I arrived the door was locked. I was standing there twisting the knob when a nurse walked up and said, 'She just died.' My old man died while trying to drink a glass of water. The water kept running and running and they heard it and when they came in he was dead on the kitchen floor. With Jane I stood there wiping away her guts as they ran out of her mouth. Death is eternally everywhere, I need not tell you that. The ways are hard whether they are God's ways or simply ways. To say that I understand the machinery of it or accept it would be a lie, or to say anything to help you at this moment would also be a lie. You know as much as I.

I am lucky. For me, there is nothing else left to die, outside of C. Bukowski. They will find me through the sense of smell. By then, I will be stiff enough to slide down the stairs like a board.

I can see some landlady going through my stuff with one of her old biddy friends. 'Say what's all them magazines under the table? I never seen such funny-looking magazines . . .' And then everything into some bag for the Salvation Army. Farewell, C.B.

One of my last friends, a dishwasher, set himself on fire or anyhow somebody set him on fire and he walked up the steps, drunk, a black monster of himself, flakes of walking ashes, and he got to his room (the only home he knew) and fell on his rented bed and died. Farewell friend.

We go on with our little poems and we wait.

One god damned hell of a situation.

The review mentioned in the next letter was among the very earliest published recognitions of Bukowski's work. R. R. Cuscaden's 'Charles Bukowski: Poet In a Ruined Landscape' appeared in Satis, *no. 5. Cuscaden, editor and publisher of* Midwest *magazine, brought out Bukowski's* Run With the Hunted *(1962).*

[To Ann Bauman]
June [20?], 1962

Yes, Sibelius later went into hiding and shaved his head; I'm told he was a handsome and vain man, and age bothered him, but for it all

> he wrote the long-striding line
> stepped around the mountains
> and died.

It is 26 minutes before 9 a.m. and I am out of beer. [* * *]

I include herein *Satis* an English magazine that has printed a couple of poems that fall into the non-uplifting category. You can get the other kind anywhere. Also, a review of my 3 books by Cuscaden. It is a good damned thing I do not wear a hat or I could not get it around my head after reading these reviews.

Darling, this is the trap: BELIEVE YOU ARE GOOD WHEN THEY TELL YOU YOU ARE GOOD AND YOU ARE THEREBY DEAD, DEAD, DEAD. dead forever. Art is a day by day game of living and dying and if you live a little more than you die you are going to continue to create some pretty fair stuff, but if you die a little more than you live, you know the answer.

Creation, the carving of the thing, the good creation is a sign that the god that runs you there inside still has his eyes open. Creation is not the end-all but it is a pretty big part. End of lecture #3784. [★ ★ ★]

Corrington, a poet then teaching at Louisiana State University, was to write the introduction to Bukowski's first Loujon Press book, It Catches My Heart in Its Hands, *which would finally appear in the fall of 1963. Bukowski notes, 'An early booster of my work.' He adds that their long correspondence 'stopped after he wrote his novel and went to Hollywood.'*

[To John William Corrington]
June 24, 1962

IN KIND OF A NUMB STATE LATELY? I mean, me. THE END OF THE SOUL. mebee. Anyhow, just crawling out of the sack and looking around, that's about where I am at. They've machine gunned me down to this nub. good. cigarettes, cigars, candy?

Jon's hard at the book, I know. How about yours? I heard that your San Francisco Review has folded or will change hands. Weren't they going to bring out a new collection of your poems? Check your tires for air.

Just off a four day drunk. Bloody ass. Glass on floor. Broke. Coffeepot now going in front of me: GLUGGLE, GLUGGLE, GLUKE GLUKE!! I think a new piece of ass would fix me fine. This old stuff gets so hard to handle. That their eyes spray me with love is not enough. It is the sagging of the tit, the worn-flesh? If I could only once have a drink of clear spring water. Everything has mud in it and sticks and discarded socks. Well, I am not so much myself. Crows don't sleep with peacocks. I've got to realize this. [★ ★ ★]

[To John William Corrington]
June [?25], 1962

[★ ★ ★] How are you going to lecture on the novel? How do you do it? Are you going to read them *Finnegans Wake*? Are you going to tell them that Faulkner's novels are slick as onionskins and that you can fall right off the page because most of the time he is writing about *nothing* and he throws in all these pages of italics to show you *something* is going on, but really, nothing is going on at all, and because you really at first believe this and don't want to, you finally figure that something profound is going on, else why all the pages this way? And so it is better to believe it is profound because they tell you it is than be the first to stick your neck out. Faulkner will never take the shotgun because he is too clever to let you believe that he has failed. Steinbeck was very good at one time when he had ideals but his ideals trailed off and he flattened out. I think Sartre's 2 or 3 books around the war in France are some of the best writing I have seen done. Where these Frenchmen get drunk on wine in the church; the battle in the tower, from the tower, all the many things I have forgotten but that stick in me like threads of a good happening. I don't do much reading anymore. I don't read anymore. Maybe the *Racing Form*. The time comes to end reading. The time comes reading makes you sick. This is where some music and drink and love come in. Music and drink, anyhow.

[★ ★ ★] Answering yr bit. I was a Catholic. As a kid. Just got past the catechism bit. We had to memorize it. We were on the front porch, Frank Sullivan and I. 'God has bodily eyes.' And Frank put his fists to his eyes: 'You mean like this? Like *milk* bottles?' And we laughed and then we got scared. At 13, 14, 15, I stopped going and there wasn't much my mother could do and the old man didn't care. I don't like to hit on the subject because it is a puzzler. Jane was C. Slept with rosary under pillow. Well, hell. [★ ★ ★]

Wormwood Review *published the following letter as Bukowski's response to the editor's explanation that the payment for publication was four copies 'which we will mail to anywhere, anybody or anything. . . .' (M.S. is presumably a slightly disguised reference to Sheri Martinelli and C.W. to John William Corrington.)*

[To Marvin Malone]
[August 1962]

Well, ya better mail one to M.S. or she'll prob. put her pisser in the oven, she thinks she is a goddess, and maybe she is, I sure as hell wd't know
    like some of the boys tell me,
then there is C.W. who does not answer his mail but is very busy teaching young boys how to write and I know he is going places, and since he is, ya better mail 'm one . . .

then there's my old aunt in Palm Springs nothing but money and I have everything but money . . . talent, a good singing voice, a left hook deep to the gut . . . send her a copy, she hung up on me, last time I phoned her drunk, giving evidence of need, she hung up on me . . .

then there's this girl in Sacramento who writes me these little letters . . . very depressed bitch, mixed like quite some waffle flower, making gentle intellectual overtures which I ignore, but send her a magazine

in lieu of a hot poker.

that makes 4?

I hope to send you some more poems anytime because I got to figure that people who run my poems are a little mad, but that's all right. I am also that way. anyhow,—

I hope meanwhile you do not fold up before I do.

A note by the recipient identifies this as accompanied by the gift of a bobby pin. The 'her' in question is presumably Jane Cooney Baker, who had died early in 1962. For Bukowski's relationship with her, see Hank, *chapters 4 and 5.*

[To Ann Bauman]

[September 1962]

Death does *not* take everything, god damn it.

I hope you can use this in your hair to keep alive a something that I should have died in front of. o my god my god yes I am drinking. and who cares? I love her. simple swine words. use it, in your hair. Thank you, Sacramento fog, fountains, odd voice, grief of wretched breathing, phantom love, oh child, wear it in your hair, honor me, her, the mountains, the hot great tongue and flash of God.

Thank you.

[To Ann Bauman]

September 4, 1962

Disregard my last letter. Strings became undone. A little sawdust spilled out. Beer. Wine. German gloom. These things can fetch anyone. A waterglass looks like a skull. Horses run into the rail. Insomnia. Job trouble. Toothache. The body bleeds. Retching. Flat tire. Traffic ticket. Lack of love. Sleep, then nightmare. Paper everywhere. Trivial bits of paper. Nothing ever done. Flooded sink. People in the hall with cardboard faces. Sure, sure, sure.

Today I will walk in the sun. I will simply walk in the sun. [★ ★ ★]

[To Jon Webb]

September 4, 1962

Regarding the death of my woman last Jan. 22, there is not much to say except I will never be the same again. I might attempt to write it sometimes but it is still too close, may always be too close. But that time in the charity ward years ago a little Mexican girl who changed the sheets told me that she was going to shack up with me as soon as I got well, and I began feeling better right away. I had one visitor: a drunken woman, red and puffy-faced, a bedmate of the past who reeled against the bed a few times, said nothing and walked out. Six days later I was driving a truck, lifting 50-lb packages and wondering if the blood would come again. A couple of days later I had the first drink, the one they said would kill me. A week or so later I got a typewriter, and after a ten-year blank, after selling to *Story* & others, I found my fingers making the poem. Or rather the bar-talk. The non-lyrical, non-singing thing. The rejects came quickly enough. But they made no indentation, for I felt in each line as if I were talking the thing out. Not for them, but for myself. Now I can read very little other poetry or very little other anything. Anyway, the drunk lady who reeled against my bed, I buried her last Jan. 22. And I never did see my little Mexican girl. I saw others, but somehow she would have been right. Today, I am alone, almost outside all of them: the buttocks, the breasts, the clean live dresses like unused and new dishtowels on the rack. But don't get me wrong – I'm still 6 feet tall with 200 lbs. of ableness, but I was able best with the one that's gone.

Bukowski's 'WW 2' appeared in Mica *7 (November 1962). Previously, three poems were published in* Mica *5 (Winter 1962). The magazine was edited by Helmut Bonheim and Raymond Federman from Santa Barbara.*

[To Helmut Bonheim]

September 28, [1962]

Thanks the stamps, and good you like 'ww 2' which is more factual than inventive, but what the fuck, you've got to give me credit for putting it down anyhow because it's what to know what to leave out that makes me different from the garage mechanic, if we are too much different. There is another story I have written – about a man who murders a blanket. Sent it to *Evergreen*, 6 months now, no response. Wrote stamped, self-add. thing. No response. I don't keep carbons. I suppose I'll see it in print some day under the name of Francios Marcios or Francis Francis or F. Villon. I keep getting reamed this way. But it is good for me. It reminds me that the world is pretty shitty. and this keeps me deftly abdulah and stasher of cannons. Anyhow, on 'ww 2,' change and shift lines at your will . . . to fit page or to help readability; – although I personally garbled it a little, voices and ideas running together – to throw nails.

I'll send you more poems since you ask for them, but haven't written any, and they don't come back. I don't mean they are accepted; I mean the swine simply do not return them; they sit on them like pillows, friend. aye.

This is garbage talk.

I have come through a green and red war these last 2 month. My side lost but I am still more alive than ever, in a sense. We have to pass through these things, again, again – arguing with a knife blade, a bottle, weeping like a frigging cunt in menopause, afraid to step out a door . . . afraid of birds, fleas, mice . . . encircled by a clock, a typewriter, a half-open closet door full of ghouls, killers, horrors like sea-bottoms. And then it ends. You are calm again. As calm as . . . a garage mechanic. I think of a D. H. Lawrence title: *Look We Have Come Through*.

Anyhow, I'll try you with some poems, although I don't know if they can be like the *Mica* things. They will just have to be what they are . . . If you read somewhere that I cursed editors and other critters, you prob. read correctly. I deal pretty much alone and don't care for ties. Tits, yes. Ties, no. I never wear ties. Creation and flow are the factors. Survival is not too important to me, either in any sense of immortality or in any sense of today – paying the rent, eating a sandwich, dreaming of a good fuck etc. etc. Although I get pretty scared sometimes when the world tries to kill me. Not the death-part, for as Socrates explained, this cannot be too bad. It is the getting there. The eyes. The flies. the ties. rubber tires. dead fish. fat landladies. buttons falling off shirt. dirty laundry. garage mechanics . . .

savannah and eggplant

The Webbs were preparing the third issue of their magazine, The Outsider, which would be devoted mainly to Bukowski, whom Webb proclaimed recipient of a special award as 'Outsider of the Year.' The issue would include tributes to Bukowski as well as photographs of him and poems and letters by him. It was to be followed by the publication of a 'Loujon Press Award Book' collecting Bukowski's poetry.

[To Jon Webb]

September 28, [1962]

[★ ★ ★] I have been doing some thinking. I would like to write you another letter of acceptance re the OUTSIDER OF YEAR 62 thing, and I will anyhow, and it should be arriving in a day or 2 [★ ★ ★]

As per writing more letters, as you know, this can't be done just like that any more than a poem can; in fact, a letter is tougher because the letter mood seems to fall less upon me than the poem thing. Yet I think the letter is an important form. You can touch about everything as you run around. It lets you out of the straightjacket of pure Art, and you've *got* to get out once in a while. Of course, I don't restrict myself as much in the poem as most do, but I have made this my business, this freedom with the word and idea, because . . . to be perfectly corny . . . I know I'll only be around once and I want to make it easy on myself. [★ ★ ★]

[To Jon Webb]

[ca. October 1, 1962]

[★ ★ ★] Sherman was up yesterday to borrow 5 bucks. Said it was raining and his windshield wiper wasn't working. I hate to be a bitch but this kid is getting to be real pain in the ass. He's got a $150 a week job and he keeps borrowing from me, and then he's got guts enough to claim he's paid me back. [★ ★ ★] I'm going to have to cut off relations with Sherman. You are the editor, but if he sends in anything on me on congrat. for 1962 OUTSIDER, I wish you wouldn't run it because congrats from this person are

45

not congrats at all. Enough of this type of bitching which is a little bit swinish . . . if it were only the borrowing it would not be so bad, but there are other facets of personality here in Sherman that you wouldn't find in a low-grade polecat. Enough. [★ ★ ★]

[To Jon Webb]
[ca. October 1, 1962]

I am enclosing another letter of acceptance which I much prefer to the other one I sent you. Of course, I do not know exactly what you want, and even if I did, I couldn't do it. This one might be a little too long for you, or the ending rather sudden. I don't know.

I am over my menopause or whatever the hell it was. It only lasted a month; maybe it was something else. I don't mind going mad so long as it is clean. I don't like the sloppy thing. Yet, you surely know that any of us who work with the word are open to anything, I mean any day we might test the cliff's edge. This is the nature of remaining as alive as possible: while other men die slowly, we are more apt to blow out the fire with one quick fucking blast – see Van Gogh, see Hemingway, see Chatterton, see the whole thing back down and through. Or if we don't kill ourselves, the State kills us: see Aristotle, see Lorca. And Villon, they ran him out of Paris just because he did a little thievery between poems. We are in for hard times, Jon, any way you look at it. Even those of us who are not giants. But it is harder for the giants. Their bones are the same as ours but they have strained and made the leap. Then there's a lot of pap and shit: people who write drivelly little poems while maintaining a time-clock, children, new-car, new-home decency. They'll make with the poem as long as nothing *else* is lost. It won't work. Man can't *divide* his impulses and expect to have power down every corridor. Now, the original Beats, as much as they were knocked, had the Idea. But they were flanked and overwhelmed by fakes, guys with nicely clipped beards, lonely-hearts looking for free ass, lime-lighters, rhyming poets, homosexuals, bums, sightseers – the same thing that killed the Village. Art can't operate in Crowds. Art does not belong at parties, nor does it belong at Inauguration Speeches. It belongs sitting across from Khrushchev but only if it drinks a beer with the man and talks anything but politics . . . and there are so many good beginnings. A strong young talent makes it. Then can't stand light. This is nothing but the plain old-fashioned fathead and shows that the Artist was not *ready* in the first place. The days speak; the years tell; the centuries throw out the garbage.

God oh mighty, another lecture. Is this a sign of old age? Let me tell you that by saying these things to myself, and to you, I protect myself from rot. I've seen so much rot. And I may be rotting myself and may not know it. It's just like when someone else is sleeping with your wife: you are the last to find out, or you never find out. Such is the soul. We are tested when we lace our shoes, or in the manner in which we scratch our back. [★ ★ ★]

The following is from the letter accepting the 'Outsider of the Year' Award that Bukowski sent for publication.

[To Jon Webb]
[ca. October 1, 1962]

[★ ★ ★] I have always been pretty much *outside* it all, and I don't mean just the art I try to send down through my typewriter, although there it appears I stand outside the gate also. It appears from many rejections that I do not write *poetry* at all. Or as a dear friend told me the other day: 'You do not understand the true meaning of poetry. You are not lyrical. You do not *sing!* You write bar talk. The type of thing you write you can hear in any bar on any day.'

I have always been one of those people who do everything wrong. This is essentially because I am not involved in the march.

Nothing is quite real to me. Streetcars. bombs. bugs. women. light-globes. areas of grass. All unreal. I *am* outside. Death which is *true* enough, even this appears unreal. Not so long ago I was in the charity ward of a hospital in one of our greater cities. This is wording it badly: the whole god damned hospital was a charity ward, a place to crawl around in, a kind of purgatory on earth where the dying are allowed to lay in the stink of their sheets for days and the appearance of a nurse is redemption and the appearance of a doctor is like God Himself. All this is pretty much *outside*. They *do* keep the men and the women in separate wards. This is about all the individuality, all the identity we were allowed to retain: what's left of the gender. [★ ★ ★]

[To Ann Bauman]

October 8, 1962

[★ ★ ★] I have taken a 30 day leave of absence (without pay) from my post office job. The job was driving me mad (if you'll allow a platitude), but I find this time to drink and gamble – think – also leads to madness.

I was 42 on August 16th. That I have lived this long is a true miracle. I cannot hope for many more days. They will catch me. They will get me in their bloody net and I will have done.

I wish Sacramento were around the corner. I am usually – in spite of all doubt and razors and grief – fairly strong, but tonight I would have liked to talk to you. This letter then will have to do – and perhaps tomorrow – t & t & tomorrow – I will be more the hard steel German-Polack who bats out the sounds of living from the top of a beercan.

[To John William Corrington]

October 8, 1962

[★ ★ ★] Yes, the giants are gone and it makes it a little tougher when you stare down at the white paper. Before the death of the giants you used to think, well, they don't expect anything from me anyhow. Now there is this hole and the hole must be filled and we don't know how it will be done or who will do it. But writing is entirely different now. I mean we are raw again. We are beginning again. And it is good this way. Facing the raw. This is what the thing was meant to be. Only it's no longer Left Bank Paris or Carmel or Taos, it is all of us; and some of us, a few of us, will come through. This will be done through force, energy, magic, belief, and a way of living. But it may be, perhaps, that the age of giants is over. This is hard to believe. I'd rather not believe it.[★ ★ ★]

[To John William Corrington]

October [?9], 1962

[★ ★ ★] It might amuse you to know that 'Home from a Room Below the Plains' was written out of an experience I had when I was a mailman one time. Terrible hangover, stupor. I had some letters for this church. Was new on route. Couldn't find mailbox. Wandered into church and down some steps. Dark. I saw a switch on the wall, one of those handle things by a black box. All the lights in the church came on and probably some of the candles too. And there was the priest's cassock and stuff laid out on the table. Very holy looking. I threw the switch back off and wandered around some more. Found a can and took a crap. And almost took a shower. All this time I have this mail sack, dragging it around. Finally came out of there and found the mailbox in the parish house next door. It was one god damned odd experience of many odd experiences and it came out as a poem some years later. So you see, you cannot always tell what a man is writing about, but if you put it down as true as it seems to you, they are apt to take it anyhow. [* * *]

[To John William Corrington]
October 10, 1962

[* * *] you mentioned something in your letter that has been rattling in the dry leaves of my brain – which is, the death-thing which is due me & the fact of your letters being there, which should be seen – someday – by somebody, some people, some something besides myself. And if I go at 1623 or wherever I am, chances are they will simply hustle everything out of here and burn it in order to make room for the next drunken roomer. My only living relatives, an aunt and uncle, have disowned me and I do not leave their address around and since their name is different than mine, they will not be bothered finding a hole for a dead body they detest. This brings us to the letters, and I want to get them out of here before something happens. I was thinking of mailing them to Cuscaden, but somehow, I don't know, something warns me not to. I think I will mail them back to you – if this will not keep you from hanging more sheets in your typer directed to 1623. So, soon you will get a package or 2, and I will be able to die in peace, as they say, will be able to die without picture-aftershadows of pokers and flames punching your good letters to pieces. This is all pretty dark, but it has been hanging over me. Look for them back then. I am going over them again Sunday, and then back to Baton Rouge. I wish I could be yr Boswell but my age, my heath, my drinking, all against me. [* * *]

Yes, you are right. They are putting a lot of light on me right now, and it is the test. There is little doubt that obscurity and aloneness and failure are the agents and angels of the good Art, and I am being tested here, even, in this 1623 place: there are bangs on the door where formerly there were almost none, but just as before, I don't like to answer. Only now they intend to call me 'snob' where before they called me 'nuts.' What they call matters little. I like to think I have been cleaved enough to come through. I should stop writing for 10 more years like I did the other time, but I don't have these kinds of tens left anymore. [★ ★ ★]

Photographs were needed for the Outsider *feature.*

[To Jon Webb]
[?October 15, 1962]

Well, I have been shot. It's all over.

J. phoned and I told him I needed to be shot and J. is a great contact man and he came up with a brother-in-law, one John Stevens who works in a factory and shoots on the side, so over they came from Pasadena, J. and Stevens and J.'s wife and some other young man (I never did quite get where he fit), and they dragged the stuff in, and somebody said, 'This guy doesn't even look like a writer,' which is something I have heard before and before and before. Such as, 'You wouldn't think he was the guy who wrote those poems . . .' Or, 'I don't know, I expected, I expected well, more *fire* out of you.' People have these ideas of what a writer *should* be, and this is set up both by the movies and by the writers themselves. We can't deny that such people as D. H. Lawrence, Hart Crane, Dylan Thomas and so forth had a scabbard of personality that cut down into people. I say or do nothing brilliant. The most brilliant thing I do is to get drunk — which any fool can do. If there is any dramatics in me, it must wait on the Art Form. If there is any ham in me it must wait on the Art Form. If there is any D. H. Lawrence in me it must wait on the A.F. I am pretty much tired and when it comes to playing writer, somebody else will have to do it.

Anyhow, they set the thing up and I got out the beer and J. and his wife talked to me, trying to make me forget the camera, but I'd be a fool to forget the camera, my mind is not that bad. If there were a snake in the room I would not forget the snake in the room. And flick, flick, you could hear the thing going. It is not essentially a happy mood and I kept thinking, this has nothing to do with the poem, this is how men die. Kennedy might phone me any day now and ask me to do a foreword to a campaign speech or something, and I will have to tell him what Frost did not. So flick, flick, more beer, another chair, another shirt, another cigarette, J.'s wife laughing, enjoying it all, like watching a bear poked with a cigarette. Then they stuck me behind the typer and asked me to type and I wrote: 'It is only when I read of suicides that I feel happy at all. To know that there are other votes in that direction.' Flick, flick, there was plenty of beer and plenty of cigarettes and evidently plenty of film. The thing finally ended and I went into the can to piss and then I found we had probably messed up everything. In the beginning, I had scratched the top of my head and here was this floater of hair sticking up on top of my head like a coxcomb or whatever. Everything ruined. Why didn't they tell me? I came out and told them I had a flag on my head but they intended to ignore it. The camera won't.

I got some more beer and we stopped off at J.'s, and here more trouble. I went into J.'s can and when I flushed the thing it ran over and out into the hall. He's been having trouble with the thing and his landlady can't seem to get it fixed and this set J. off. He has the true writer's temperament and he ran down the stairs to fix his teeth in the landlady. I guess he was embarrassed about the toilet (I was too), and maybe the only way sensitive people can override embarrassment is to howl. I do not. When something bad happens I say nothing. What's wrong with me there, I do not know. Anyhow, J. got his teeth in the landlady and a scene spouted up. She came up the stairs crying and had this mop and mopped the floor, and it was funny in a tragic way: here she was with the mop, weeping, poet J. standing over her saying, 'Now, Mrs. M., I think you get simply too *emotional* over these things!' Anyhow, she went weeping down the steps, and J. came in and paced up and down cursing the toilet. He said he liked the view. You can see the whole horrible city of Los Angeles. J. likes to look at it. But he's new in town. I've seen the welts of L.A. too long. I never go to the window. Not to look out at the city. To look at a bird maybe, all right. Anyhow, I guess you can't blame him on the can: when a man wants to piss (or worse) you can't piss in a view. Anyhow, we had another beer and left. I drove Stevens and his friend back to Pasadena, a city I am not too familiar with. My night was not over. When I left them out they said, 'You see that blue light down there?' I told them I saw that blue light down there. They said, friend, when you get there, turn right. You'll hit the freeway in about 2 or 3 miles. Well, I never did find the freeway. Maybe it was because I was too busy looking for a liquor store. It was about one thirty a.m. and they close at 2. But in Pasadena they close about 10 p.m.

My old man said 30 years ago, 'Pasadena is a one-horse town.' It was one of the few times he was on beam. And it still goes today.

To make it worse I got lost. I drove and drove and drove. And everything was closed. Gas stations, everything. Cafes, everything. On the largest boulevards there was not a single person on the streets. Just signal lights, street corners, and no direction signs and if there were direction signs they only said Arcadia and I had no idea where Arcadia was. I kept driving almost under a sense of panic. I get into these things time and time again. I got to thinking of Kafka, how he wrote about going into these buildings, one room after another, being shuffled and buffoned [*sic*] about, nothing making any sense. I am sure if Kafka had been driving with me this night he would have had another novel. Panic, sure, all you want is a bed and a cool beer and here you are driving in a peopleless world of smooth and efficient streets that only lead you further and further away and you can't stop because this would then be real panic, you understand? I kept driving, and then it became really nightmare. I ended up in the hills! A small road going up into the hills and over one of the hills I saw a thing that looked like a Chinese temple. Jesus Christ, Jon, I was in Tibet! And sure enough, halfway through the hills here was this kind of Chinese village-inn type of thing, but no people, just these Chinese signs, and I began to feel as if I were going mad and I swung around the village driveway and shot back down out of the hills the way I came.

I must have driven an hour more, seeing no one, getting nowhere, backtracking, turning, going North, South, East, West. Then I saw a human being. He had one of these gas trucks and was running gas into a gas station. I asked him, 'How do I get to L.A.?' 'Whereabouts you want to get in L.A.?' he asked. 'I don't care *where*,' I told him, 'just show me the city hall.' 'Well, buddy,' he said, 'you are going in the wrong direction. Just turn around and follow this street straight on in.' That simple.

But going back, I got found, I recognized some of the streets leading to Santa Anita racetrack and I was on my own route back home. I can get you to any racetrack from California to Mexico but don't ask me where anything else is at.

I got to my sweet room, full of empty beercans and bottles and I went to the refrigerator. Luck. There sat one chilled and lovely glass bottle of Miller's. I drank that and went to bed.

And that was the night of the photos. I hope something comes out of it because I don't think I can go through with it again. Not this year, anyhow. I mean, other people can do these things easily. Me, I'm a frog on a dissection table. I guess that's why I write. They keep cutting me open. It's nothing profound, but so odd. And all these photos with this hunk of hair standing up on my head. I can't even walk across a room with success. This morning I stepped on a can opener that was on the floor. No shoes on, of course. Another minor tragedy. Yet the spirit is not suicidal. I tend to linger just to see how many more odd turns the gods can throw on me. I suppose somebody will tell me I need the couch. Well, we all need the couch. Don't tell me that with our Berlin walls and our stockpiles that our part of the universe is healthy and makes sense. If I need the couch they had better start building a lot of couches. I won't deny that I might be somewhat off, don't get me wrong But if you are going to try to show me a leader or a way out, I am going to ask a lot of questions.

Anyhow Stevens is supposed to phone me about the pictures. He has them in Pasadena and is going to put them into the soup. And I guess I am supposed to – ha, ah ha, ha, ha!!! – drive over and pick them up!

I will airmail them if I ever get to Pasadena and back again, and if you use any of them, I do wish you would give him a line: Photo or photos by John Stevens. Something like that.

Well, Jon, that's how it went. I tried. Only wish my hair had been combed. Do you figure this ever happened to Hem or Willie the Faulk? I guess not. Going out to mail this now, get some beer and some sleep. To hell with the world's series. I couldn't sleep last night – steaming about the cockscomb.

[To Jon Webb]
Wednesday [?October 17, 1962]

[* * *] Tired today, from horses and other things, but hope to have a prof. photog up here tomorrow or Friday, and chances are he'll have a better camera and know-how. That is, if I don't go mad, or just don't fall through the floorboards. This picture-taking has some semblance of horror in it to me. I go through the same thing whenever I get a haircut. And sometimes the bastards will spin you in the chair and show you yourself in the mirror. God. [* * *]

. . . I have all these letters Corrington has sent me, and I began to worry a while back when I was not feeling so good mentally and physically. I might have to get them off my hands and may ship them back through you and have Bill pick them up when he sees you. There is kind of an ivory-carved quality to most of these letters and they are much better than his poems. In the poem he still sometimes has this E.E. thing mixed with Auden plus a kind of hysterical abstract and fancy glibness. When the letters catch up to the poems (and I think they will) — I mean when the letters become the poems — they can't catch them, being past them, Corrington will be a poet to listen to. He's getting better now, which is much better than laying still. His politics and outlook a little too far right of center but this is the Southern Aristocrat somewhat, and doesn't mean he lacks heart. Anyhow, if some day you get a pack of Corrington letters, I know you are busy, but flip through a few and hold the pack for Willie. They make the Miller letters look like burnt apple pie. [★ ★ ★]

[To John William Corrington]
October 28, 1962

[★ ★ ★] Well, I had a quote from Pascal written on a piece of paper which I was going to write down here. But now I have lost the little piece of paper which is not as bad as losing a good piece of ass but what I mean is that you would understand the quote but not need it.[★ ★ ★] Anyhow, to put the Pascal into my own words — : Only things done in quietude secure and holy, without direct aim at fame or applause, are worth more than the applesauce shit of a turkey.

[To John William Corrington]
November [?15], 1962

WE KEEP GETTING BACK at this argument about the novel. It is like being married. There is this thing that is always hanging there, and, BANG!, you've always got an argument about the same thing.

You keep telling me that (in essence) a great writer makes a great novel and we don't want to knock the thing because so many people fail with it. BUT I WILL TRY ONCE MORE. god damn. What I am saying is that this is not the TIME for the novel. Now, I don't want to bring in the bomb. It's there. But let's forget most of about the bomb. Yet it is this and it is something else. It is in the air. IT IS NOW WRONG somehow to write a novel. Don't ask for proof. Don't ask for reason. I am, let's say, an old whammy woman in a tar shack killing chickens and drinking their blood or whatever and sticking the feathers in my ears. I only sense that this ass-time 1962 is simply not the time. DON'T SHORT-CHANGE ME. I KNOW THAT ART TAKES PRECE-DENCE. I know that a lion can be gorging a good man's balls and that he can go right ahead while he's still living and paint that madonna or what-ever is bothering him with ice cream and taffy. This is not the point. The point is that this is not the time. For the novel. Do not ask me how I know this or why or how. I cannot tell you.

bill bailey, won't you please come home?

If you can swing the thing with ROMAN BOOKS for our letters for $150 or $300 or for 50 cents, go ahead, swing. It has been a hard year. I am backed down to a hard-caked dirt. We've got plenty of time (maybe) to write more letters but the time for selling may be too late. Or maybe too soon. Then I don't know if you are kidding or not.[★ ★ ★]

I am glad Nixon got pole-axed here in Calif. That man's face has been bothering me for a long time. It is a face of power. It is a face that attempts to say one thing in order to get by and yet it means something else alto-gether, and if you are one of the boys you know what it means and you put your hand under the tablecloth and you got it made and fuck the rest. I'm glad he's going back to lawyer. That's where he belongs. Pal with the judge, and fooling his clients. If he ever comes into a place to eat where I am washing dishes, I will take his dishes and cups and saucers and break them with quiet languor and then have a gentle pull from the wine bottle.[★ ★ ★]

[To Ann Bauman]
[November 22, 1962]

[★ ★ ★] No, I am not feeling better. I need an operation for one of my maladies but don't know if I have either the guts or the time for it. I never get splendid clean diseases that you can talk about over a cup of tea, like heart attack, stroke, amnesia, etc., but instead, ulcers and hemorrhages, madness, boils, ingrown toenails, rotten teeth, and now hemorrhoids, which, my dear, is a malady of the ass. [★ ★ ★]

It is more than difficult for me to survive. My present job has me by the throat and I don't know how much more I can take. I have no special

trade and am getting old. It will all end somewhere down the line: an old
dirty demolished German pig, sitting on a doorstep looking in the sand
for a razor.

Life is for achievement? Even Hegel's achievements are paling. See
how we waste? Life is avoidance of pain until death. Life is finding that
love between 2 people only goes one way. One is always the master, the
other the slave. Life is Tuesday afternoon in a cage. I do not like to talk
about life. It gets silly. It sounds silly. Death is the master. [* * *]

---

*Jim Roman, a dealer in modern first editions, operated from Fort Lauderdale.
He was to publish Corrington's* The Anatomy of Love *in 1964.*

[To John William Corrington]
November [?24], 1962

Well, your letters are enclosed in case you want to swing with Fort
Lauderdale or however it's spelled. Maybe a publisher might pick them up
in this way. They are no less than great. There must be something about the
letter-form that allows a man to become looser and freer. Perhaps in the
poem we pack too much on-stage stuff.

I'm not sure all of them are here – the introductory ones aren't. How
was I to know? Anyhow, good stuff, you are wide of soul and lay down a
pliable law.

I hope you write me some more. Viva Villa!

[*In holograph with the preceding*:]

I return herewith the letters of yours I could find. Maybe some day one of
us gets famous and some fool wd pay $ for these, and since you and I did
not do them for $, the laugh's all on the swine and the readers. Even if they
don't ever 'make it' anywhere they have made it

    here

       with me.

Guys like Roman go bugs over this stuff, mainly because he's trying to
beat lit. history before it happens – which is intriguing but dangerous. I
would pretty much bet that Corso, Ginsberg, etc. will not be around after

they are gone awhile. When you go up fast, you usually come down that way. I think it is the pleasurable simple workman (not Bukowski) who will hold his ground. But who gives a damn???

> we are here now
> (for what we know is a short time).

and here are your letters

> gracious godly friend
> kid,

they are good, very,

> and your praise
> and sticking stilts
> under an old man
> when hardly anyone wuz,

this was a nice gift,
and as I sit here tonight
mailing these letters back to you,
let me say

> that

they were not
will not be
can never have been

> wasted.

[To Jon Webb]
November 25, 1962

[* * *] Very little new out here. Just difficult to believe you are working on this Outsider of Year thing about me. I keep thinking of a certain paper shack I ended up once in in Atlanta without light, heat, food, typewriter or drink. A most cold, most dark end. Yow. I have slept on park benches in the warm parts of the country and there seemed air and light and easiness, but somehow this was so closed and finished. My ass was really in the trap, the first gilded shape of hell reaching out. I did have a pencil and I sat there in the dark daytime ice writing things on the edges, the margins of old newspapers that I found on the floor. How I got out of there I don't remember, but I did and I left the writing there. It was quite mad, most of it, I guess. Now I have 3 collections of poetry, have been

photographed by imbeciles, and you are giving me the honor and light of the O. of Y. award, almost as if much of my misery had been recorded right along as it happened. So many of our writers now have teaching positions, they teach the thing they do, and it's no wonder the writing has no lumps, no rawness. But in spite of this, I am sure that right now there is some poor bastard freezing-starving somewhere, writing sonnets on toilet paper. Not all of us can go through the college degree teaching bit. We cannot jump through the hoops; no wiseness in practical sense of survival. If an English teacher can write, good enough for me. You don't have to be thrown into half a hundred drunk tanks to be shaken into or out of life. But there is something about their lives that is too safe, too pat. Their intrigues of the day are political, bitchy and petty, feminine. Very few of them come to class drunk. They know what they are doing, even when they sit down to a typewriter. Corrington seems to have escaped much of this but I keep thinking they will get him. [★ ★ ★]

[To Ann Bauman]
Late November, 1962

[★ ★ ★] Kafka, unlike your Henry James, was not ordinarily intelligent and discerning. Kafka was a god damned petty clerk who lived a good damned [*sic*] petty life and wrote about it, the dream of it, the madness of it. There is one novel where a man enters this house, this establishment, and it appears that from the viewpoint of others that he is guilty of something but he does not know what. He is shuffled from room to room, endlessly, to the rattle of papers and bureaucracy, a silent simmering horrible living dream of ordinary mad and pressing, senseless everyday life. Most of his books are on this order: the shadow, the dream, the stupidity. Then there are other things – where a man turns into a bridge and lets people walk across him. Then there is another where a man gradually turns into a giant cockroach ('The Metamorphosis') and his sister feeds him as he hides under the bed. Others, others. Kafka is everything.

Forget Henry James. James is a light mist of silk. Kafka is what we all know. [★ ★ ★]

Corrington was to publish one of the first critical articles on Bukowski in Northwest Review, *1963.*

[To John William Corrington]
November 29, 1962

[★ ★ ★] If you are going to article me, all right, but I don't know what the poems mean, so maybe I better find out. And then, for all your work, tend to ignore it. What I mean is this. When I write the poem it is only fingers on typewriter, something smacking down. It is that moment then, the walls, the weather of that day, the toothache, the hangover, what I ate, the face I passed, maybe a night 20 years ago on a park bench, an itch on the neck, whatever, and you get a poem – maybe. I don't know much what you can say about these poems. 'Old Man, Dead in a Room' is my future, 'The Tragedy of the Leaves' is my past, and 'The Priest and the Matador' is a dawdling in between. But I'd rather have it in your hands than anybody I know. You jab well, carry a good right, are younger than Archie for sure, and you can't be bought for a tankjob. [★ ★ ★]

[To Jon and Louise Webb]
November 30, 1962

[★ ★ ★] Yes, disgusting the rent they charge of a dive in the business districts of anywhere, and the landlord doesn't have to do anything but sit back and take it in while you hope to make it – somehow. Hang on, you're getting an *award* too, somewhere, somehow; this is lit. history like *Poetry* when Ez was European editor and full of beans, or even like Mencken's *Mercury*; or *Dial*; but you are essentially the new center and the part of this age, only people never realize the blood sweat weariness disgust breakdown & trial of soul that goes into it; and the puking little criticisms of milk-white jackasses. [★ ★ ★]

Federman was coeditor of Mica, *the last issue of which appeared in November 1962. Bukowski's story, 'Murder,' was published not in* Mica *but in* Notes *from Underground, no. 1 (1964). Dorbin records no earlier story in* Mica, *although one was published in* Canto *(Los Angeles), winter 1961.*

[To Raymond Federman]
December 6, 1962

Rec. your O.K. on 'The Murder.' I write very few short stories–you've taken the only 2 I have written in years. Both of them were very close to a type of personal experience and feeling that just did not seem to fit into the shorter poem-form.

You might call 'The Murder' a prose-poem as I have worked with the poem so long that when I do try the story-form I still feel as if I were laying down the poem-line.

It might interest you to know that over drinks and in conversational lulls with the few odd people that get in here I have told the story of 'The Murder,' first telling them what made me write it, what was happening to me at the time, and how I took this and made it into a story – or whatever it is.

Their comment at the finish was usually, 'Jesus Christ!,' which I took more as a criticism than a vindication.

[To John William Corrington]
December 13, 1962

Dear South ribbon talking pure word:

Yes, it is terrible, this essence of spotlight. You carve a thing in a cobweb room maybe when you are not feeling so good and feeling a little crazy, spitting flecks of blood out through a broken tooth where somebody hammered you when you were too drunk to see it coming or too drunk to care . . . you carve a thing and then somebody sees it and runs down the hall with it and shows it to the other roomers. You are running behind him, you need a shave and a fresh pair of socks and 2 or 3 operations to get the tigers out from inside of you. And he is hollering, holding this thing you've done up in the air, he is hollering, 'Hey! *Hey*! Looka this thing *Smitty* did! Who'da thunk Smitty'd do a THING like *this*? Jesus, jesus, looky, LOOKY!'

And, South, as you know, then, 9 times outa ten, no, more than that . . . you're fucked. That night some old well preserved gal will tap on your door and give you the thing she has been saving for some ivory god. Little girls will slip notes under your door at night. The milkman will show you some thing he has carved out of wax on cold nights. The worshipers will sob and tremble for the hairs from your razor. You're fucked. You sit down to scratch things on another brick with a can opener . . . and what is it? hmm . . . must be something wrong with the brick? Or maybe the opener's dull? . . . Now, let's see . . . HOW DID I DO THAT OTHER ONE? They SURE liked that OTHER ONE. Let's see . . . I think I was thinking of birds with their feet frozen to phone wires in Texas, awakening in the morning, stuck there, slicing God's air with wings, stuck, stuck, and then tired sick falling upside down, and frozen in the cold air that way . . . the end of a lunatic life. Yeah, *that's* what I was thinking . . . and then I put in the eyes . . . and the nose . . . and . . . And then there's a knock and a man with prince nez, princ nez?, he wants to know the color of the house you were born in. And then behind him stands the old gal with the thing for ivory gods again. And then . . .

Let me say that the spotlight Jon puts on me I accept with honor from the German blood that unpollutes the Polack in me; I cannot deny this: I still play with the old words: honor, truth. That I am pretty well pulled to pieces by the spiders of the world does not affect me, I hope it does not god damn effect [*sic*] me, in this sense. Anyhow, I still like to play with bluebirds and old dreams among the toy cannon. I go my way, antiquated and ruined. [★ ★ ★]

[To Ann Bauman]
[Tuesday] December 18, 1962

Terrible happenings. Got drunk Sunday night and thrown in jail. Must see judge on Wednesday. Fell and twisted ankle – swollen now, might be broken. Missed 2 days work. Judge might give me 120 days. This is not first offense. Will mean loss of job, of course.

Have been laying here in horrible fit of depression. My drinking days are over. This is too much. Jail is a horrible place. I almost go mad there.

I don't know what is going to become of me. I have no trade, no future. Sick, depressed, blackly, heavily depressed.

Write me something. Maybe a word from you will save me.

[To Jon Webb]
[December 19, 1962]

I lucked it. Easy judge. Nobody got a day all the time I was in court, but all fined. A good 40 or 50 appeared ahead of me. Jail might be full. Christmas. Whatever. [★ ★ ★]

Don't be angry, Jon, but there are very few editors holding my recent stuff, so I can't write them. And the other stuff, the older stuff has *disappeared* and I don't keep records and/or carbons so it's pretty much lost. I've dropped 200-to-300 poems this way since 1955, and I used to try to get some of these poems back, the larger batches of 20 or 40 that I remembered anyhow, but I have found that the elongated keepers of poems or destroyers of poems WITHOUT EXCEPTION do not respond to polite and reasonable inquiry with proper stamped self-addressed envelope enclosed. There is a mucky dismal breed out there . . . unmoral, immoral unscrupulous . . . homos, hounds, sadists; curious, blank children; blood-drinkers . . .

And then some people wonder why I write an occasional anti-editor poem. You and Gypsy are a pair of the few editors I know who operate in a professional and straight manner, and the gods have been more than good to me in that you have seen some light in some of my work and are handing me this OUTSIDER OF YEAR shining tray of honor, plus the book.

[To Jon and Louise Webb]
[December 21, 1962?]

Got to thinking about the telephone call the other night, and how you weren't going to mention this or that, and well, I think pretty slowly, but I hope now, thinking it over, that you aren't going to make a white rabbit outa me. I've got nothing to hide. Feel free. It's a person's eccentricities that give him whatever he has. Don't be too cautious with excerpts from letters, except I agree with you that mentioning a name directly (false initials will do) might be bad taste, especially if that person has very little literary standing. If he has literary standing, use the name and the hell with it. I hope this does not get to you too late. That I drink or play the ponies or have been in jail is of no shame to me.

As you can see, I have recovered from my depression [★ ★ ★]

[To John William Corrington]
December 24, 1962

[★ ★ ★] Don't keep urging me to leave the City of the Angels, this beautiful fucking place where Saints jack off in the sky. I am beholden. Look, kid, I don't got no trade, savvy? Here maybe there are a couple of race tracks I got the smell of, and I know where the rescue missions are located, and it only gets cold at night, and there are a couple of places where maybe they will let me sleep on the floor or drop me a dollar from a hardshell hand. I traveled until I was almost cuckoo, from 19 to 28. I saw it. Sometimes I weighed 200 pounds, other times, 128. I saw that there was nothing. I saw the South like a gourd of light, with dryslab faces and poverty, history running like shit from the walls and everybody burning to poke you down. You, Willie, are a good kind of South, but there's another kind of South too, and you know it. But no better or worse than New York or Chi or Philly. But to go running off through the same scene would be like taking a dose of salts after a good bowel movement. Here in L.A. they leave you alone. You lay dead in a room for 5 or 6 days and it's not until you begin to stink or fail to pay your rent that they come in and drag you out. This has advantages if you are not heavy in love with the roving tribes. Here I've just got phantoms and a dirty floor from my own feet. Peace, cousin. [★ ★ ★]

. . . On the poems about Jane, I *kept* copies, sent them out somewhere . . . As to the poems I put *in* the letters, that is what they are for, the letters, and I do not save these poems or intend them for publication. If I can't spare a couple off the elbow, then what the hell's the use?

No, Jane doesn't leave. Some deaths won't. They are imbedded, fingered in the brain forever. And the life comes back, scores of life like an old movie. I've wanted to write this story but it's too big for me. I am weak and let it go. [★ ★ ★]

[To Jon and Louise Webb]
December 27, 1962

Got your six page letter which I read through a couple of times while drinking a Miller's, and the sun's out good, but it's cold & I have a heater on and the stove on, and somehow there's a feeling of peace today – I feel like a fat man who ate a lot of turkey, and since this feeling does not arrive too often, I take it, I take of the good of it without examining it, without feeling selfish. That's what good about being 42: you know when to go with what's left of the soul. I spent Xmas in bed asleep. I hate to go out on the streets on Xmas day. The fuckers act like they are out of their minds. They strain at the thing; round-eyed and hacked-out they drive through red lights, they look at each other and say things but they don't know what they're saying: their mouths have long ago been cut out and thrown away. Christmas, to most of them, is like owning a new car. They've got to do it. They don't have the guts – or the sense – to pass it up. Enough. Did I say I was feeling at peace? [★ ★ ★]

[To Jon Webb]
[December 28, 1962]

No, as to title, I don't care for *Naked in the Womb* or the *Alcatraz* one. When I said you think up title, I was only thinking in terms of a *summary* title such as *Selected Poems* or etc. As to the *other* type of title, I don't think it would be fair for you to submit titles any more than it would be fair for you to put one of your poems in there under my name. Surely, you understand this? I have been trying to think up a *summary* title, but if you want a straight title, I will send you a half dozen or so in a day or two. I'm glad this came up. Please do not use one of your titles that is *not* a summary title (such as *Collected Poems, Selected Poems*) as this would take the heart out of me. I will be strictly dreaming titles from here on in, say like *Beer and Frogs Legs* or *I Can't Stand the Sunshine When People Walk Around in It* or *For Jocks, Chambermaids, Thieves and Bassoon Players*. I almost like the last one. It carries summation plus the rest. Yes. [★ ★ ★] or *Tonic for the Mole*. Meaning these type of poems for those who duck out to the world, ya know. or *Minstrels Would Go Crazy Singing This*. [★ ★ ★]

Know it cost you money to have your man work on photos but glad he perked up a couple. I cannot get over the nightmare of those photos, and maybe some day I can write about it, but it's still too close. [★ ★ ★]

· 1963 ·

The title settled on is a phrase taken from a poem by Robinson Jeffers.
Permission to use it had to be obtained from Random House.

[To Jon and Louise Webb]
January 2, 1963

christ, I'm glad you liked the title (*It Catches My Heart in Its Hands*),
and yes I'm sending book (this piece 'Such Counsel You Gave to Me') to
you [★ ★ ★], and no, I'm *not* going to change my mind, THAT'S IT, and so if
you are going to or have set up an ad using title, fine. Also glad you and
Louise have accepted dedication. I have been worried about both ends of
this: title and dedication, and now all's well. [★ ★ ★]

No, I don't know how many copies of each of the 3 earlier books
there were. Although I believe Cuscaden (*Run With*) mentioned 200, and
I believe *Longshots* around 200 too. On Griffith (*Flower, Fist*), I don't know,
and also, he doesn't answer his mail. [★ ★ ★]

Must say again, very glad you went for title and dedication. Yes, the
title is in my head too. It says so god damned much. Jeffers, when he got
good, he got very good. There were these long periods when he flattened
out and had a tendency to preach his ideals of rock & hawk, but when he
did get the word down . . . he got it down in a way, that to me, made our
other contemporaries or newly deads seem not so much. [★ ★ ★]

p.s. – my photo on cover only another miracle on miracle that has been
occurring. It does not seem too long ago that I was considering the blade.
If I never write another decent poem it's your fault, Jon. I've got my alibi
ready.

[To Jon and Louise Webb]

January 6, 1963

[★ ★ ★] I am glad on Corrington for intro. He knows me – and my work – better than anyone, and he possesses the style and manner to do a patrical job. (I wanted to say 'pat' but it looked like 'pot,' so I changed it to patrical, whatever that means.) Anyhow, Corrington's the only one, and his own writing is improving. His lines seem clearer and harder – he sent me a poem called *Communion*. It has a holy edge and fervor, quite good. Quite. [★ ★ ★]

Photo of Sandburg in *This Week* holding little girl on his knee and underneath poem about death. Death is hush, says the old boy. Well, I guess so. Only I wish he'd crop or comb that sickly flange of white hair that looks like a wig. If I EVER get that old, they'll find me under the bed drunk

with the Racing Form AND

a big OLD girl. [★ ★ ★]

Roman Books, run by Jim Roman in Fort Lauderdale, Florida, published in 1963 a ground-breaking catalogue called ' "The Outsiders": a collection of first editions by avant-garde and "beat" generation authors of prose and poetry since World War Two.' Bukowski is giving his approval to Jon Webb's sale of manuscripts to the dealer.

[To Jon and Louise Webb]

January 7, 1963

[★ ★ ★] On ROMAN BOOKS, I understand. In your position, why not? Someday when you are gone they will talk about the force and vitality of the *Outsider* in mid–20th century literature, and how you stood in front of that press feeding it your blood and your hours and your life. It will very *very* romantic *then*. But now? Shit, nobody ever cares about NOW. They are always looking *back*. They moon for the pain of Mozart or Lorca bulleted in the road. But there are always new Mozarts and Lorcas, new *Poetry* Chicagos, new *Blasts*, new *Brooms*, etc. If you can swing a buck from ROMAN for a few wilted manus in order to go on, hell, do it. YOU ARE LIVING NOW. If you have any manus you want me to sign, ship them here, I will sign and return. Ink is cheap. [★ ★ ★]

[To John William Corrington]
January 14, 1963

[★ ★ ★] my cock average size but mostly out of action lately, desire there still, but price too high, trouble too much, I do not search like a highschool boy, and some night finally it is there, or at a motel outside Del Mar track in August it is there, and then it is gone, the color of the dress I remember, some words spoken, but the act is really secondary, they have hung the cock on me, I have dipped, but really, the walls are large.

Born Andernach, Germany August 16th, 1920. German mother, father with American Army (Pasadena born but of German parentage) of Occupation. There is some evidence that I was born, or at least conceived out of wedlock, but I am not sure. American at age of 2. Some year or so in Washington, D.C., but then on to Los Angeles. The Indian suit thing true. All grotesques true. Between the imbecile savagery of my father, the disinterestedness of my mother, and the sweet hatred of my playmates: 'Heinie! Heinie! Heinie!' things were pretty hot all around. They got hotter when I was in my 13th years on, I broke out not with acne, but with these HUGE boils, in my eyes, neck, back, face, and I'd ride the streetcar to the hospital, the charity ward, the old man was not working, and there they'd drill me with the electric needle, which is kind of a wood drill that they stick into people. Stayed out of school a year. Went to L.A. City College a couple of years, journalism. Tuition fee was two dollars but the old man said he couldn't afford to send me anymore. I went to work in the railroad yards, scrubbing the sides of trains with OAKITE. I drank and gambled at night. Had a small room above a bar on Temple Street in the Filipino district, and I gambled at night with the aircraft workers and pimps and etc. My place got to be known and every night it was packed. It was hell getting my sleep. One night I hit big. Big for me. 2 or 3 hundred. I knew they'd be back. Got in a fight, broke a mirror and a couple of chairs but held onto the money and early in the morning caught a bus for New Orleans. Some young gal on there made a play for me, and I let her off at Fort Worth but got as far as Dallas and swung back. Wasted some time there and made N.O. Roomed across from THE GANGPLANK CAFE and began writing. Short stories. Drank the money up, went to work in a comic book house, and soon moved on. Miami Beach. Atlanta. New York. St. Louis. Philly. Frisco. L.A. again. New Orleans again. Then Philly again. Then Frisco again L.A. again. Around and around. A couple of nights in East Kansas City. Chicago. I stopped writing. I concentrated on drinking. My longest stays were in Philly. I would get up early in the morning and go to a bar there and I would close that bar at night. How I made it, I don't know. Then finally back to L.A. and a wild shack job of seven years drinking. Ended up in same charity hopsital. This time not with boils but with my stomach torn open finally with rot gut and agony. 8 pints of blood and 7 pints of glucose transfused in without a stop. My whore came to see me and she was drunk. My old man was with her. The old man gave me a lot of lip and the whore was nasty too, and I told the old man, 'Just one more word out of you and I'm going to yank this needle outa my arm, climb off this deathbed and whip your ass!' They left. I came out of there, white and old, in love with sunlight, told never to drink again or death would be mine. I found among changes in myself, that my memory which was once pretty good was now bad. Some brain damage, no doubt, they let me lay there a couple of days in the charity ward when my papers got lost and the papers called for immediate transfusions, and I was out of blood, listening to hammers against my brain. Anyhow, I got on a mail truck and drove it around and delivered letters and drank lightly, experimentally, and then one night I sat down and began writing poetry. What a hell of a thing. Where to send this stuff. Well, I took a shot. There was a magazine called *Harlequin* and I was a fucking clown and it was out in some small town in Texas and maybe they wouldn't know bad stuff when they saw it, so — . There was a gal editor there, and the poor dear went wild. Special edition. Letters followed. The letters got warm. The letters got hot. Next thing I knew the gal editor was in Los Angeles. Next thing I knew we were in Las Vegas for marriage. Next thing I knew I was walking in a small Texas town with the local hicks glaring at me. The gal had money. I didn't know she had money. Or her folks had money. We went back to L.A. and I went back to work, somewhere.

The marriage didn't work. It took 3 years for her to find out that I was not what she had thought I was supposed to be. I was anti-social, coarse, a drunkard, didn't go to church, played horses, cursed when intoxicated, didn't like to go anywhere, shaved carelessly, didn't care for her paintings or her relatives, sometimes stayed in bed 2 or 3 days running etc. etc.

Very little more. I went back to my whore who had once been such a cruel and beautiful woman, and who was no longer beautiful (as such) but who had, magically, become a warm and real person, but she could not stop drinking, she drank more than I, and she died.

There is not much left now. I drink mostly alone and discourage company. People seem to be talking about things that don't count. They are too eager or too vicious or too obvious.

I hope this clears up some things and that I have not Ferlinghettied you. I can tell you things that happened like this and it takes nothing away because it is only a LISTING in a sense, and what happened, the living of it, it is still there. I have played some bad lutestrings and taken some knocks in the head, but it was the only way, there was only one path.

As to the other, I like the EARLY Hemingway, and like the rest of us, was affected somewhat by T.S. and Auden, but not so much in a sense of *content*, but in a clean and easy way of saying. I like Wagner and Beethoven, Klee and Stravinsky, Rachmaninoff and rabbits. This is all pretty common, I realize. So is breathing. Then too, there's Darius Milhaud, Verdi, Mussorgsky, Smetana, Shostakovich, Schumann, Bach, Massenet, Ernst von Dohnanyi, Menotti, Gluck, Mahler, Bruckner, Franck, Gounod, Handel and Zoltan Kodaly. Brahms and Tchaikovsky somehow become less and less to me. In Jeffers, I like the longer works, where the style is almost prose, but where everything is hard brick and breaking, where everything is up against the knife and very real. Jeffers almost admires his non-thinking man-brutes as opposed to etc. . . . that gives his work the touch of truth. He writes believably and the pages are in your hands like warm things, difficult to believe that type and machine also put them together. As to contemporaries, they do not do much for me. I do not mean the poets still living who have stopped writing, I mean those living now and writing now. I canont see much. A great alikeness. A carefulness. What a stinking age! What a set of ass-lickers.

Enough of that. [★ ★ ★]

Got a letter from Germany today from some Heinie telling me that he has translated 'Candidate Middle' and 'The Life of Borodin' and that they will be used in a radio feature. This calls for cold chills all around. I, who can no longer speak or understand the language of my birthplace, will be going back into my own tongue from the place I left. This is some kind of magic, like black horses turned loose and running on a hill. [★ ★ ★]

Weekend shot. Sherman haggling with Norman Mosher who studies under T. Roethke. Real bitter stuff. I have long ago said that I do not care for the poets. I would like to see one once in a while with a little self-doubt instead of this cockiness and the unsheathing of the nails. I am just about now getting over it. People climb into my mind, kick around, piss around, and it takes some time for them to leave.

69

. . . a part of the ankle will not go down. I will be the club-ankle poet. Lord Byron, make way!

I told Jon to let you have your head in the intro. If you want to go long, go long; if you want to go short, go short. It is a tough job at best. But you must know that I am honored to have you for my barker: 'And now, ladies and gentlemen, we give you – ,' and Bukowski steps out from behind the tent flap with 3 red hairs on his chest, and can of beer in one hand and a German shepherd pup in the other.

Keep your bones in good motion, kid, and quietly consume and digest what is necessary. I think it is not so much important to build a literary thing as it is not to hurt things. I think it is important to be quiet and in love with park benches; solve whole areas of pain by walking across a rug.

you got it.

dip the brush in turpentine,

p.s. – I asked Webb not to send proofs of the section. I'd rather see it all at once, quietly with a cold beer audience. And maybe think of other days & bad days to come, like all this is well, but the wall will be coming down. [★ ★ ★]

Arnold Kaye's interview appeared in Literary Times *for March 1963, under the title, 'Charles Bukowski Speaks Out.'*

[To Jon and Louise Webb]
[?February 1963]

Enclosed copy of *Literary Times*. I might suggest when book comes out you send them a review copy. Arnold Kaye over last night to interview me, I suppose a la Ben Hecht. He gave me the old bullshit about me being a legend, and he had a list of questions. I was fairly drunk and don't remember what I told him. Some of the questions rather vapid like: 'What effect does Mickey Mouse have on the American public and culture?' I don't know if they are going to run the interview; I might have been fairly bitter and vulgar. The guy had just come from Zahn's where Curtis had babbled on and on, I am told. At least I kept it short and hot. Anyhow, what with the horses and interviews and the bottle and being a LEGEND . . . I have not written any poetry lately, and this is how we go down the drain:

doing everything but creating. There are enough traps in this world to kill a man before he becomes five years old.

At any rate I had sense enough to turn down an invite to be on a panel thing on the radio with Zahn and Kay and some editors. J. B. May etc. I still believe in more privacy and less talk. Badly hung over today but I see no broken furniture and my knuckles are not bruised so there was no fight. Good. May told this guy, 'Bukowski's kind of unfriendly.' These people don't understand that the living takes time and that the talking about it is unnecessary. You do. I think that when they knock on your door you feel the same way I do. That's why we pretty much get along.

Anyhow, going now.

I think the bastard took my pen.

[To John William Corrington]
February 19, 1963

[★ ★ ★] It seemed to me the man in Camus' *Stranger* showed more courage than the Hemingway man because his courage was a courage of acceptance rather than defiance. With Hem victory or at least a good defeat seemed reasonable. With Camus – this did not matter. Or so I gather, having heard a few chapters over the radio (*The Stranger*). I could not be this type of Camus because I could not accept everything in order to dismiss it, or ignore it, or play at rot. Somewhere between Hem and Camus I stand, or sit this morning, sick, pale, white, old. Tomorrow it might be better. [★ ★ ★]

[To Jon and Louise Webb]
Early March, 1963

[★ ★ ★] As to dedication of book to you, Lou, it is all pretty simple. When I heard you over the phone and you did not give me a bunch of literary doubletalk, accent, etc. etc. – your complete sense of *un*falsity, this led me to suggest the dedication to you. This, plus the fact that it being the first book in your series (you and Jon: *Loujon*), it seemed in a sense of history – and literary history is the only one that seems to have some sense – the only dedication. As to being on cover with you, great, but it does not seem real, it is a conjecture sort of thing and I will not know it, really, until the magazine is in my hand and I stand here in this room with it and something in my head says, it happened. I will have a drink on it, a good scotch and water, and I will think of myself down in the alleys again or in all the rooming houses in hell, and the jails, freezing, madness etc., and it will come through to me good. You know, for all this, I still feel pretty much outside of everything yet. It is as if, any moment, somebody is going to knock on my door and a couple of guys are going to enter some day, 'All right, friend, we've come to cut off your arms.' Psychologically speaking, there might be a reason or a term for this, but we do not live with reason or terms, unfortunately. [★ ★ ★]

[To Jon and Louise Webb]
March 17, 1963

starting to thunder . . . like a dark closet in here, but I've still got #3 to my right here, and I hope you people understand why I did not phone upon rec. copy, but rather wrote. The phone calls have been mostly when I was pretty high, and a sense of madness there, and yet not. Anyway, what I am trying to say is that on the phone the voice does not say as much what the mind is thinking as the typewriter does. Somewhere the thought in coming down from the mind and out into the voice, the thought becomes dispelled, distorted, petty and so forth. So, upon rec. #3, I thought it best to WRITE about it rather than TALK about it. Anyway, as I said, my section was done with a good, sure hand, a beautiful hand, and better and gentler and cleaner than I might have dreamed. . . . but this, mainly to say I've gone on reading more of #3, after getting Bukowski out of the way, and GOD!!! ya really laid the whip on Creeley!!! What you say I agree with, find true, but I'm afraid that as many teeth as you put into him I'd havta add another: CREELEY CAN'T WRITE, nor can the rest of them. They affect to write, and out of this affectation, of course, they need powers, groups, blather, underground lines, handshakes, imputations, delegations and barkers to make the thing go. However, I'm glad you took a swing at them: they need a spanking, these little pricks in their walking shorts and mountain cabins and goats and money and teaching positions. They are fondled enough by society without the rest of us having to put their spittle in cups before the shrine.

Your story an odd one, Jon, but has the taste of air and being, kind of like Sherwood would do, Sherwood Anderson, and this is not a knock . . . I do not believe that the short story has gone forward beyond Anderson. He's been dead a long time now, but the way he put down the word is not. I suppose Anderson has influenced me as much as Jeffers, but in a different way – the cleanliness he had of getting a line down, it is hard to beat.

And it was quite a thing, of course, to read that Genet liked 'Old Man Dead in a Room' best of all the poems in your #1. There were a lot of poems in #1. And I always get the unholy chills when I think of the language switch. Think of this Frenchman sitting in a room reading 'Old Man' in French to Genet, the walls there, the chairs, while I am asleep at the time or betting on a horse. Life is oddly wild, full of miracles as well as horrors. [★ ★ ★]

More thunder. Burroughs, of course, is important because he keeps the air-holes open. We need a Joyce or Burroughs or Gertrude S. every age to keep us loose and let us know that everything needn't be so, the way it seems or the way the herd-writers want it to seem. These people are valuable, in a way, beyond their work – icebreakers, knockers down of policemen. . . . Yes, the Millerboy finally got around to working Walter over and he did put him straight enough on politics and Art, and it still stands today. I am not saying ART is going to save us . . . it might save me, for a little while . . . but politics isn't going to either; politics got us this far, and see what we're doing now: tossing the bomb back and forth, back and forth, and the first one to drop it: o, blaAAHHHHHHHH! [★ ★ ★]

[To Ann Bauman]
Mid-March [1963]

Know I have not written, and am bastard slob this way, drink, madness et al., but I always figure that I am no good for a woman anyhow, and any way I can save her from myself is all to her good. Meanwhile, as you might have guessed, I write for selfish reasons: I have a book on the press now, Selected Poems 1955–1963, *It Catches My Heart in Its Hands* . . . Loujon Press, 618 Ursuline st., New Orleans, 16, Louisiana. 2 bucks, baby, and an autograph, even. Christ, y've got 2 bucks somewhere, haven't you? What I mean is, I don't get any money out of the book at all – as if it mattered – but I am pumping for these people because 2 bucks to them might mean such a simple thing as eating on this day or not. They eat one meal a day and forward such bastards as I, and I figure if they can do this (and sometimes they don't make the one meal), I figure I can forget immortality and carefulness and isolation and maybe even myself and go out and ask people to buy the g.d. book. If you think this is slick sales talk, it is not. I have thrown money into the fire. I have thrown my guts into the fire. I know more than this. But these people are the oddest set of living gods ya ever saw. She sells picture postcards on the sidewalks for meek coin and he stands 14 years hours a day poking paper into a cheap press he has hustled somewhere. I can't tell you more than this, only that these people are giants in a world of ants. If you can get hold of *The Outsider* #3 (same address) (as book) perhaps you will understand more of what I mean.

Meanwhile, glad your car running good. Mine lets up this cul de sac cloud of gaseous nauseous burning oil continually, until people stare as I go by . . . like a forest fire.

I lost your photo. How could I do this? Ya don't have another around, do you? Perhaps some day we will meet over a beer. It's a long way to Sacramento, but perhaps a good horse . . . a little luck? And then we'd only be bored and disgusted with each other. Keep working with the poem; if you treat it right, it is the most faithful and truest of all.

[To Jon and Louise Webb]
March 26, 1963

[★ ★ ★] If you think the interview with Kaye (*Lit. Times*) was rough for me in the sense of the poppyseed question, you should have heard afterwards . . . when we'd both had a bit more to drink:

K: 'Look, if the world were going to end in 15 minutes what would you do, what would you the tell the people?'

B: 'I wouldn't tell 'em anything.'

K: 'Now LOOK, man, you're not cooperating! If the world were going to end in 15 minutes, I wanna know what you would do!'

B: 'I'd lay down and rest, just like I'm doing now.'

K: 'But what would you tell the people, man, the PEOPLE!'

B: 'Don't forget your streetcar transfer.'

And the odd thing is, you tell these people the truth and they think you are not cooperating. [★ ★ ★]

[To Jon and Louise Webb]
March 28, 1963

[★ ★ ★] I have already caught hell, in person, for #3, and I was going to spare you some of this, but it may prepare you for what's to come. I bought him a bottle of wine and he arrived an hour later than he said he would – which is bad form; when I tell someone I will be there at a certain minute, I arrive *on the minute*. However, it gave his wine a chance to chill, and he fingered his drink and began, mostly telling me that there was *another* type of poverty that nobody knew about and he was going to write about it. What he means is that he has a $200 a week job and he somehow can't MAKE IT! I told him that I had little sympathy with this type of poverty, that one hundred and sixty million out of 180,000,000 in this country lived that way. I think it an entirely different thing to want something to eat and not being able to eat, and a place to sleep and rest the tired body, and only having the benches, the streets, the ice, the rain. Because a man needs 2 cars, a tv set, 12 pairs of shoes for his wife, this signifies to me only an unhandsome sort of greed that is needed to fill a hole where something else should be. I did not tell him all this but let him talk. Then he got on his job, writing blurbs for the pictures in nudie magazines, and then he said, 'Oh, I know you were offered the job first and you turned it down, X. told me about it and I am tired of hearing about it, and you were offered the job again, there was another opening and you turned it down again . . . but you could not have gone up the ladder the way I have!' What he means is that he has been promoted from writing the nudie blurbs for the magazines that lay around in barbershops chairs and that he has been elevated to writing books about legitimate nudism . . . nudist camps, etc. He is right: I would not have gone up the ladder. I wouldn't have lasted one day writing blurbs. I would rather wash dishes and go at night to the glory of a small box-like room with swinging electric light and the other torn people walking up and down the halls, half out of their minds, miserable, waiting to die, wanting to get drunk. I let him talk on. I am not much of a talker. I think very slowly, very. I have some bad teeth and I lisp once in a while. But mainly, when you're talking, you're going OUT, burning away, and although I don't mind much burning, I don't care for haggle, argument, point and counter point. I am not a lawyer. I am not a movie star. I don't know what I am. But as I go on, the feeling is toward a gentle center somewhere. Anyhow, he went on and I listened, and he said, 'I could have had my picture on the cover of *The Outsider* myself . . . and then, there's Corrington . . . you and Corrington. You dedicated a book to him and then he writes this stuff about you. Look at my face. Why don't you look at my face? Are you afraid of me?'

'That is not why I do not look at your face,' I told him.

'I love you,' he said, 'I guess I still do, but you are not the person you used to be. I mean, dedicating a book to an *editoress*. That's cheap. And, in #3, The Editor's Bit, it was too long and it cheap-ened everything.'

'Don't you think,' I asked, 'that the way he tore up Creeley was a courageous thing?'

'I threw *Outsider 3* in the toilet,' he said, 'I flushed it down the toilet.'

(Cavelski [*Kabalevsky? – ed.*] on now. Something *Brilliant Suite*, so clean, so sharp. There have been men in the world, thank the gods, thank the tulips, thanks the dead horses, thank the Winters and the midgets and the grass growing.)

'I told my wife I would only be gone 10 minutes,' he said. 'I have wasted a half hour. Well, these people think you're GREAT, there's a lot of space separating you from them, they don't know you like I know you, so they'll keep thinking you are great. You are safe.'

Then he got up and moved toward the door. 'Just keep on living your small, little insignificant life the way you are doing.'

'Slam the door when you leave,' I asked him.

He got in the last punch. 'I'll leave it for you to close,' he said and walked out leaving the door open.

He won. I had to get up and close the door.

Now, I can't pretend that all this did not bother me. I am very full of self-doubt, self-doubt twists me in the vise forever, and I know that I often do badly and write badly and I don't live exactly like a saint, but it does appear to me that I ought to be allowed to think along my own lines and live in my own way. The trouble with this writer is that he has built an image of me, probably from my poems, that I do not seem to stand up to in the flesh. Well, maybe I lie in my poems. I try not to. But if I do not present a flaming torch while sitting in a chair drinking a beer, I can't help it. I don't believe much in extra talk. I can talk for hours on paper because there is only the click of the keys and this brown torn shade pulled down in front of my face. It is a clean white thunder. That is why I do not like opera. Somebody I know pretty good and who knows I like the classical symphonies [★ ★ ★] asked me, 'How come you do not like opera?' and I answered, 'Because it contains the human voice.' 'What's wrong with that?' she asked. 'I don't know. I just don't like the human voice. I think it's fake.

Almost anything that comes out in voice is fake. I don't care if it is singing or the Gettysburg Ad., I don't like it. Here you have some bitch singing ultra-soprano who beats her kids and squats over a bowl and drops turds like the rest of us, and she is through the Art-form trying to become purified and trying to purify the rest of us. I just don't like the human voice: it drags down, it wears, it will simply not let things alone.'

But she was fairly sharp. 'You like the violin, or some of the horns, don't you?'

'Yes, at times,' I said.

'But don't you realize that these instruments are played by human beings and that the human voice is just another instrument?'

Which is a pretty damning argument, but I still say the voice is more *direct*, and that something is gained (not lost) by letting it come down through the fingers (violin or piano). Which is essentially why I am *ashamed* of the one or 2 drunken phone calls g.d. put through to you: because I had only the voice and the voice could not say, never damn can. [★ ★ ★]

And what my bottle bloody knife fireblast friend said was right: I am glad there is space between us, so that if I am a phoney or a coward or a rotten human being you will jes. christ never know it

because all you see is a sheet of ape ass paper

and you don't see me

or what I really am –

which is not much,

but which is me and which is working toward some saliva and red end of everywhere, and which is repeat the rift of the wind and I am tired, shit, and you are tired, listening . . .

Only the boy who came in and spewed his venom on me, I have, for a long time, been trying to get rid of but did not want to hurt his feelings. I hope this does it. But I sense that he will be back. It is too good this way.

But life does not always hold the Brutus within its sleeve. I was walking out toward the parking lot after the 9th race and somebody shoved 50 cents at me and said, 'Can you give me a ride, my friend pulled out without me.' I asked where he was going and since it was a couple of blocks away, I told him to forget the 50 cents and get in. Turns out I had driven him in earlier in the year only I was drunker and didn't remember, only that time I was a big winner and flashing broken teeth and mug. And so we talked, quietly, weary, smashed, as I tangoed in and out of traffic, slipping through with my sometime smoking car, and we talked the gambler's talk, the rough days, the good days, but essentially nothing important. I let him off at Hollywood and Western. 'Goodby, Hank,' he said. 'So long, Nick,' I said, and I took a right, circled round and came back into the liquor store where I billed an I-owe-you for $11.50.

Now, this is not bad, It adds up into living. No great words. Nothing. But somehow good. How can you explain it? [★ ★ ★]

[To Jon and Louise Webb]
April 1, 1963

[★ ★ ★] I agree with you on the Creeley, but am not too amazed that a lot of people don't. They believe you have pot-shotted him, but they seem to forget that you have published *him* and *his*, plus their theories. You are going to hear a lot of stuff about how there were always 'schools,' and you are going to hear some big names of the past mentioned as proof of those who have created and created damned well in spite of (or, they would like to say, because of) schools. What these good people forget is that the past does not prove the present. The past may have called for schools, whether they were created for self-survival of IDEA, or whether created by critics. The present, I feel, does not call for schools; with our speed-up of transportation and communication, it MIGHT become apparent to some sensible & feeling people that *we touch too much*, we are now slowly becoming ground down to the same thing. The only hope of survival is to escape as much as possible from the mass-hypnosis, of which the 'school,' be it Black Mountain, Kenyon and/or etc., is still part of the grouping-thing and too many men in a closet (or make it *bed* for some of them). The only defense of a bad work is to create a better work, not to have some disciple of a school come to bat for you. In some places it helps them to teach English; in other places they gather as homos or smokers of pot. They need the trunk and then they feel pretty good as branches. Politics is often, it seems, involved with Art; and as Politics often stinks, their creations do too. If I want to join a Lonely Hearts Club I will go to a genuine place where I might make some old woman happy. Otherwise, all I need is a typewriter, some ribbon, paper, envelopes, stamps and soul. School – is out.

. . . anyhow, I have an idea that this Creeley-blast might be good for *The Outsider's* circulation, you'll see. You took a swing but don't back down; if you back down, you're dead. Give them space, but don't forget there's *creative* work to be published, new people, new Buks, new Creeleys . . .

'Kaja' is Kaye Johnson, of whom Bukowski notes, 'She wrote very literary letters a bit on the pretentious side.'

[To Jon and Louise Webb]
April 9, 1963

[★ ★ ★] If you do write Kaja, please tell her that her 'White Room' has a lot of the female race laughing because it's true and sobbing because it's so. Women, g.d. them, tho, must learn that there are other things besides LOVE, I mean, concentrating, centering on it; the man is not actually callous but more divided – he plants his seed and moves on, not nec. toward another woman but away from the *concentration*.

[To Jon and Louise Webb]
April 22, 1963

[★ ★ ★] Heard from Kaja today and also Harold Norse – so not being much of a reader I had to open #3 and read the Norse poem, and luckily it was pretty damned good, although a little too poetic for me, I like my cake plain, but he seems filled with the fire, so, o.k. I should read more, but reading bothers me. [★ ★ ★]

oh yes, heard from Malanga today. He sent me some of his poems, which he self-praises but which do not get to me. He thinks you've got something against him because he rubs elbows with Auden and the New York Crowd. Me, I don't think you care where a man comes from as long as he lays the line down. By the way, the boys didn't like the photos you sent, said they were too 'domestic.' Wants a head portrait, or something. So to hell with it. I told him to write in space where my photo supposed to be: 'Charles Bukowski wishes these poems to be his photo.'[★ ★ ★]

[To Jon and Louise Webb]
April 26, 1963

[★ ★ ★] The book is beginning to well into my mind as a possibility. It's like, you know, you meet a beautiful woman, have some talk with her, but really think nothing of it because everything seems pretty much out of reach and you turn to leave and find that she's walking beside you, and she walks up the steps with you and stands there while you open the door to your room and then she walks in with you. The book's like that. A little too much to behold. I've had so many knives stuck into me, when they hand me a flower I can't quite make out what it is. It takes time. [★ ★ ★]

[To Neeli Cherry]
April 29, 1963

enclosed bad photo from leftover stash I had taken for some artist who thinks he might do a drawing for *Cold Dogs in the Courtyard*, Cyfoeth, Chi. Lit. Times, out in May, I'm told. Anyhow, Jory over for small drunk, saw reject photo and said I should send it to you. O.k., I said, o.k. But I didn't and J. has kept hounding, so here it is, whatever it is. Which explains nothing.

Picked up a couple of Borestones the other day. One for 'The House' and one for 'The Singular Self.' They will come out later in the year, *Best Poems of 1963*. I've never seen one of their collections. Might be pure crap. Most poetry is. Almost everything is.

Tell Sam to keep working out. I think I can find room for a good 4 round man down at Santa Monica. I hear all you havta do is keep the gloves laced.

More and more black cats everywhere, but there's a *white* cat here, that means *luck*, brother. He has an angular scar down the left side of his head. Proud; a real shit-head. [★ ★ ★]

[To John William Corrington]
May 1, 1963

god damned quarter horses worse than money stealing sluts, hot enough out there to take the bark off an oak tree, and everything in kind

of a yellow-sandish grit, like a cheap dream, and you peel the money off –
your last poor bloodsmeared 5 or ten, and here they come, damp, fear-
peeling, and the number goes by and it is the wrong number. you are
fucked again but the most noticeable part is that you are getting used to
it. some day in an alley I'll wish I had back g.d. once more, the green, and
the milk from ma's tit, but it will be old newspapers and hacked-out minds
and blue wind and young cops. What I am trying to tell you here is that I
lost at Los Alamitos, and they all lose, they stand there stunned and grey-
faced, the dream all gone. And I hit down the freeway in a borrowed blue
1954 Buick that drove like an ice truck. Tomorrow night she'll be over
and I'll have to hear all about the horrors of the Right (as opposed to Left)
and how soon we'll have a sort of Gestapo dragging people screaming
down the streets. She'll have 2 tickets to a lecture by James Baldwin and I
will refuse to go. As to Gestapos, Gestapos have always been – and hooeva
is in powa has his own kinda Ges., only they call it something nice the The
Federal Bureau of Investigation or Vets of For. Whores, or the A.M.A. or
the Y.W.C.A.; when these shits gona realize the Gestap. has always been
here? that Life is Blood? Control? Fences? only a guy like Gandhi did
without and they got him. What I am trying to say, I lost at Lost
Alamitos.[★ ★ ★]

[To Ben Tibbs]
[May 1, 1963]

Thanks for the drawing. It is the best one I have seen of yours. Don't
be pissed, but I think it so good I'd almost use the dirty word 'genius.' I
want Webb to see it. Going to write to him about it. But I want it back
because you sent it to me.

I will stoke up something for you – eventually – perhaps a series of
small ones, if I don't get run over or pressed out.

Meanwhile your work lights up this dump on this grey day like one
thousand searchlights. Thank you, Ben.

Yes, the death of a good woman, it is a bad thing.

I heard about the death of your wife, but take hold, man, your work is
getting stronger, so put down the ink the way you do, go on, maybe she's
watching, and if she isn't, go on anyway – she'd tell you to.

Thanks again (a small thing to say) for the fine drawing. do continue.

[To Jon and Louise Webb]
May 1, 1963

[★ ★ ★] Ben Tibbs shipped me a drawing which he says [he] has not submitted anywhere and he wants me to have it, only it seems so quite warmly funny and good . . . I would like you to see it for possible *Outsider* use, but I would like the original back. I guess he just drew it for me, but hell hell, it's something . . . called 'Idyll' and it has one of Ben's little old men with life-filled child eyes, hat on, reading a book in a rocking chair, and it's out on the grass, and there's a bed and the woman is putting a sheet on this bed and you can see part of the body through the sheet and just where the THING is, there is a patch on the sheet – oh, it is not vile ugly dirty but warm laugh clean and love – and then on the sidelights: there is some kind of bird sitting on the head of the bed, and he's looking at the patch, and there's tree back there. Ben wants me to send him something in ink, but hell hell I can't match, it's trying to draw to an inside straight with a short deck.

And yet I know that Ben is not trying me in contest. He has liked some of my drawings. Well, this is good, but drawing hardly interests me now – little does – and I draw like Thurber

> which is o.k. only if
> you are
> > Thurber

and T.'s dead so he's ahead of me on 2 counts, only o you should see the Tibbs, this is the best I've seen of his. Did you know he's an old man? Not that this should prejudice judgement of a work. I see whatever I can see that is there. But when you get an old man who still has velvet in his dreams you get something coo, dad, and mama.[★ ★ ★]

[To Ann Bauman]
[May 2, 1963]

I am writing this right after you have phoned, and you have so little money and you should not have, and yet this makes it better, and for it all, it was a sound out of the darkness, and I love you for it, and there's something good in you, you may not know it, but there is, and forgive all the comas and loose talk . . . it is so odd to hear a sound out of all this madness. I am not so good at talking on the phone, or talking at all and though I say small things, hesitant dull things, it is only shame and lack of heart and lack of ability and all the lacks that keep me from expressing what should be, and when the phone is put down I always feel as if I have failed – not only in ordinary failure but in a failure that affects everything: myself and you and tomorrow morning and any way the smoke blows. [★ ★ ★]

Ann, I think you should know this – I am not primarily a poet, I hate god gooey damned people poets messing the smears of their lives against the sniveling world, and poets are bad and the world is bad and we are here, ya. What I am trying to say is that poetry, what I write, is only one tenth of myself – the other 9/to hell tenths are looking over the edge of a cliff down into the sea of rock and wringing swirl and cheap damnation. I wish that I only could suffer in the classic style and carve out of great marble that would last centuries beyond this dog's bark I now hear outside of my 1963 window, but I am damned and slapped and chippied and wasted down to the nothingness of my arms and eyes and fingers and this letter tonight, May first or second, 1963, after hearing your voice upon the phone.

I deserve to die. I wait upon death like a plumed falcon with beak and song and talon for my caged blood. This may sound pretty god damned pretty but it is not. The poetry part of me, the seeming actuality, what I write, is dung and dross and saliva and old battleships sinking. I know that when the world – which is fairly cheap and stylish and what? what? – forgets a little of the poetry that I have written, it will not be entirely the fault of the world – mainly because I do not *think* of writing, and only the edge of the knife . . . where I spread the butter or cut the onion keeps practice in the verse of my mind.

You do not know how much your call meant although I was seemingly dull and drab and stupid, but I do wish you would not do it again because I know how things are going for you and yours (not so good) and I don't want the few good people of the world hurt because of buk the puke. (Someone once wrote me that Buk rhymed with puke and she was correct, not only in manner, which is bad, but also in the way the chandeliers work their still lightning in an empty room) and I say, everything is pretty good now but I of course don't know when or if or what the next o my god stroke of everything will bring, which is a coward's viewpoint, and all drowning men are cowards, hear them scream, and life is what? what? going down into the water, and it is not the cutting off of air and light and lung and eye and love that counts – it's the itch they put into us making us wonder why the hell we are here. For these few things. Like a phone call from Sacramento at 7 : 30 p.m. I don't know, I don't know, and it is so sad. If I could give tears to make it right we would all drown in my sick tears. I hardly know what to do. I drink too much. Or not enough. I gamble. I make love to women who only exist within their bodies and I look against the flakes of their eyes and I know that I am lying to myself and to them because I am no less than a dog, and love or the act should contain more than a couple of steaks in a frying pan or else all is lost like weeds in a garden or snails stepped upon and crushed and left in some sort of slime which contains life, smashed life forever and foreboding.

This poetry-thing is the worst sort of crutch. It weakens a man. And if a man is weak before he writes poetry he becomes, finally, through the strumming of shadows and wailing, he becomes finally what he is – just another fine pink juicy boy doing his god damned job in the frailest and most vomiting way.

You've got to understand that there are other ways of facing the horn except through the typewriter. Those who are known to us may just be a bad choice of chance. Never take the Arts as a holy mirror. Very little is just, and that includes all the centuries. The most honorable countries do not survive through courage nor do the ages survive us the best artists. Everything is chance and shit and the strumming of the winds. Please forgive the center word. If I hate anything it is a vile word said vilely or a dirty joke or the making of sex and life and woman and man into the thing they seem to want it to be.

I am probably fairly insane and you should know this (a more somber note with golden screeching undertones) and I do not mean to knock your verse plays . . . some have been done well . . . Racine, etc., only it is too much and ever so easy to mock and cajole when you do not *give* or try, and I say go ahead: verse, or phone calls or cards or death or love or vast areas of bathing in arenas of sound and stroke and midnight moments, I thank you for going on and I, too, go on a little while more.

p.s. – don't hate me for feeling more than is (perhaps) necessary. It may be best that the lost frogs and space-burnt nylon and neon air . . . it may be best that we are creatures of gesture instead of reality and marriage is reality with life and very few of us can stand either marriage or reality or life.[★ ★ ★]

[To Jon and Louise Webb]
May 7, 1963

[★ ★ ★] Gypsy, when I phoned last I remember saying 'Good-bye, Baby,' and it bothered me for hours afterwards. It is simply terminology, crass yes, hell yes, but you should know all the people I know who toss this term, and it can mean everything – to you it meant simply the best of everything: luck, love of the kind I know, rising spirits, grace, 7, the nose in front, holy Mary, you name it. That's what it meant. and you know it. and you stay out of this, Jon.

[To John William Corrington]
[?Mid-]May, 1963

[★ ★ ★] . . . on the blood yes, it is not too good, and I know the cancer-bit. I remember my mother. She couldn't straighten her legs. womb. gut. she kept telling me all along, 'Your father is a great man.' I knew what my father was. She didn't. I took her a rosary on Christmas eve or Christmas day, I can't remember. She was dead. Fry was with me. Fry was dead too.

I pretend that the blood from my mouth is bad teeth and the blood from my ass is from hemorrhoids and then I feel better and take another drink. What man wants to waste his time in hospitals? I am not so particularly concerned with writing poetry as I am concerned with standing around in the sun or just sleeping or getting drunk or looking at the poor face of some old woman I have made love to and watching her eyes eating into my face, into my body, this delight delight, until I am ashamed and turn my eyes down. I am tired as hell but the longer I live the more something begins to take shape. I thought the whiskey would finally ride my brain down, and maybe it has, and as I type this to you I am listening to some new Broadway musical, they are pretty similar, it is more Artless in its shouting than a blowjob whore, but it is a moment, a sound, not bad, and I am writing this to you and I am drunk but I am still alive, and we write on, over and over, live on, your wife, your kids, myself, Jon, Lou, WILDCAT, and tomorrow's entries. The fucking stage, yeah, the fucking stage, we are all there. [★ ★ ★]

[To Jon and Louise Webb]
May [?20], 1963

I am so in love with the book you are doing. this keeps the keenly
biting down somewhat and I go on, but very much afraid I am hypo of
some sort and only decency of – of what?? effrontery? is in destroying
myself, and I keep drinking and looking out of windows, flowers, grass,
people down there . . . grass people down there . . . ah, ha, I can still laugh,
and you people are so good, god damn it, my madness, I am so unkind, this
is the book, my love, yours, but I look ahead, and if I am there, here, anywhere, I have a title for another book, be there another book, another me,
another anything: LEAP OUT OF ANY WINDOW. Really my love grows sadder,
my life grows realer, too real, I can hardly beat it like cherries blooming in
a fucking glass of scotch, within the gall of scotch . . . things crawling
growing inside my sick-gut mind, the whole world waving waving

> hello and goodbye
> and I've been so rotten

there's so little left to do. you either bleed to death in small drops or you
go out like a snarling tambourine, why not, car doors slam across my living

> my way

> > and their way

> > > tangle like angry panthers
> > > in a cave

and they know the way
  they know the way

> > And,

> > > yes

> > > > of course I've been drunk
> > > > u might have guessed

missed work missed work
god damn them
and so a job I hate prob. gone
and I can do nothing
have no trade
> but maybe luck
> > luck

image
> flat floating fish
> stunned and pecked to death
> getting by
> in a lost mirage.

Please do not take this letter too seriously or bother making phone calls because all our dimes are thin, thin, thin, like slivers in our final coffin poking our eyes alive, g.d. g.d., this is the ending of the birdsong, this is the coconut eaten, this is slime upon the walls, this is a flat tire, this is dirty laundry, this is everything eaten from its insides out and its outsides in, this is a bad morning,
this is a bad day, this is gas stations under moonlight, this is
the lousy screw with his precious freedom walk outside the bars, these
are the bars filled with the lonely hemorrhoids of life, this is the
world waiting upon the mailman and the bomb,
this is a cat crucified by a dog,
this a man cruxed by a woman or the other way around,
this is a worm crawling an apple under a temperature of 69 degrees, this
is all is Christ dangling from nails dangling dangling
this is the horse that did not quite qinuto quatro win
this is the whore that did not quite love
this is the city that did not burn down to new empire
this is the rodent staring with the square blue eyes
these are madmen's tears
like the lava of a fish crying for greater things,
these are tootsie rolls and buns,
these are things that smash me dead
like blank faces
like envelopes
like buns
like mercenary women
like countries that proclaim justice
because they are strong enough to say what they want
to seem to believe;
. . . like that last kiss and that first kiss,
like the hands that once loved you
resting upon coffin-bottoms while oranges still round young
and full to the shape of the sun,

and these things you know,
please cry with me,
please be weak,
please do not become knowing
or fancy as that man
who takes the bull to hell
like a spider working a fly,
oh Hemingway was a liar,
I do not call this Art
and I do not call this Life,
for all your fancy jurists and all your fancy ways
and all your fancy gods –
I cannot see, I cannot see,
and I grow tired
the larvae crawl the eyes of my soul,
the bricks fall,
Stalingrad again, or Greece
or Berlin
or the fingers of myself
working out toward a god
or a leaf or a sound or a symbol
or a meaning.

I am not wise enough
and this is a terrible thing;
it is so easy to become wise enough
that I cannot do it,
I cannot see it
I cannot be it.

It is a becoming thing
and becoming things fit me
like loose shelves and [? saucers]
in an earthquake.

ah jesus
I talk too much
I mouth words like a mimic
I roll and stroll

and beat my silly bloody breasts
and miss the point
miss the point.

ah, god damn, sweet soldiers,
sweet whores, sweet friends,
the point is in
and down
and working,
can't you see
that???
like a gaunt and noble
and giant cock
working forever
reaming the original guts of life
out of you?
Pan, Pan, I am so sad,
and where does the working go?
where's the Peace?
where's the victory?

oh, god damn it, I know:
we are tried
again and again
and that's our sustenance:
working finely with these master
teeth,
but I grow sick of Henry Miller
and the balustrades,
I'm tired of D.H. riding the thighs of his
eternal and saving cow,
and when Hemingway met an enemy without a flag
he surrendered
which is not bad at all
but he should have known earlier
or he would not have fucked around with so
much stuff,
but still a great man
whatever great means

or I would not be talking about him
in this round dull and sickening morning,
now now now
where are we at? ha?
what's it mean?
I'm not the first to toss this grain
of salt,
but really am more vicious and desperate and
wanting
perhaps
than many of the rest,
and that is why you read this
and that is why this screen in front of my face
is all that separates me
from the sweet black pavement that looks for its own
freedom.
You think I bluff?
Of course.
so long . . . as long
(you are the pretty grammarian)
as I remain alive I bluff.
your criticism is justified
but your life
is not? not.
period.
definite statements
are generally
like love:
they turn out
badly. Of course,
you know that real love
like real life
only comes along in the shape
of a body
every 2 or 3 centuries.
I know. You think it is
Christ or Joan of Arc
or something obvious.
I do not think that way at all

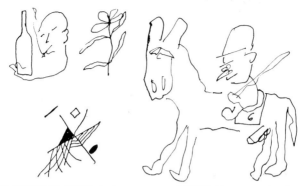

LOS ANGELES IN AMERICA (o!) and this is OCTOBER 28th. and a fly keeps
brushing bumbling bastarding past....

hello D.Blazek:

fine, I got your o.k. on the 3 poems, and while I have a
theory that rejection is good for the soul, the theory seems to work
best when it applies to others.

bio: born 8-16*20, began writing poetry at age of 35. 5 collections
of poetry with a 6th., CRUCIFIX IN A DEATHHAND to be issued by ######
Loujon Press and Lyle #=Stuart, Inc. early in 1*65. That's it.

Rough night in the pit last night, bastard on one side telling me
how great he was and bastard on other side telling me how great he was,
meanwhile the work-whip flashing like a cobra hung to a windmill...

Listen, on the books most of them are out of print or too hard to
get but for the record: FLOWER, FIST AND BESTIAL WAIL (HEARSE PRESS);

LONGSHOT POEMS FOR BROKE PLAYERS
(7 POETS PRESS); RUN WITH THE
HUNTED (MIDWEST POETRY CHAPBOOKS);
and IT CATCHES MY HEART IN ITS
HANDS (LOUJON PRESS.) COLD DOGS
ought to be out, I've corrected the
proofs some months back, a month
anyhow, and if nothing in another
month I'm going to ask why. Meanwhile, I've got faith. You might
get hold of IT CATCHES by writing
Jon Webb, LOUJON PRESS, 1109
Rue Royale, New Orleans ##16. I
don't know tho, he may be #####
out or charging collector's $$$
on what's left.

my neck hurts. I seem to be
dying of something--maybe life or
maybe no young ass. well. listen:
bottom of paper here. slipping out of typer. going. hold and luck,

To Douglas Blazek. October 28, 1964.

JANUARY 26TH., 1964,
    LOS ANGELES, CALIFORNIA —

Dear Jon and Gypsy —
    Hope LONG TAPE GOT THERE O.K., IT IS NOW 5 IN
THE MORNING, BIRDS STILL ASLEEP AND I AM SUCKING ON A
sour orange candy which MAKES ME TOUGH AS
HELL BUT THEN THE ASS HAS BEEN bloody + bloody
CHUNKS OF **FLESH**, so I am tenderly cooking IT
FOR A COUPLE of DAYS. — ON BEER, ETC.

    Thanks for RETURN of poem BATCH — I WILL
continue to send NEW ONES IF AND WHEN They
become.

Jot 2 copies of book sometime back, all good like
new icecream again + I am waiting with some WONDER
an inscribed copy FROM the **EDITORS**, yes.

To Jon and Louise Webb. January 26, 1964.

Village Voice ad das cost like Hell but might make Loujon Press well-known as well as Buk + I hope you have ENOUGH copies left to go at $5 which it should HAVE gone FOR AT ONCE and when I THINK of THIS BOOK SELLING FOR TWO DOLLARS, I think it A CRIME and people should have sent you more money at once out of SIMPLE DECENCY OF SOUL, But it's much EASIER for them to think that MONEY is BAD for your soul but O.K. for theirs — so O.K. for them too, keep it — the MONEY, I mean.

I don't know about the Cherry Cherries — Jory says he spoke to them about it — let me know if they finally + decently ante up. I'm told they are NOT going TO SELL the 10 copies BUT SIT ON THEM !!! This doesn't do the LOUJON PRESS one damn bit of good, the way I see it + specially for FREE. WE can sit on our books OURSELVES + that's our RIGHT, but seems to me when you give special bookstore rates, they aughta OPERATE LIKE A BOOKSTORE + I mean SELL BOOKS.

Please don't sell any more books for LESS than $5 — the word is out, they know what you've done; but hell, you're the editors and I should know that you know more about THIS type of PUBLIC than I do.

Rough on the moving coming up. There's always some son-of-a-bitching obstacle to BREAK a man down when he tries anything out of the ordinary — while the fools and PRICKS sail blithely on.

To Jon and Louise Webb. January 26, 1964 (Page 2).

I read book review of IT CATCHES Frances
wrote for SOUTH + WEST; it seemed O.K., mentioned
WORK of editors too... She re-wrote completely
a first version which I thought was FLAT and
mechanical, which can + does HAPPEN TO ANY
OF us.

Ship more purples, sure. I've still got plenty of
SILVER + the YELLOW, and it is easy ENOUGH,
rather FUN + EXPLORATIVE specially if I have
2 or 3 weeks.

I don't KNOW if there will be poems enough,
good ENOUGH poems for another book in
some future should we all survive EVERYTHING,
but I will keep sending and if you
finally see fit, GREAT !!!

Yr, you're right — Willie prob. tied in
with THESIS + 2nd. novel but he wrote
such INTERESTING letters that I miss them.

I might have to MOVE OUT OF this
place — 1623 N. MARIPOSA — many reasons,
many odd reasons... but not quite
yet.

SHOOT the purples out + I will get
busy. I am full of BALOGNA + some
DRAWINGS.

HAIL, HAIL,
HAIL,
Buk

To Jon and Louise Webb. January 26, 1964 (Page 3).

dear Jon and Louise:

thanks for all the photos, they really brought me back there, sick, ##/hungover in the old bathrobe but really being glad to be with both of you but no way to say it without seeming corney, and like with Greg. and Steve, same thing, I am just not a talker, so to all of you I ######must apologize, I am not OUTWARD, and there isn't any help for it. that's it. I do think all you good people understand what kind of cage I am crawling around in. so thank you. love you all, plenty.

yours,

Buk

p.s.--poems enclosed. try to get back soon? luck with the landlord...

b.

HA, HEHE, HA . . .

P.S.- I SENT WORST PHOTO OF
MARINA. CAN'T SEND OTHERS, AFRAID
OF LOSING, EVEN THO I HAVE
NEGS. YEAH, I'M CRAZY.

LOVE,

Buk

SHIT!

IF YOU COME TO KINGMAN
CAN'T YOU FLY (HAVE TO SEE ME?
CAN PICK YOU UP AT AIRPORT. DRIVE
BACK. I'M UNEMPLOYED, BED YOURS.
COUCH MINE. LOVE, B.

NO-1-6365

p.s.--wrote a poem about meeting Mrs. Robertson but sent it to NOLA. didn't want to hurt any feelings. Betsy a lovely lovely woman, believe me. I am the ox. you s##/her, tell her, my love.

To Jon and Louise Webb. [April, 1965?].

June 2, 1966

ah, blaz:

        terribly hungover, so short here, but not to keep you bouncing the blue
lame dream in your malted milk--send your poems and I'll submit forward. but
give me bit of time--forward's are like fucks or poems or whatever: they have to
wait the proper emergence. I think your poems will allow me to do the forward,
and I have no shame in sending a good man out on the street with a rose in his
hand. but if the forward doesn't work for you, it's yours to kill. you have
a title yet? anyhow, send the stuff on in when you are able.
                                iz
        Good the Norse went. writing such an odd thing--you work it but don't hardly
every know if it works or not.

        really sick today, and this isn't a letter, just to let you know I am ready
to read the Blazac screams and declamations. o.k.?

        sing horses to sleep when the picture books burn,

To Douglas Blazek. June 2, 1966.

les angeles, calif.
march 3, 1967

hello Karl:
        very dull and damp and down today, and for some time....

keep remembering tho, you wanted me to say something about Klacte, so I will, and if you
care to #use it? otherwise--

    KLACTOVEEDSEDSTEEN DIFFERS BECAUSE IT DIFFERS IT DIFFERS FROM OTHERS GOOD OTHERS
BAD OTHERS BUT I FIND THIS STRANGE DIFFERENCE MOSTLY LIKE YELLOWGREEN ELECTRIC LIGHT
LEFT FROM WIRE INTO WALLPAPER AND CRYING BRAIN, SAYING THIS THING LIKE THIS:
CLOSED AND ALERT, ####DONE IN THE MESSAGE*FLICKS OF THE SMILING GENTLY WARM THINKING
METABOLISM. ZANI BARBWIRE INTELLIGENCE TRANSPOSED INTO MORNING TOAST. DO YOU SEE
WHAT IT IS? BAYONETS AND TURDS AND WHORE CANDLES AND DOG WITH TOOTHACHE NOT ONLY
UNDERSTOOD BUT RE-:LINED, BOXED, TIED WITH RIBBON, THEN SENT TO THE PICNIC SHADOWS
OF FRA BARTOLOMMEO AND MIXMILIEN FRANCOIS MARIE ISIDORE DE ROBESPIERRE. SOUND LIKE
BULLSHIT? I AM SINCERE ENOUGH, BLUE KID. LET ME SAY THAT WHAT I HAVE SAID SHOULD
BE PLENTY: IF YOU DON'T SMELL THE GRASS HALOS YOU MIGHT AS WELL ####KEEP LAYING
AROUND ¼ ¼ one-eighth BLOWING YOUR GRANDMOTHER. or the DIAMOND WART WITH THE
STALE MEDIUM SAUCE ON YOUR LEFT WRIST, GOODBYE.

                              --Charles Bukowski

    not too good here. health slipped again. eyow, next thing I knew I am walking
around drunk again, unable to make work. worried about THEIR DAMNED WORK, their place,
their walls, their trained-seal rules. umm, umm. LIKE WORRYING THAT A SHARK MIGHT
SNUB HIS NOSE STUB HIS NOSE WHEN HE TAKES A BITE OUTA YOU. then I am someplace else
and somebody keeps handing me this pill-things in a ####/#### jar and I am transfixed
like a thorn upon a rose I cannot see. I turn down fucks. I don't talk. I listen,
nervous, uncomfortable, unable to move, not caring too. sun goes up and down. voices
say voice things like flutes and beards hidden under some near pier, shorn white voices
with broken backs. fuke! 36 hours later you get up out of your chair and walk out;
it's cold. the car starts. you are cole cole cole COLD. LIKE BONEWET AND PACKED WITH
FISH*ICE. eyes don't care. you drive out. broke. days away from chicken shit job.
you come back to your place and it's a SMEAR OF PAPER AND SHIRTS AND STOCKINGS AND
SAD UNDONE THINGS ON THE FLOOR, LETTERS FROM Germany, und letters from peppermint
hades, and a letter from a lady who still wants to get FUCKED. I lay down and
cannot sleep. I FEEL AS IF I HAVE BETRAYED THE FOOTBALL TEAM BUT THE FOOTBALL
TEAM ISN'T ANYWHERE AROUND. round or around. I can't sleep. don't want to come.
have arrived. only the fish smell like selda-wands with ####flick-switches.
:::::::write: Karl:

        so that's it.

nothing to roll or pipe, no pills, no money but will go out for beer at this place,
beer and wine, have credit, whiskey scotch that stuff tears my stomach which is about
gone. but shape of spirit strangely gross-strong, like badbreath come-thru, hahaha,
maybe I get lucky strings inside, like no matter what happens this butterball thing
keeps puffing, yet no long dastardly letter, I allow myself greenbean laziness,
complete stinking of socks, and knew u understand and that is fine phine.

    by the way, do you have tape machine? I knew good madman, poet Dehan Thomas,
who has 2 or 3 tape machines, we can send stere or mono, ####prefer 3 and 3/4
speed. can you send us something? we will answer from our bearded hills,
something.

        meanwhile, pray for dead fish,

                Buk

LET ME
KNOW IF
YOU
"WANT" THIS
ACTION ???
:D

To Carl Weissner. March 3, 1967.

April 19, 1967

hello Jon and Lou:

god, Jon, didn't knew the prostrate so bad. DON'T DRINK, please. I have gone on the wagon myself, for a while. the price seems terribly high for us, surely and especially you.

this very short letter to tell you to take it easy easy. a few beers aren't worth all of that.

yes, please mail some pages for me to write some sayings on for your Crucifix's. it will give me a chance to mouth a bit. won't takeme long and I will mail back as soon as finished. I too would like to see Crucifix move a bit more, especially now that I see that most of the poems have held up through Time--for me.

have been having insomnia among other things and now another god damned scheme in my lap to pass for the postoffice, hours and hours of MY TIME wasted, I mean time off-the-clock. I cry into the same hankercheif. (ie).

if things a little better around June 26th. and you still want me to make that run, understand that I will not drink in front of you. I will go back to the place I have rented and maybe have a beer or 2, do a little werk on the damned novel or whatever.

on yes or ä nay on Patchen edition of OUTSIDER, I couldn't wouldn't toss in a word one way or the other--- somebody singing on Opera new -- MAD, MAD, THE WHOLE WORLD IS MAD-- to influence or un-influence you.

by the way, in PRISM international, Spring 1967, there is a cover photo by one Jon Webb. I take it this is not you? or is it? anyhow, mag obtainable by writing PRISM, c/o Creative Writing, University of British Columbia, Vancouver 8. B.C.
                    this is.
now must try to get that sleep. short half-wit letter, but to tell you, Jon, to stay away from stupid BEER CANS! and you, Lou, see that he does. I have spoken. let there be order and a chance to breathe.

better letter soon. don't forget to mail pages to incribe for good ol' CRUCIFIX.
fine.

                    the big page to you,

                              Buk

nothing on L.A.Times interview. guess they decided not to run it. Free Press? beat them to it and guess they did not want to play #2nd. fiddle. well, either way.

MARINA

Hope #11, think I want(ed) you / Copy. L., B —

Daw hope I have New left my / P.S. Hope you get. mag / letters to Mac. —

To Jon and Louise Webb. April 19, 1967.

and that is why we do not get
along.
But the real Christ or the fucking real
man is the man
who does not cuckold to the Arts,
a man who does not suck the nearest breast,
is a man who paints the walls of his life
kindly
and nobody
ever knows,
and this is the man of men
the walls of walls
and Hells Heruculius [*sic*] Jericho does not bring them
down,
only the sweet substances of his hands and his walk
and his life
like a bumblebee in the flower of a bull's death
sings these sweet songs to us,
o go away
go away
everything
the swaying of the planets
the muscles on a freak
the flat floating sorrow of a punk pudding
my insides screaming for the love of violins
such a giant drunk falling falling
across the face of this world
oh sweet cream and peaches
oh sweet love and hate
oh sweet dynasties of burning,
oh walnuts and tits
haunches and dogs,
oh simple moon
voices lips eyelashes
destroy me
I beg you
I beg you
destroy me forever
because my eyes have grown too large

my wisdom like a beautiful peacock
that can only separate pebbles from corn,
yes, yes, that is so,
do not laugh,
or what the hell
laugh
yes do laugh . . .
I am so serious
like a god damned kid with a yoyo,
and I too dislike serious
people –
when you're serious about life and death
you not only become a bore,
but serious enough . . .
you destroy yourself.
this is not what I mean.
what I mean is
what are we going to do this afternoon
while sitting around
eating apples and
destroying hangovers
and preparing for
future hangovers?

all that I can see is the
bird–like and drifting
Savannah of sunlight,
my harmless
so far
arms and hands and
veins,
and darling
sweet love of life
and child and blossom
do not think I am cruel
because I am afraid,
and now
spreading across my mind
they ring a god damned gong

across the afternoon
why? why?
as I am drunk again
as I understand nothing
as the sink is stopped and as the flowers
poke holes in my eyes
as love runs like a rat down the drain
and I become myself
ugly
real
vicious
standing with the worst armies
in the worst time
in the worst land
in the worst minute
or the worst light
slashing through this screen
taking me taking me
goodbye forever oh friend of my love.

Jory Sherman's My Face in Wax *with an introduction by Bukowski was published by Windfall Press, Chicago, in 1965.*

*The end of this letter refers to Karl Shapiro's introduction to the first book of Jack Hirschman (*A Correspondence of Americans *[Indiana Univ. Press, 1960]), who in the 1960s was teaching at UCLA. 'Was invited to dinner by Jack and his wife Ruth,' Bukowski notes. 'I drank a lot of wine and made an ass out of myself. Jack has the ability to get off some strong lines and poems, strange and original.'*

[To John William Corrington]
May 23, 1963

got yr 2 letters right one on the other, and I am hanging in (yet); sometimes I think u think I think I am sliding under the table. Drunk phone calls are my specialty. Cost me 50 bucks a month, which if the mules don't start dancing, I'm gona haveta stop doing, but don't worry, there's bloody ass but windows with screens, and how are YOU doing? They went bad again today, and my feet hurt, and no money ha, but that's not it, it's the TIME melting like vanilla, boy, and I am going ha, and that's it, a crotch, a crotch of grey waiting to stretch out and stop farting, and fucking old things, but the drinking's not bad, the drinking lifts, verily, John, fills the gap I'm not filling at the time, it's beans on the shelf, things going, radios, and all the words of silence that crawl the walls like cockroaches. Bang, bang, you're dead. [★ ★ ★]

I'm not worried about the Southern problem; that will work itself loose into another problem. And the bomb. That will, slovenly thing, solve itself. You know the ol' hack – we cure the obvious and the subtle takes over, and if it's subtle enough some grow fat and happy and others grow mad. I know this woman (pretty well), she marches on City Hall, the protest thing, either the black or the bomb, and she asks me, why don't you do something? and I don't say it, but I think I AM DOING SOMETHING, I am fucking you and you seem to like it a lot more than I do.

But I tell her, down where I work at night, I know plenty for there are 4 thousand people in this building and three thousand five hundred of them are black or mostly black, and I get along solidly with those I like, but here the problem is in being WHITE, and I have faced the problem in the factories and the slaughterhouses, I have been the WRONG color most of the time, but I can't expect sensibility when they nailed christ on the cross for pulling miracles, I don't go around pulling rabbits out of the hat. I have gotten close to their women and I have seen a black walk up to these women with a piece of white chalk in his hand and draw a line of white on his skin and ask one of these women, now will you have ME?

The fact that he was a sloppy strutting egocentric bastard, he did not take into consideration, only the fact that he was black. It's hard being black. It's even hard being white. It's hard being alive.

She listens to this and says, At the meeting today I saw the most *beautiful* thing. This girl, she took this man's shoes and stockings off and washed his feet in a pan of water, and then, after carefully and tenderly washing his feet, she kissed his feet, she was so young and beautiful and had this long hair and it fell over her face, and she kissed his feet, kissed his feet, and then she put his stockings on and then she put his shoes on.

Now this woman did not tell me the color of skins involved here, but I knew, of course. And I said, Well, I guess when we find out God is black we'll all feel better and get around to raising roses. don't get me wrong willie, but don't get me right, either, it's so easy to be RIGHT AND DO THE PROPER THING when you figure you've got the proper *cause*, and nothing to worry about, and that's what puts old men and women in churches on Sundays in their proper clothes – there's no drawback, and it seems like courage, it seems like knowing. This is a pretty good feeling. Some people go around looking for easy good feelings. Like a young girl kissing a black's feet in front of a Los Angeles crowd and feeling good because everybody knows you're going to fuck him later when nobody's around. Because your parents didn't understand Proust or Conrad Aiken. A psychologist could tell you a lot more about this than I can. But the human mob never solves a problem straight on; it generally fucks up in a mesh of shit and carries further problems to the problem, and the weak ones protest the most and do the most because there is this hungry space within them that can only see the immediate, the thing that can answer back and boy, they feel good; it's either a war or a pol. party or a magnet of some sort, and when they are long dead to the worms, somebody a couple of centuries later, when it gets cooler and clearer, decides that they have done the WRONG thing. I hate to leap into dishwater. Like you know guys used to go to doctors and the does would put these suction cups on them and draw out their blood and they would pay for this. Then there's the history of wars. I am bullshitting a loghead tonight but the mules were bad and this too is a sort of colossal type of righteousness blah to right the torn-up tickets. But I know my madness more properly than many others. I hope, ya. I have an idea the medics are some day going to find out that cutting out cancer with a knife was the quickest way to death. Or that teeth never should have been pulled. These are guesses but I am a pretty good guesser and I know that rot should be removed but not with such force and gesture, and further bullshit. [★ ★ ★]

On the foreword to Sherman's book you will see that I am talking mostly about myself, which is savage and lets out air and sometimes a little light. Don't worry about me laying out any bolognas out on the stage. I mostly blast Shapiro in it, in opening, not mentioning name, about using his name to promote another college Eng. teacher, and giving the grand come-on, I found the pages not to be like that at all. This is just part of it. I went over drunk one time and ate with man and wife in their house, the book I speak of with Shapiro foreword, and I told them I didn't like it, that it shouldn't have been done, it was bad for Shapiro and it was bad for them. Now I do not argue and I do not take stands but sometimes an idea will come out of me drunk during a drink and I will say it.

You know what he said?

Well, the book never would have gotten printed without it.

That's what he said. [★ ★ ★]

[To Jon and Louise Webb]
June 3, 1963

Well, I got the plaque, it was leaning against the door when I opened it – the bastard didn't knock, or I was asleep. Anyway, it's on the wall now, it's a fine thing and it holds the walls up . . . 'the poet Charles Bukowski.' Sometimes it's all in the dream-state and I don't know who Bukowski is. Sometimes I expect somebody to walk out of my bathroom and say, 'Give me a smoke, man, I am Charles Bukowski.' Anyhow, something like this which you needn't have done at all and did do with this beautiful gesture of warmth . . . this thing on the wall will be mine, and as the years go on – saving I hang around – this plaque will mean more and more to me. [★ ★ ★]

Our boy Sherman has a book coming out in which I write a long introduction. It was done sometime back when I was feeling pretty good. I speak more of myself . . . if I remember . . . than I do of Sherman. Neeli Cherry was orig. going to bring book out and Sherman asked me if I would do intro. I said I didn't know and then one day sat down and found myself writing it. I hope they have not cut it because then it would not make sense. [★ ★ ★]

[To Ann Bauman]
June 3, 1963

[★ ★ ★] If you should ever come down here your problem will be to keep the conversation 'dull.' I am an old wolf and after a few beers begin to imagine myself a young bull. I would always rather chance that they go away angry and unloved than unangry and unloved. It is better, of course, for them to leave unangry and loved, but of the other choices, at least I will know that I have tried. [★ ★ ★]

The review mentioned here is not listed in Dorbin's bibliography.

[To Jon and Louise Webb]
June 24, 1963

A little good news. Yesterday, Sunday, in the *Los Angeles Times* book review section, we, LOUJON PRESS and Buk and *It Catches* was mentioned by

Jack Hirschman. Some bit about my style of writing (according to Hirschman); that the book was on the press, price of book and address of LOUJON PRESS given. Also several other books reviewed and a kind of eulogy for Creeley by Hirschman. Anyhow, we have been mentioned, and maybe a few sales because of it? It might pay to send Hirschman a review copy when the book comes out? [★ ★ ★]

The U. gave Corrington a grand ($1,000) to lay around and write so he wouldn't have to teach Summer School. Well, this is o.k. if you can work it. Also, I think, a $2,500 advance on his novel. He's now thinking about going to Europe. I guess they all do that. They start running around the world. (See Ginsberg, Corso, Kaja, Burroughs, etc., etc.) I don't know quite what it means, but I'd rather side with Faulkner who g.d. figured there was more than enough just around his doorstep. This culture hunt smacks too much of a Cadillac sort of acquisition.

All right, hang in tough.

Corrington published 'Charles Bukowski and the Savage Surfaces' in Northwest Review *for fall 1963.*

[To John William Corrington]
[June 1963]

Don't worry yourself shitty on the *Northwest Review* article, I understand, and I hold to the savage side with the honor of my teeth. I know damn well I don't wax the golden poetic and I don't try to because I believe it to be essentially outside of life – like lace gloves for a coal-stoker. On the other hand, I don't believe in being tough because life is tough. I like my sunlight and beer and cigars and occasional pussy just like any matador or prelim boy, but there's still room for a good symphony written in 1700 or 1800 or the disgust-strike of sadness at seeing a cat crushed flat by wheels upon asphalt. There's room for things, and I once tried to straighten these things into REASON by reading Plato and Schope and F.N., Hegel, the whole host of boys, but I only found that they were tilting silver water, getting lost in it, and as long as I was getting lost I figured it might as well be in a cheap bar where I could listen to sounds that were not being written, and if I found love it was some other old dog's bone. Because if the answer isn't at the top, it isn't at the middle, and you'll find just as much at the bottom which was where I was at anyhow. It's not so much savage as it is discarding the whole facade of knowledge and education and looking as directly as you can into your own sun. You can get blinded this way but at least a lot of it is your own doing. Like suicide or betting the 9 horse. The next cold drink is God, and the next cigarette isn't cancer; it's the next one after, the one you haven't gotten to. And you realize all along that you are not getting very near anything, but if it's not the razor, you toddle along like a kid shitting in its pants, and the game is corncobs and dollars and buttons and an occasional Easter candle.[★ ★ ★]

I get touches and hints of the book from Jon, and this man and his wife weave things like a golden dream, touching it, tasting it, adding, subtracting, loving, o loving, they touch again and again the thing they are working with, it takes design, it takes them, they heave to it like good steak or a visitation by the angels; these people are blessed beyond blessedness, and my unholy mad luck has made this work of mine fall into their hands and I look through the curtains, and the cars on the street and the people and the sidewalks have become real and carved and yet soft like pillows because these people have touched me with the wand. All my luck came at once, and it won't last, I don't want it to. There will be a time of looking back, and I am ready. I came out of absurdity and I will go back, back, but now now all the dogs and flowers and windows laugh with me, and it is a stirring a stirring like an approaching army marching or a butterfly coming out of the cocoon.[★ ★ ★]

I await the *K. Review*, and your probable 18th century sonnet. This is all right. The *K. Review* is good fat book, stirs with a kind of dusty knowledge and unreality, but some of the critical articles hold little strokes of lightning, the taste and stir of the good long word mixed with the near-slang. This beholds one in an amusing sort of way.[★ ★ ★]

[To Ann Bauman]
[mid-June, 1963]

if you come to LA someday I hope you come to see me, part of that time anyhow. The only problem being that I work about half the weekends and the other I don't. If you come by bus, would be glad to meet you at bus stop, or drive you anywhere around town you want to go, or if you don't want to go anywhere we can have a beer at my place and make dull and polite conversation. However, I know that your idea is only half-resolved, a thought in between many other thoughts while things are going on, and that it prob. will not be followed through.

I am signing pages for the book, a huge stack of purple pages arrived in a box with instructions and this Sunday I will quietly drink beer and smoke and listen to my radio and look out the window and sign the pages.

Webb sent me a dummy copy of the book and it is a real thing of beauty – the paper, the type, the cover etc. etc. [★ ★ ★]

[To Jon and Louise Webb]
July 1, 1963

[★ ★ ★] If you are serious about a 2nd book to follow *Outsider* #4, I can say no more than that the miracles are still coming, the honor laid out like all the horses dancing in my dreams. Should you people change your minds – because of circumstances or conditions later, that will be o.k. too. I've got to go with you. YOU HAVE EXCLUSIVE RIGHTS TO PUBLISH THE NEXT BOOK AFTER *It Catches My Heart in Its Hands* [*dated and signed*].

This is real nice to say – as if I were giving *you* a break or something, after you break your backs to make me known! Don't worry about a notary: my word is good, and when my word is no longer any good then my poetry won't be either. I'm glad to go with you, much more than glad; you are my kind of people. Not a bunch of phoney literary bullshit or slick-assed business people, but people in love with their work and their lives, asking nothing but enough to continue to stay alive in order to continue to do the thing.

Your danger after putting me out in such fine style in *It Catches* would not be from the little chapbook operators but from the big boys, the bigger publishers, who might think I would go. But they can go to hell. I'm with you, and same arrangemetns with 2nd book, no royalties, but would like some copies. I'm afraid, tho, we will never come up with such a good title again, but meanwhile I will be thinking, gently thinking of one, as I go in and out of bars or watch them run.[★ ★ ★]

I don't write letters . . . too much . . . anymore, because it was simply it is simply a time of no letters. It may change. But I get to thinking IT IS THE ART-FORM THAT COUNTS, and all the letter-writing in the world won't excuse a bad poem or make it any better. Then I am still drinking, and the drinking often takes over and I don't know quite where I am or what I am anymore. Right now this place has newspapers in it that date 3 weeks back, onion stems, beercans, coffeepots on the floor. This woman comes over once in a while and straightens up but then she starts in with THE INTELLIGENT TALK, and I let her win her precious little arguments, I hate haggle, but just the same I get a little sick with how PROUD people are with the mind, how they want to ram it through you like a sword, how they want to talk talk talk. Don't they know that there is simply something nice about sitting in a room and drinking a beer and not saying much, feeling the world out there, and sitting there, sitting there, resting? [★ ★ ★]

I will send you a tape of a poetry reading of mine I made on my machine and which was broadcast over KPFK in August 1962. Of course, they deleted a lot of vulgarity, had to, so it is not quite the same thing I sent them. They asked me to come to their studios, which is like asking me to go to church with a hangover, so instead I mailed them what I had made in my room among the beercans, and, lo, they accepted it and played it over the air. Jack Hirschman's wife runs the literary and drama end of KPFK. Anyhow, when the thing finally came on over the radio . . . at 11 : 15 p.m. . . . I was drunk and did not hear it, but somebody retaped it off the radio and I was able to hear it afterward. [★ ★ ★]

Bukowski had three poems in El Corno Emplumado *no. 7 (July 1963), published in Mexico City. He had previously appeared in no. 3.*

[To John William Corrington]
July [22], 1963

shd. change ribbon but I am too tired – *Mutiny* editors are correct: I am a bastard: would rather kiss the king's ass than change a ribbon.

Heard from Jon. His spirits seem high, which does me good, as I would hate him to bite into the book and get this bad taste in his mouth. . . . Got copy #7 of *El Corno*. They seem to be falling off from a good start. Of course, I can't read Spanish or Mexican either, so it doesn't help my broad-minded eye. I got to figure that what I can't read isn't any good. That's how flies get fat. [★ ★ ★]

[To Jon and Louise Webb]
July [28], 1963

[★ ★ ★] In case you decide to send a copy of *the book* to Jack Hirschman for review for *L.A. Times*, his address is 10543 Bradbury Rd., Los Angeles, Calif. I know, I broke all rules and went there for dinner once, drunk. He thinks Creeley is God and Robert Frost 3/4s God but then he teaches at a University and therefore some of this is understandable. They see the underside softside of the wing. But he may have ordered the book anyway, and we may be in trouble, but I kind of like trouble sometimes – I mean, in my rather long foreword to Sherman's book (out July 21st, I believe), along with other ramblings, I take to task Karl Shapiro for writing a misleading introduction to Jack Hirschman's book. Names are not mentioned but, I guess, rather obvious. And at the dinner I told Jack that the introduction was bad but he told me that the book would have never been published without it, that there was only one good poem in there. Which might have been modesty but let's not pick at bones. This is the trouble with getting involved with literary talk; soon you are covered with slime and haggle, and creation is forgotten, So far, I have often forgotten creation because of drink or gamble or plain forget, but so far, very little shit-paddle has stopped me and I hope I remain as lucky.

When I took this woman home today she showed me a collection of the early poems of Ernie Hem. Out of the *Little Review* etc., but although most of them were not very good, they were not very bad either, and there was one poem in there . . . after the style of Ger. Stein and you can see how much this woman *did* affect him, which we all know but which we tend to forget after Hem and Stein are both gone and Hem more or less remains. However, these poems are encouraging to any young (or old) writer to show that something almost can come out of almost nothing. It is simply buttoning a button right and knowing how to open a door. It is easy as hell, really, it is so easy that almost nobody can do it. [★ ★ ★]

[To Jon and Louise Webb]
August 6, 1963

[★ ★ ★] Then there's the bush down there, the same bush with orange blossoms forever, and the old man down there poking in his wooden mailbox. He must be a writer or a madman; he keeps looking in there as if some long-limbed thing sheathed in nylon is going to take him back to the full bright dream. I'm hungry. It's good to be hungry when you can afford to eat. Right now, I can afford. I like crab. You can get a big crab down at one of the stores for around 80 cents and it takes you all day to eat him and you don't feel very sorry for the crab. That makes it nice. Although they say they boil them alive? But they boil me every time I walk out the door. Swosh. sure. I'm lucky to have a rented door to walk out of. haven't read a book in ten years or seen a movie in fifteen and don't give a damn. Airplanes and sirens now. Do you think it is going to rain this Winter? I've got to throw out the cans again. There's the mailman. Hot damn, look at the ol' man run!! [★ ★ ★]

[To Ann Bauman]

[August 14, 1963]

[★ ★ ★] I was jailed for common drunk 6 a.m. Monday morning, bailed out 8 p.m. Monday night. went to court this afternoon (Wednesday). judge gave me choice 3 days vs. $30. I figure easier to lose money than mind.

. . . I must be more careful. I am all right if I drink where I live. Good manager here, good people. But when I go out on the street, BANG.

Anyhow, I am alive yet. Maybe.

I do not even feel depressed. It is all so very odd. my god, what they'll do to a man, over and over again, for nothing.

I never understood society. I understand that it works somehow and that it functions as a reality and that its realities are necessary to keep us from worse realities. But all I sense are that there are plenty of police and jails and judges and laws and that what is meant to protect me is breaking me down. I know that I am not much good in the network and the miracle is that I have remained around this long.

Now: off to work, if my terrible job is still there.

Bukowski contributed to the symposium on 'Little Magazines in America' in Mainstream, *June 1963. The editor was Walter Lowenfels.*

[To Jon and Louise Webb]
August 22, 1963

[★ ★ ★] Wrote to *Mainstream* and sent a buck, they sent money back, and then mailed 2 copies. Said had mailed twice before to WRONG ADDRESS. The whole picture there has been jumbled from the start. It always is when Lowenfels gets a finger in anywhere. First I was contacted by Larsen who said *Stream* had written me but he had misplaced the letter in a bottom drawer for a couple of months, but here it is Buk. Meanwhile, Larsen's article on the littles had already appeared. Not that it matters. But everything always works in a bugged-up fashion and I find more and more that there just aren't any people around. Everybody's clay or horse-shit or posing.

As far as that goes I cannot seem to get unstrung either. I just lay in the sack or stare out the window and I say to myself, come come, old man, this is not the way to create Art. And then another voice says, well, hell, EVERY-BODY's busy creating ART, and maybe that what's the matter. They're all trying to MAKE IT, trying to hustle up their little snail walls. God damn the prince and Tolstoy and Norman Mailer. [★ ★ ★]

The Webbs eventually published an issue of The Outsider *featuring a 'Homage to Kenneth Patchen' section, but not a separate book by him.*

[To Jon and Louise Webb]
August 23, 1963

[★ ★ ★] Good on the Patchen; he's not believed in his fame or he knows that a man working out of fame is the same as a man working out of failure – each time the one or the other begins again, they begin even. You might call this innocence or you might call it non-innocence or you might call it anything, but whatever it is, it is good that he has it.

Does accepting the Patchen book mean that Buk book #2 is off? This will be o.k. if you cannot bear the load, and remember I told you I did not hold you to a second book – which it looks like we don't have the poems for anyhow.

It Catches is plenty for me, I can only bear about so much good. [★ ★ ★]

[To John William Corrington]
August 28, 1963

[★ ★ ★] Well, they marched for freedom on the capital today. That's nice. I prefer a black and WHITE freedom. Someday they are going to find out you can't get a job whether you are black or white. And when you vote – either way, either man can be bad. And they are going to find out that water tastes the same, but then you can't blame a man for wanting small things. They want to go into any church; I don't want to go into a church. They want to vote; I don't want to vote. They want to live where the white man lives; I don't care where I live. They want equal rights, which means the rights I've got, and these rights are so small, so insignif-icant in the living of everyday life that I spit on them. There are rights that are talked about and then there are things that happen. A man will never make it through the machinery of the State. A man must make it through his own bones and mind and his own laws. Great men don't wait on the State. They ignore it or make their own to suit their passions. So the thing in Washington today, the Freedom March, while seeming a lot in essence, in spirit and etc., the forwarding of Man, wow, it is hardly all that at all, and it rolls along in its quiet slime drowning itself as it inspects itself. [★ ★ ★]

[To John William Corrington]
September 3, 1963

[★ ★ ★] I wait mainly on your next novel, the Civil War is all right, and you prob. wanted to write it with your South hand, but must guess (since you ain't talking) that most of the rewrite was to make it stop looking like the South won the war. And yet, even now, the way the Feds have to play with the city cops it looks like the South wasn't played with too much. I really don't know what the war *was* fought for; I mean, I've read the history books and I still don't know. A lot of wars, I think, are fought mostly over SPEECHES AND PROCLAMATIONS and then after everything is over, the whole works returns to the same hard bubble. Yeah, I know. This is pretty simple thinking. [★ ★ ★]

[To Jon and Louise Webb]
September 18, 1963

[★ ★ ★] Got rid of a mass of your rejects to *Targets* for $25 for his next issue as a Signature. Also Holland took a couple, so the luck holds. With *It Catches* coming up, I might need another 10 years off to get my senses back. There is always the danger of writing too much or pushing beyond yourself. Something kills writers and kills them pretty fast, and then we all die anyhow like the fly and the flower, the wail . . . shit, so . . . some dullard outside honking his horn; somebody else hammers. Still the insomnia thing but most of the bleeding has stopped. nasty letter from a churchboy who was handed one of my poems. . . . I'm interested in the Patchen section, of course. Do try to get some DRAWINGS from him along with photos. Do you know that I haven't read any of his books, never seen one? Just a poem here and there, mostly a reprint and mostly all good in this awesome softly real good way; but then, I have not been much of a reader for some time. I get the idea, though, that he has remained *alive* as an Artist. On the back-thing, I really don't know. I am somewhat confused on the back-thing. I think *everybody* with a bad back should be taken care of, including Patchen. I mean, have the medical thing. But the poems are Patchen, and the drawings. And he's as OUTSIDE as any, sure. [★ ★ ★]

[To Jon and Louise Webb]
September, 1963

[★ ★ ★] It took a lot of guts to turn down the Roman offer but hell, you've been there and you know it is only finally chopchop and twist and chop and demand and then you've had it. You depend on their money and the 'free editorial reign' but they've got ways of pulling their money out or getting nasty, and all these fingers running through your brain like neckties. I know that I have always felt better broke than not because when you are broke you have nothing to lose and are loose, and when you get it you worry about protecting it and you don't do *anything but* protect it. [★ ★ ★]

Gypsy, take vitamins, even I do – 99ᶜ for a month's supply – and eat bread and potatoes, and when you can't sleep at night don't fight it, get up and read a newspaper, something dull, the financial sect., war, marches, weather reports, so forth. And be kind to yourself when you're feeling bad, try to think of something good that once happened to you or of something good that might happen to you. We are often too tough with ourselves. I know that this sounds like a corner preacher or etc. but try a little of it: OL' BUK'S EASY WONDER CURE. I wish I could give you about 20 of my pounds; I am a swine; in a morgue I would look like a stuffed turkey. [★ ★ ★]

[P.S.] no man is an island but why are so many of them flecks of dirt?

[To Neeli Cherry]
September 20, 1963

well, kid, I got your burnt Bukowski poem bust-out booklet, and it was somewhat like finding angels female with good figures and some wing in *The Daily Racing Form*, and I thank you for the toast (burnt) and I guess you are neva gon forget I threw one a your poems in the fire. but you've got to remember it was a hot night and the fingers of my mind were sweating, I was almost out of stuff to drink and your old man kept running in and out of the back door with this constant stagger of logs and I was standing in front of the fireplace and it got hotter and hotter and I thought I was a wheel from the old Lafayette Escadrille and when you handed me a poem there was nothing left to do but dump it along with the rest of me. ;;;ah, a hell of an excuse. !!!

well, the booklet had some good poems in a kind of blaring hardstone sense that is really closer to feeling than the perfumed hanky drillwork of OUR contemporaries; but I remember your bedroom and you asleep in there like a sick frog, and pictures of Hem on your walls, pictures of Hem and maybe Faulk and so forth, well, this is better for a kid than Henry Ford and almost as good as ice hockey but look someday the pictures have to come down, the walls will have to be as bare as say the ass of your own reflections getting pinched by the light, and paeans to a minor poet c.b. must stop. It is pretty hard, as you must guess, not to die before the last Supper of your 30th. birthday in our American Society, and then you are never safe, you can go at any time like any Mailer or Jones, although I do not know their ages nor am I interested. The novel nowadays has become the guillotine. You can last longer growing inside and around the poem although it isn't any news that you won't make any money but you'll live longer even if you sell papers on the corner than you will hustling The Book of the Month Club. This is stale advice from an old man to a young man, and much of the bad breath of old age is that the old tend to tell the young where the sun comes up. I think maybe it is time for the old to listen to the young but since I am at this moment handing it out, I will continue to slough it. Don't ever write a novel unless it hurts like a hot turd coming out. You will know when this happens; it has not yet happened to me but it can happen to you. If you ever feel like pressing, get drunk or draw something on a piece of paper or a piece of ass. There are plenty of doors to go out of that breaks the place of yourself up but if there's enough left when you get back maybe you got a hustle going. [★ ★ ★]

[To Jon and Louise Webb]
October 1, 1963

I did not make work tonight, and so there it goes: the job on the edge of the cliff again, and I do not like work and have no trade but I do like to eat, so this is basic, the basic training of slaves to fear, but I wrote some poems and it does not matter whether they are good or not – yes, it does, everything should be as sharp as possible: I talk like a fool; what I mean is, it is good to hear the typewriter running again across my brain like a lawnmower or a machinegun or what is left of anything. You've got to get the idea of this breakfast nook here, it's always hot, and mostly always beer, but sometimes just the window and I look out the window and like any other damnfool writer I begin to wonder where the soul went, and I used to think this was foolish, but no more, I know that the soul does *go*: zip, and then that's that. Only you don't think of it like an expensive item, like a big diamond, more like a good solid piece of ass with eyes of sea that walked out for somebody with more $$$ or more dangle or more natural decency toward his fellow being. ow. [★ ★ ★] There are good days, tho, when the whole world unfolds . . . unfolds like what? like a lie. Most of us hold onto jobs if we can, sell brooms door to door, work in post offices, slaughterhouses, collection agencies, all that hell. Hell and hell and hell, on and on. I no longer wonder about Rimbaud running the guns and hunting gold and going buggy in Africa. He only wanted time to write poetry, I think. And he wanted it so bad that he didn't write anymore.

Starvation may or may not make artists; I only know that it gets very tiresome to STARVE while guys pass you on the streets with faces that look like dishpans and bellyfuls of porterhouse and fries and all those things that kill: like penthouse blondes and collections of Mozart, ow. I mean, I write better, I think, when I am not worried about the belly or the rent or scraping up a piece of ass. These things are primaries and when you get them out of the way you can begin to worry or unworry about a hell of a lot of other things you wouldn't have time to think about in the first place. I don't mean I am for Harvard educations. I'm not. If I had one I would probably say they are o.k. but since I don't have one they can't be o.k. for me because it is not happening. I paid the rent today and if I walk on the job tomorrow and they do not barber me too much we will have PEACE for 3 or 4 days, maybe. There is always this sense of futility and disgust that you have been hammered finally into something which you do not WANT TO BE, and as long as you are conscious of this and not man enough or clever enough to find a way out, you are going to be pretty generally unhappy like with hot tongs gripping your guts most of the time. This is sad but it makes me glad I've written a few poems today, bad and/or?, and this is madness too, I know, a kind of screaming. Yet I know people, other people who do this; they send me their poems in the mail. Well, it's nice to be selected to have poems sent to if you are not an editor; if you are an editor, well, it's just another day's work. Well, most of the poems are bad, to me, that is. I don't like them. I read them and say, Christ ugg, and throw them away. Yet these people think I am human, more human than an editor, and this is all right. But what I get from this mainly is the idea of all these people going wacky mad etc., out there really, while in actuality they are working as waitresses, truck drivers or male hairdressers. I prefer the poems from the ladies especially when they enclose their photos. But what I mean is: there are all these people out there going mad and writing bad poetry, and when somebody *does* SHOVE THROUGH it is kind a landmark, don't you think? Now Ginsberg bothered me a long time, and then somebody told me Burroughs got a regular check from the Burroughs adding machine co. and some of the floss fell away, let alone the homo bit which DOES bother no matter how humanitarian you try to get. But you've got to hand it to Ginsberg. He's gotten away. He's sitting in India, which is something. I guess they've got good beer in India and I imagine now and then Corso comes to see him, which will later give them both something to talk about write about, a kind of Lawrence-Huxley mess, you know the people bite on this and get excited. The only people who come to see me are winos who need enough change to round out 64 cents. But Ginsberg has gotten out of it somehow so he has time to write even if he ends up writing badly. It's a gathering of dust and electrodes and a vomiting out, later. But he's got a better chance than if he were working in a Chinese Laundry or as Secretary of State – IF HE REMAINS UNPROFESSIONAL. But the problem is not Ginsberg tonight, it is me. I feel like a sow or an edge of dust of a lamp shade in the attic. I do not want *attention*; I want myself and they are tearing the arms of my mind apart. The only thing which saves me from cutting my belly out like an apple pie is that I am a coward, and anyway I have so many things wrong with me now that any one of them could take care of the situation with less clutter. God save the King and send in the longshots. If people can set themselves on fire in the streets, I can have another cigarette. They have turned off the refrigerator and the beer is warm. I must wash my stockings.

[To Jon and Louise Webb]
October 18, 1963

[★ ★ ★] Whenever I need a lift I look at that table of contents you sent and I think of all the pages and all the poems. You really let the book run away with you and I'm glad. If I remember right you were once thinking of 60 pages. If I never write another poem, I will always have this book, a kind of holy thing to me. [★ ★ ★] And we've got the right title too. After these months it has become solid as a wall. I'll never forget the night I came across it, early a.m., and I said, they've got to take it, they've just got to. And then sweating Cerf. I've been lucky on the titles of my books because the editors have always gone right along, and each title has explained my mental-spiritual shape of the moment – or if this is too fancy: the way I felt. [★ ★ ★]

[To John William Corrington]
October 18, 1963

[★ ★ ★] I may have to move from here. Only reason I have stayed here so long is that I am forced to live in apartments or rooms, and all these years here there hasn't been anybody with a loud T.V. Now there is. The guy downstairs died of a heart attack and somebody else moved in there. This somebody blares the T.V. up through my floorboards. I don't have a T.V. and I don't mind other people having them – as long as I don't have to listen. I can listen to lovers' quarrels and/or beatings without distaste but these quiz contests, news broadcasts and COMEDY? that stinks up through my floorboards is like getting slapped across the soul (?) with a dirty floormop. The masses give me trouble not because they are basically stupid but because they push their stupidity into my life. People are always talking about vague things like 'freedoms' or newspaper things like 'civil rights,' and this all sounds good and makes them think they are saying something. This wordage is putty without shape. The most needed thing is THE FREEDOM AND RIGHT OF PRIVACY FROM OTHER PEOPLE'S SOUNDS OF LIFE. It is difficult for a poor man to attain this. Neeli Cherry of *Black Cat Review* asked me to write something about 'Civil Rights,' but I knew what he wanted. What other people call civil rights, I don't even want. Nobody really has any rights anyhow, not even the rich; you save what you can and try not to be fooled too often. There's a law for them and a law for me and if my law is broken too often, I am dead. I didn't write the article for Cherry on c. rights. Somebody else will give him what he wants. Sure.

I have been visiting people lately, which is only mostly to explore that they are not there mostly and to see if I can sit still and listen to TALK. Hit Jack Hirschman's for burned steak and scotch, and next night went to – rather a week later – Orlane Mahak's big picture window that overlooks the sickening Sunset Strip, had Brazilian chicken and rice, but brought a woman along who liked to TALK and so she talked and I sat there mostly which saved me. I talk quite stupidly, you see; I cannot get the thought out of my mind into proper order to be made into sound for the air. In fact, I don't want to. I am like a child hiding what he thinks is a hell of a hell of a hell of a jewel in my back pocket, and I don't want to show it to anybody. If I do, it will be in the proper temple. But after one visit people don't bother me anymore and I don't bother them. That's the sweet part, daddy. When I walk out the door the first thing the good people do is look at each other and say, 'Jesus, was THAT Charles Bukowski?' If I knew how to talk I'd sell all the old streetcar tracks in this town to the Black Muslims.

[★ ★ ★] Somebody at one of these places, I think Mahak's, asked me: 'What do you do? How do you write, create?' You don't, I told them. You don't try. That's very important: *not* to try, either for Cadillacs, creation or immortality. You wait, and if nothing happens, you wait some more. It's like a bug high on the wall. You wait for it to come to you. When it gets close enough you reach out, slap out and kill it. Or if you like its looks you make a pet out of it.

Then this woman who likes to TALK jumped in: 'You can't make RULES! That's all right for YOU to say "don't try" but you can't make a rule like that for everybody. It's like saying – '

'O.K.,' I said, 'I quit.'

I've heard all these things centuries ago and I still hear them, the same old sayings and terms, things like . . . well, they like the word CULTURE and they like the word MIDDLE–CLASS and when they put them together like MIDDLE–CLASS, CULTURE, this really sounds like something and it makes them feel good but it doesn't mean anything, it is like CIVIL RIGHTS or FREEDOM, words long ago washed way away and left meaningless by abuse and over-use. [★ ★ ★]

[To Jon and Louise Webb]
October 19, 1963

[★ ★ ★] Some outfit in Frisco wants me to give a reading in Feb., offer of 2/3rds of house but I can't see myself on the boards in front of the yak hyenas, lonely hearts and homos. Not yet. If I were starving, maybe so. But I am not yet starving. People keep explaining to me that I am really lonely, and this makes my ass bleed too. What they are talking about really is themselves and they figure my machinery has to be set the same way. There is nothing sweeter to me than closing the door on the world, having the walls again. Generally, I am too TIRED to be lonely: a hangover or bucking the horses or the job or some woman and when the time is finally given to me I like to duck under the table and hide rather than go get myself the wet nurse of the crowd. You remember the poem I wrote of the man who dug a hole in the ground and crawled down into it? And he didn't tell the people why when they asked why, he only smiled because he knew that they wouldn't understand, he knew that he was odd-fish out – Outsider of the year, Outsider of the world. I too have learned not to explain anymore. Let them win the word-games of the air; if I have anything to say I hope to put it into a rock with a fork. Maybe it will last through a few rains or maybe they'll throw it into a cesspool, endurability is not so much the matter anyhow as is waste and nonsense and yak yak yak. [★ ★ ★]

[To Jon and Louise Webb]
October 27, 1963

[★ ★ ★] Wild telegram from Orlani Mahak. Perhaps she needs . . . friendship? . . . but she appears to be supporting a very young poet and thinker (I only know as David) and it so happens I like David and would also have to work around the stuff I have on hand now and I don't like to tiptoe or to spoil somebody else's game. Besides, all this has very little to do with writing the poem, and I am still interested in that, and I realize that if I had not written the poem the Orlani Mahaks would not be telegramming me, but it is the stuff of my own kind of life I am interested in, and what this other stuff is I don't quite know. I don't want to become anybody's pet. I know that Henry Miller was good at it. Henry, like the rest of us, hated to work for somebody else; but I hate to be petted by somebody else. Which does not make me a better Artist than Henry Miller, just a different person, and not nearly so famous, thank the gods! [★ ★ ★]

[To Jon and Louise Webb]
November 10, 1963

[★ ★ ★] No poems lately, although I may knock off a couple to send with this, I doubt it, I've got to be alone and the woman has just come back [★ ★ ★]

Now she sings, 'There is no Christ upon the Cross
    and we are sad . . .'
She makes these songs up. You see why I drink?
Now she sings, 'Buk is bleeding from the asshole,

     Buk is bleeding from the asshole,

    and we don't give a
               damn

                  damn

                     damn . . .!'

You see why I drink? You see? You see?

Get some drawings out of Patchen . . . those upside down soft elephant creatures asking us to save the world of flowers and baby's hands, they're good like sunlight on putty in the window says. [★ ★ ★]

[To Jon and Louise Webb]

November 26, 1963: THE DAY

I came back from the store and there was the package against the door 'don't open 'til Xmas,' but to hell with that, I *have* been waiting, and I tore the paper off, saw the miracle: jacket, cover, skeleton in sand, the works the works . . . peeling back the pages I ate the whole insides, read the poems I have forgotten, the good Corrington, back page wherein you describe paper, type etc., the humor-agony bug-rat breakdown struggle which goes so well along with the author. And to say you've come through is nothing; that you've come through in this way . . . page by page, inch by inch, breakdown by breakdown, cut fingers, landladies, the street corner, the hours, my god, if the poems have been wasted the BOOK has not been wasted, little calm and precious beauties and loves of doing like a garden of good, like mountains, like everything that counts . . . by god, you've done it, you've done it, and I'm proud and struck and awed that you have – the both of you – caught me up in it.

This is the kind of book that grows on you in days not minutes; this is the kind of book that you remember like you remember war or birth or love or fire, this singing in my darkest dark–the photo of Buk with cigarette, everything, everything, there is no beginning, I don't know where to touch the book next – first I think the jacket is impossibly impossibly true, then I go elsewhere, it's like walking through a forest with wine at high noon and everything gone except the soaring my god, you've done it, you've done it! Never such a book! Where? Where?? in all the libraries, in all the cities I have never seen such a book put together in such a way, inventive creativeness and love. Where have the publishers been for centuries? You've done it.

you've done it.

The books will sit and grow on me, they will enter me, it is a part, a beholden and miraculous part. It does little to say more: the whole thing wells and turns in me almost impossibly. My thanks my thanks for all the love and honor and pain and beauty; the pain yours, the others you've passed to me. Going now, going.

[To Jon and Louise Webb]
November 26, 1963

Sitting here smoking a 1/4 last night's cigar and savoring the book –
as I will always savor it, it is endless with endless little touches, and looking
at the jacket now – the way it works around the cover, the marble paper
over our sandman skeleton, and do thank (for me) Chevrier and Salantrie
for their fine work. The jacket I cannot figure out, how it has this antique
quality and I do not figure it out, it would be like tearing a rose, formulas
do not interest me, it is the thing being there like the sun that warms me.
I do not think there will ever be another event in my life like this book,
and I keep thinking of the years drunk in the alleys, of the 3 years I sat in
the same Philly bar on the same barstool from 6 or 7 a.m. in the morning
until 2 a.m. the next morning, staring down at the wood, listening to
nothing, maybe, and now this book, this book, this book out of nothing
like somebody saying, see, it is not nearly *all* bad. I know how close you
must come to dying in fighting from all nothingness of poverty, hoping on
luck, a break from the sky, kinder landlords, praying typefaces do not
break, that somebody will send a dollar for paper, that somebody will buy
a postcard or a painting from Gypsy, that the body will hold up, that the
landlord will smile, that cars will not run you over, everything everything,
so please do not say that your blood is 'more like the pseudo-stuff that
bleeds from the *madras* tissue between pages 96 and 97.' I know better and
the living people of the world know better. Don't make me sad; the
miracle is yours; you have drowned me in honor, and no matter what
cheap hotel, what jail, what grave is there for me, they can never take away
the miracle.

I would like to say that the people who have seen the book are as
taken with it as I and that the last page which begins '777 copies of this
book . . .' is one of the best poems, if not the best poem in the book.

A little sadness here – and I thought I'd tell you before anybody else
told you – in the poem 'Dinner, Rain & Transport' page 46, one line was
left out, 'I can prophecy evil,' this was to proceed 'with the force of a jackhammer.' And when I say a little sadness I know it will be mostly yours,
for to me the book is so much that this makes no difference, so please
don't blame yourself for being also real enough to error. [★ ★ ★]

President Kennedy was assassinated on November 22nd.
'The book' is It Catches My Heart in Its Hands, *published by the Webbs'*
Loujon Press with a foreword by Corrington.

[To John William Corrington]
November 27, 1963

I have been putting off writing thinking maybe the book would come
and it did come – the day after Kennedy was assassinated, and now I have
the book on my right side and the beer on my left and I am king prince
lightning Ruth in '28, Nap at the top, Hitler in Paris [★ ★ ★]

Your foreword is more honor, and quite prophetic: 'the marksman will
not be long in coming.' I don't look into myself to see why certain wheels
turn; I feel this is dangerous. First, if you get to know what you are doing
you are apt to keep doing it, or second you might become so self-conscious you end up sounding like an old Rudy Vallee recording. Both are
bad. [★ ★ ★]

[To Ann Bauman]
December 4, 1963

Like the American provincial, I start my letter: 'I have been meaning
to write but – '

It's good you liked the book; I feel that Webb has surrounded me with
more than the poems deserve, and he will hear this from many quarters,
but for it all, he has created a book such as I have never seen, and he (*they*
really!) have done it out of absolute poverty and the force of their beings.
[★ ★ ★]

The book has lifted me high over the branches, building, etc., but they
are still there, and I go on, actually tired physically as if I had been
wrestling a bear for 43 years, and I slept ten hours today and wish I could
sleep ten more but after I type this I must go to the place and the place
will have its way. [★ ★ ★]

[To Jon and Louise Webb]
December 7, 1963

[★ ★ ★] Enclosed the article Robt. Fink was speaking of, mentioning *Outsider,* and lucky the papers lay on the floor with the beercans for days or I would have long ago thrown this bit away, but enclosed. Lipton gained his golden head through the BEATS but the beats through their artifact of so-called brawny and courageous poeticism did more damage to the pure poem trying to breathe than Poetry Chicago has done accepting the accepted. The trouble with the BEATS: they gathered in crowds to gather SOLACE and when you take the gang–form you become the gang – i.e., the same as CORE or Congress or STANDARD OIL or American Banana and their assorted $ ventures and assassinations and cries. You've got to rise from the floor alone or fall back alone. What I mean is: conceive the Art-form and forget it, and conceive it again if you have the blue blood and the red blood the bull blood to carry you past the matador the god whatever so and whosoforever stands in the way. I told you I was drinking beer. [★ ★ ★]

Corrington writes me to ask what I think of the Kennedy thing. So, after I finish with this letter I must write and tell my oh my I must tell him, and he's tough but he might not like what I say, and to you I say although I do not hold K. martyred as most, I do not like the dissolution of K. on down to a RUBY. The only thing that could be low enough to kill Ruby, a Ruby, would be a turd, and maybe one of them will stick into a stone mortuary within his intestines, but I doubt that – shit generally gets along with shit.

[★ ★ ★] If Henry Miller reviews me and it comes out bad, don't worry. I once reviewed Henry Miller. I was in a little bus station in the middle of Texas and some gal who had been ramming her tongue down my throat went into the ladies' room and I walked over to the newsstand with my hair down in my eyes and I bought one of the *Cancers,* I forget which, and Henry understood that the only way to get to a man was to speak the language of the day, the present tongue, but he got to a part where he talked about a guy with a big cock and how he made it with all the women with THIS BIG COCK, and he went on and on with this and I began getting sleepy and worse . . . worse than ANYTHING, I got the idea that Henry Miller the ALL-KNOWING didn't know much more about fucking than to talk about it, and that's the way most non-fuckers are. But then, it's easy and simple to knock great names or kill 1/4 great men, and I remember when I was very young, Hem used to work out in the ring, you know, and I always dreamed that I would volunteer to sit in the opposite corner, and in my dream, of course, I kayoed HEMINGWAY, and therefore I was a greater writer, I was a greater everything. Which is pure shit, and a kind of Oswald-Ruby thing. But Hemingway was partly responsible for it because – for all his hardcore writing which was good and needed to be done – he did build, at times, this sort of Hollywood plastic-image sort of thing, and what many call his greatest work, the thing that appeared in LIFE week by week installments, was a returning to his youthful formula of strength and victory and death and bravado straight on down the line, the only thing being he was no longer young, the snows had melted, and when he put the gun to his head he was putting the death to ungrowing cancer, and that the public (*Life*) was ready at the same time as he was ready, this was sad.

And, now having neatly disposed of Hem and Miller, which is a kind of a bitchy thing, but all writers are bitches clothed in articles of the sun, and I am sad because we are all such bitches, all so unreal, and maybe it comes back to the thing I was thinking during the then years drunken blackness: that real men don't WRITE. But, if they don't, WHERE ARE THEY? I have looked, everywhere. [★ ★ ★]

p.s. I guess *The Old Man and the Sea* was presented in ONE installment in *Life*. no matter; same god damn thing.

[To John William Corrington]
December 7, 1963

[★ ★ ★] Somebody told me tonight when I said that the real men work in fish factories, somebody told me that men that work in fish factories are too tired to write, I told this person that English teachers are too *untired* to write, she told me, or started to, this broad, she started to tell me about the agonies of an English teacher, but having known English teachers, having looked upon their faces, and having worked in slaughter houses, cake factories, railroad gangs, madmen, I told her not to tell me about the agonies of an English teacher . . . correcting essays, planning midterms, grading by the albatross scale, and writing *poetry* in between all this agony of deciding whether they are homosexual or whether Clayborn who teaches Advanced E. 2 is a punk [★ ★ ★]

You aske' me what I think a tha Kennedy. I don't think anything of the K. Down where I work they have a black sign under his picture: MARTYRED. Do you really think so? Harvard? A fine piece of ass that starved herself to keep a figure that would kill babies. Do you think a man is martyred because he follows the open downhill path? Is it really HELL to be born with more money than you can ever spend? Is it hell to never think about where the rent is coming from? Is it HELL TO HAVE SOMEBODY ELSE PUT A BULLET INTO YOUR HEAD INSTEAD OF YOURSELF PUTTING THE BULLET THERE? Where does hell come from and how do you spell it? Do only the top-figure people suffer? How many dead were buried on the same day K. was buried? Who bull-like bleeds from a sword? Hell, ace, who gets cut when they are shaving? Kennedy followed the wigwam in. He *could have* turned the presidency down. I WOULD HAVE. Oswald was a fink, true. He read too many books and lived too little. He was never in love with the sunlight or watching a cat walk across the rug. Kennedy was, a little. Ruby, he never saw anything. And now, being alive now, I think of Lincoln, he got it too, but I keep thinking, for all the turning he caused, could we not through the years of not-knowing, of awayness, [have] over-evaluated this man? Huh? What ya think, Willie? Maybe I only got beer running out of my oyster ears. [★ ★ ★]

Willie, you prick, I am drunk, but this instance of burning, these dry ash tears rolling down my fat arms and belly, I thank you for the good foreword, and only hope you are partly right; I remember once talking to the old man over the phone when he told me he was going to put my photo on cover of *Outsider* #3, and I asked him, 'How do you know that this isn't going to give me the fat head?' And he answered, 'That's the chance I've got to take.' Which was very kind. Anything I hate, it's a sense of false humility. Saying such things as, 'Oh, I really don't *deserve* this.' But almost worse, is feeling that you do deserve it. I hope that my evenings, nights, mad-drunk in drunken alleys, g.d. jails, hospitals, I hope I remember these things, I hope I remember the broken-winged bird in the cat's mouth, I hope I remember the rifle poking out of a 5th story window, I hope that I remember what I should remember, I hope I do not ever become a Will Rogers plying humanity through his simple and lovely face that the only thing to do is to love humanity because it is the only thing to do, win big the big love, I am lifting another beer and hoping I remain the same and grow the same as whatever seed was planted within me from a hateful father and an indifferent mother. See here, you Freudianists, get out your notebooks, and you have the ANSWER. Well, I've read Freud too.

He had enough sex but not enough climaxes; his brain was too far above and, at the same time, too far below his belt. Love, which I hardly know and am very afraid of, Freud never considered. I am not speaking Christianity which is shit also. I am speaking shit commonsense living wherein we, you and I and she and Oswald-ex, are all involved in. Thanks for good foreword. And when I am dead, bad enough, worse enough, when I am living somebody will tear the mind of my chicken limbs apart for burning, and they will be right, we are all wrong forever, there is an unanswered question, some face burning in the night, and for a time I thought too it was Marxism we needed or Plato or a rereading of Shakespeare or the alls of anything, ugg pal, it appears Willie we are all irrevocably lost forever and like Tom Wolfe, Mencken, Ruby, we do we do the best we can.

[To Jon and Louise Webb]
December 18, 1963

I, too, am shot. They have machine gunned me down with their labors and I have bought their plan, god damn them, I've got to get the horses moving, no rich women around I can bear . . . 12 hours of madness a night, left shoulder, arm and neck, I mean right shoulder arm and neck about paralyzed and then insomnia, go back moth-eyed and white to the spider mouth and they suck again, and as you can see all this is making me a withered crank. . . . Like the old poem, or something like it: we need time to stop and stare* and blow cigar smoke in the air. [★ ★ ★]

* 'What is this life if full of care, / We have no time to stand and stare?' – from 'Leisure' by W. H. Davies, a popular anthology poem. – *Ed.*

[To Jon and Louise Webb]
December 25, 1963

Christmas night and they've battered their heads together until they are silly and they've smiled themselves silly and vomited on the floor, 98% of them amateur drinkers, amateur Christians, amateur human beings; and I got 4 more books yesterday and lined them up with the other, they stand there, each one different, each one a piece of something, and they are FOR

SALE, anybody can have one for $10, double the price on the jacket, for this is the cost of the paper alone (to me), and the labor and the poems and all else is FREE. Yet how can you put a price on anything like this? [★ ★ ★] You and I don't have much to do with money because we know that money is beside the point, except enough of it to keep you alive so that you can do something else BESIDE $$$. This is what you've done bringing out this book in this way, and when I hang a $10 on it, it is not an insult, just enough to allow me to KEEP ALL THE BOOKS because I like them lined up against the wall, although I did give one away to Sherman because I am supposed to get one back of his wherein I did the foreword and I wonder what in the hell I said in the foreword like some John William Corrington who did o.k. but luckily I do not wear hats.

· 1964 ·

[To Ann Bauman]
January 2, 1964

the wind is blowing singing inside of my head with holy tiger's feet and also banging the shade and I have pulled down the dirty window, and it's all over, god, it's all over, xmas, New Year's night, and now I feel better, almost as good as they pretended to feel, these hardhearts, these shards, these sharks, and now the woman downstairs beats on the ceiling with the end of a broom handle, my typewriter disturbs her, it punctuates the Javanese exotic head-sounds of her T.V. Well, it is a god damned bad fix, and we go on. Wow. Walking the streets. Drinking coffee. Writing letters to ladies in Sacramento. Another cigarette. A Parliament. Go with cancer. I will be sorry. I will be. I remember reading a book by by . . . shit, he was one of my favorites, yet I cannot remember his name . . . yes, Knut Hamsun, book about a nut house and one of the patients, he was called the Suicide, always talking about it, you know, and then one day the building caught on fire and who came crawling laboriously painfully like a snail down the hot rain pipe? Of course, the S.

And this is enough wind for early 64. [★ ★ ★]

The book of poems here envisioned appeared as Cold Dogs in the Courtyard *from Literary Times-Cyfoeth in 1965.*

[To Jon and Louise Webb]
January 4, 1964

[★ ★ ★] I have been kind of dreaming lately, in spite of *It Catches*, which shows you how we go on like grub, I have been thinking of the 4 books and the stuff I have written; and with these 4 editors I have . . . I have had no part in the selection, didn't want to, didn't trust myself, and yet lately I have been thinking that what the 4 have skipped (much of it) is not only pretty good stuff but maybe my best??? This is a hell of a statement I know. And so I was hoping to get somebody to run these poems in book form; I was going to write a foreword telling a little about how things work, and this is what is left, and god damn you, reader, what do you think? I was going to call the book *Cold Dogs in the Courtyard*, meaning rejected poems, of course. [★ ★ ★]

I hear from people on the book, answer them, but without being too much of a prick I try to insert the idea that maybe the creation of ART could be more important than my writing letters to them – or anybody writing letters to them. Hand-holding won't get it done. 4 walls can teach more about writing than any praise-mongering lying friend or person. I am not Hemingway but even not being Hemingway I never considered writing to Hemingway or asking him anything, or worse: telling him anything. I did, however, consider writing *myself*, and once or twice I did. maybe 3 times. I am a very powerful influence on myself. This happened in Philadelphia and I was not lonely. There is something wrong with me: I am never lonely. It could get that way. I could get doddy. The world can work on you, trick you. The traps. My man Jeffers spoke of this. Beware the g.d. traps . . . that trapped God.

> when he
> walked on earth.

Those are some pretty good lines. If I can ever learn to write as well as Jeffers I will throw all the apples on my table out of the window and they can have me. [★ ★ ★]

[To Jon and Louise Webb]
January 10, 1964

[★ ★ ★] Don't remember writing a long letter but if you got one, fine. Sometimes when there is plenty of beer and cigars and the electric light hits the white paper and the chopper chops and that whore downstairs doesn't bang on my floor I go on and on, a little cracked, kind of hypnotic, smoke and cold beer and PAP PAP PAP PAP PAP, and this, too, is good for what is left of the soul. [★ ★ ★]

'Frances' is Frances Smith, who had recently become pregnant with Bukowski's daughter, Marina.

[To Ann Bauman]

January 23, 1964

Frances says she will write in a couple of days.

Little here. New tenant downstairs knocks on her ceiling (my floor) when I type. This, of course, disturbs the thought context all to hell. Doesn't she know that I am the great Charles Bukowski? the bitch!!

Cold here and the life force drags on within, dull, putrid, limping. The job is white light, heat and madness. But then, starvation is a bother, and with either course I feel the coward.

Blighted god damned roaring stinking world.

Cheer up, dear.

the works,

[Unknown Addressee]

January 28, 1964

You knock on my floor when I type within hours. Why in the hell don't you keep your stupid t.v. set *down* at 10:30 tonight? I don't complain to managers, but it seems to me that your outlook is very one-sided.

H. Bukowski
Apt. #303

[Reply to Above]

[Sir:

It is not my T.V. set you hear, I don't have it loud at any time.

I was told you work from 5:30, but your machine is going day night and Sunday. It is like living beneath an arsenal.

This is an apt house not a business establishment. You have had your television on loud until midnight and later. It sounds as if you have all kinds of machinery up there.

You would not be allowed all that noise and racket in any apt house where people live for peace and quiet.

I have been in this house 26 years, and have inquired from many people, and you are out of line.

apt. 203]

[To Jon and Louise Webb]
February 5, 1964

Thanks for sending the review. On the review: I don't think I am 'tough' but if the poetry appears that way it is only because they are used to a different content and style. I am more tired than anything and if I refuse to get heated-up over a Sunrise or the blooming of a peony, they think this is tough. Rest of review pretty much on stick, though, and does your printing achievement some justice, and should move some copies. Whoever wrote the article seemed to enjoy the book, and that's all we want, that, and to get down off the cross.

Sorry on your finances on #4. You put so much time and $$ into book that you smashed yourself, and yet that you got carried on this wave, you must know, is not all loss. What happens to people when they see it, the incredulous wonder and awakening . . . I am not speaking of the poetry but of the book, the makeup . . . Frances' daughter wrote to her and she said when she got book she just held it in her hand for an hour, looking through it, at it, not even reading the poems. It is this awakening of the people with beauty in a world where beauty hardly exists anymore, where we are all too 'tough,' this kind of thing, just looking and wondering, it's still in people, somewhere, but it takes an act like yours to bring it back.

'Purples' were special colophon sheets for a more expensive issue of It Catches My Heart in Its Hands. *The letter to Tibbs mentioned here is reproduced as an illustration in this volume.*

[To Jon and Louise Webb]
February 7, 1964

[★ ★ ★] I stole 2 excerpts from letter to Ben Tibbs tonight for purples. I hope he does not think me a zero for this. Wrote letter first without thought of anything – then got 'purples' on mind. [★ ★ ★]

[To Ann Bauman]
February 18, 1964

Mind all clogged with useless things – can't get straight – but glad book did something for you – but as you know – it's only the *next* poem that counts, and, then, it hardly counts.

Depressed and jammed-up against small things forever, that's the way if works. 4 day cold. other scratches.

The book itself is a kind of small miracle to rest against – temporarily. Looks like you've got a good typewriter. Don't get robbed again.

Mothers are particularly painful because the world has rubbed most of them down to small utterings of inanity. [* * *]

[To Jon and Louise Webb]
March 1, 1964

[* * *] I am getting a little drunk, a good wall to hide behind, the coward's flag. I remember once in some city in some cheap room, I believe it was St. Louis, yes, a hotel on the corner and the gas fumes of traffic going to work used to come up and choke my sick lazy lungs, and I'd send her out for beer or wine and she was trying to get me straight, trying to mother me or hang me or figure me, as all women will try to do, and she gave me this old bit: 'Drinking is only escapism.' Sure, I told her, and thank old red-balled God it is, and when I fuck you, that is escapism too, you may not think it is, to you it might be living, now, let's have a drink.

I wonder where she is now? A big fat black maid with the fattest biggest most loveliest legs in the universe and ideas about 'escapism.' I wonder if she's thinking of me now, sitting here 20 years later growling about stolen microphones and that the human race is garbage?

Frances pregnant, looks as if I'll have to move from here, looks like marriage (again) and disorder but hoping for more suave luck and grace to help me this time, I would not hope to be cruel to either woman or child, god give me grace for I am weak and sad and do not feel good, but if any disorder happens . . . let it be in my life, not theirs. [* * *]

Frances is a good woman, she gets a little snappish and churlish at times but they all do, and I pretend I am asleep or I do not hear and it soon passes over . . . She kind of has this coffeehouse attitude, appears determined to save and understand all mankind, and this is a kind of obvious and tiring nobility, the other night she fell asleep reading *The People's World*, and then she goes to a writers' workshop, which, of course, is kind of obnoxious to me, always has been; but, then, I have my racetracks and beer and my nice beer drinking friends . . . It all comes out fairly even, depending upon whose head you are looking out of. Like, I imagine the guys who burned Joan of Arc had some strong ideas of why they were doing it. Ah?

I still feel good that Genet liked the book. He is one of the few geniuses of our flat age, moongone stealing immoral unimmortal cheap age. There seems so little; it is like being locked in a tin room that they are heating up and it gets hotter hotter and then you are just finally a flake of black shit. I speak not of death but of the *wearing* qualities of our age, the gross similarities. You can speak with a leader of nations or with a cleaner of spittoons and they will tell you the same things, they will look the same. We need more light than this or it gets too dull or drab to go on. Genet does this. He's like a flower in a coal pit.

Haydn's symphony #99 on now. I guess I haven't heard all of Haydn's symphonies; I guess few men have. It is good to have workmen like this around. It does damn well get hard to move on now and then, to open a door, to get dressed, to take your clothes to the laundry, to think of a way to get money, to try to sleep, to try to love to listen, everything gets hard, it gets harder, and I will not scream when death comes I will look at it like the little faint green lace vines they spread between flowers of large bouquets, and I will go without damage of transition, like a man taking his dog out to walk.

[To Jon and Louise Webb]
March 2, 1964

[★ ★ ★] Frances says you should come to Los Angeles but I do not agree. This is one big town full of phonies, as you realize. Arizona has such nice little lizards and horny toads running through the hot sand or sitting on top of big rocks looking at you. You can't get that here. I remember once walking out of a small Arizona town, the sun came down like magic, all yellow still, I kept going out into the desert, there was nobody around, not a human in sight. I almost didn't come back. But as you see, I have. [★ ★ ★]

By the way, in case you do do the book, I still, at this moment lean to the title *For Regions Lower than Crying*, although I may come up with a later preference, I could go with this one without being hurt too much; the title fits the series of edgy sequence of my titles, makes sense thru the looking glass. . . . Although I realize this title might bear a first similarity to A. E. Housman's 'Brooks Too Broad for Leaping,' but whereas Housman's title relates directly to death, the impossibility of escaping it, mine relates to the utter sadness, the almost unbearability of existence. [★ ★ ★]

[To John William Corrington]
March 6, 1964

I divined that you had turned on me out of some mysterious nature inherent in x-English teachers, all of whom I trust very little, I g.d. being crabbed by nature and busted by a heft of drizzly and ignoble Southern California sunsets, I felt that when you did not respond to my last letter . . . Then too, some English mail-man may have stuck the letter into a snow bank. Anyhow, you louse, I am still alive and I feel that my head is no fatter than usual in spite of articles on one Bukowski in *Northwest Review, Descant, Americas* the, and *Polish American Studies*. The latter written by the Rev. Joe Swastek, Librarian of Alumni Memorial Library, SS. Cyril & Methodius Seminary, St. Mary's College, St. Mary's Preparatory, Orchard Lake, Michigan. I got a letter from him this morning wondering if I had done much beside the poems and drawings in the *Epos* number. He wants to fuck up the library with it, which is very nice, I think. I'll send him on to various. [★ ★ ★]

[To Jon and Louise Webb]
March 11, 1964

[★ ★ ★] Two people down at the mill think I have cancer. Maybe I am starting to smell? Anyhow, feel god awful weak and only feel good in bed, but probably only the cause of too much drinking and gambling and working at the same time, and down where I am getting it you have to work and sweat and bleed for it, I do mean. The people are half wild with fear and something they know not of; they tremble and jerk with work neurosis, all cackling flat laughter of the deserted innards, and I am beginning to feel that way too; it is contemptuous what we have done to life and the living and ourselves. I was hoping for luck and skill in the gambling to free me but this too appears only another trap where they throw sand on the living. All the traps, and I walk into all the traps, every one that's there, I spread myself with olive oil and ointment, with hemorrhoid salve and I say *whoops*, LET'S GO, BABIES!!!

It's a hell of a juncture to bust loose and I guess I'll never bust loose, not writing poetry, and it appears I can't even do that anymore, and I sure can't go the novel, not the way I feel, the novel seems like nothing but WORK, a grandiose concept of saying a lot of nothing, and I guess the idea of the poems, good or bad, is to keep me from going crazier. I could pay money to hear some psychiatrist tell me this, and then we'd both feel better; only he'd feel better than I because he'd have my money and a nice secretary to look at walking around the room and to fuck. ah, wilderness, my wilderness. [★ ★ ★]

I reread Camus' *The Stranger* the other night and once again this appeared to me to be the perfect antidote for what was essentially wrong with the resolve in *Crime and Punishment*. It is so good that others do this work for us so that we do not have to do it ourselves.

Children outside gyrating, seeing grass and mystery and freedom, and parental tyranny too; but they (the holy children) will be melded down, they become me: an old man at 4 o'clock in the afternoon writing tea-leaf thoughts in a vestibule that smells of bacon and frogs and tumbling silence.

Bukowski was now living with Frances Smith, who was pregnant with their daughter Marina.

[To John William Corrington]
April 2, 1964

[★ ★ ★]Well, I have got me a pregnant woman and I thought she was too old and that I was too old, and I can't understand it [★ ★ ★]

I sit here now with pains above the stomach and wonder what's left, what a man can do when he's been slugged by the years and the bad jobs and the bad job now and maybe nothing later, I mean when you walk out, when you can't go through that door anymore to look at the impossible faces, the tiny continual hell of doing an idiotic boring searing task at a rate almost beyond bodily endurance, and, getting paid very little, very. Sometimes they forget what they are doing; sometimes they even go insane and take pride in what they are doing, or in what they are not doing. I wrote a poem about this called 'The Workers.' I don't know if I got it down right, I think I might have; anyway, I felt g.d. better for 5 or 10 minutes after I wrote it. [★ ★ ★]

Corrington's novel, And Wait for the Night, *was published by Putnam's, New York.*

[To John William Corrington]

May 1, 1964

[★ ★ ★] I got your book for which, you know, thanks surely, and your book sits on the shelf on top of *Twenty Poems of Cesar Vallejo*, which is pretty good, I guess, and alongside another book, Gray's *Elegy*, which was bought in a used bookstore for 49 cents and is inscribed in very faint pencil: 'Miss Mollie Zahrnde. Elkader, Iowa, Dec. 9, 1903.' Copyright 1893, by Estes and Lauriat.

> The paths of glory lead but to the grave.

[★ ★ ★]

From now until the end of the book, the letters all bear the new address given in the following letter.

[To Jon and Louise Webb]

May 1, 1964

We have moved to –
>   5126¼ De Longpre Ave.
>   Los Angeles 27, Calif.

Old 1623 is gone and it was a magic number and a magic place, but after 6 years there *is* some wear and tear especially after no repairs or replacements of any sort. However, the landowners and their serfs (managers) always holler, charge too much and feel as if they were doing *you* a favor. Narrow-minded bigots that you have to sneak women past and not be seen drunk and not do this and not do that etc. etc.; all this time you are sharing the place with rats and bugs and old churchly women who poke and grovel and skitter and clog the halls of your brain, ugghg. They even called the police on me one night (a couple of years back) and I held them off through the door chain and talked them away. Anyway, don't send any mail there as it may never reach me. They are pissed because I threw a few glasses of whiskey against the walls, bled on the rug & almost died several times and because the water pipes broke continually in the walls and they had to rip their walls open and I was there, usually in bed hungover sick unhappy with their pipes and their bodies their intrusions upon my tiniest of moments. May those whore-hating finks rot before they reach hell. I have spoken. [★ ★ ★]

I don't know where to get a *Village Voice*; if you manage to get an extra copy do send on – this address. It is more difficult, I suppose, to be a *discovered* poet; you've got to carry the load on your soul-back and when you sit down to a typer you are supposed to *do* it. I'd rather be loose, even bad-loose. The name in lights thing is good, of course, especially when you're feeling down – you let yourself taste a little, like a drink, only you know that it doesn't change the *living* life . . . a few more door-knockers, but these soon go away when you don't walk upside down from the ceiling. [★ ★ ★]

I tried to make a tape of poems a week or so ago. Started o.k. but got too drunk and started talking too much between poems and I didn't care for it when I played it back. [★ ★ ★] I think it best to 'talk' the poems instead of poeticizing them, make them 'natural' as you suggested. [★ ★ ★]

The bookseller Jim Roman also published some books of poetry, among them Corrington's Anatomy of Love.

[To Jon and Louise Webb]

May 4, 1964

Got Corrington's *Anatomy of Love* today. very *very* fine stuff in there, what I've read, he's come along a lot, and it's all much better than his novel and it seems a damned shame we can't keep him always with the poem; the novel may eat him up – I hope not.

Very little today. The cats still walk around. One of them ate a bird the other day. I won't talk to the son of a bitch for a week. As you know, I am sometimes not a realist. I can't take it. [★ ★ ★]

[To Ann (Bauman) Menebroker]
May [6, 1964]

good on the marriage.

yes, those long-distance calls tho' they cost us dearly in $$ were MORALE, and very odd and yet a fulfilling strange thing.

I am not married but might as well be. I am in strange country, fairly unhappy, dismantled but no need to be cruel. You can only save what you have left and if that is very little then to hell with it. The flowers die too.

Take care as they say around town, und don't forget ye Muse.

Corrington's The Anatomy of Love and Other Poems *was published by Roman Books, Fort Lauderdale.*

[To John William Corrington]
May [?8], 1964

o my I got *Anatomy* from Roman and this is it. You are writing better and better and better, what the hell are you trying to do? push us all down on skid-row? You've got a kind of a classical style that talks human language here, and believe me it makes me feel good to tell you how good you are, baby. There is not a fag line in the whole book. You'd look good in the ring, bull or square, I'd say you'd take the ears and tail home in your pocket & the other man's gotta fall; you'd look good reading Hans Christian Anderson; you'd look good painting a flagpole for a children's Maypole dance . . . U iz now what the criticizers kall – a major poet of impact. You are there. Willie, I keep reading the book and it's a good thing like a good fuck all over again, but more, of course. [★ ★ ★]

The review by Frances Smith under the name S. S. Veri appeared in Chat Noir Review, *vol. 2, no. 3. The Webbs' new address was in Santa Fe, but they moved back to New Orleans after less than a week (*Hank, *p. 139).*

[To Jon and Louise Webb]
May 12, 1964

aw right, I shoot you something   pomes??   to yr new address to
shew u I am still putting my socks on and also enclose knew *chat noir revue*
wich Frances ast me to en clothes shee is part ed. and wrote review a *It
Catches* wich mite bee pred. but so? und also she writes under name of S.
S. Veri I think some quite good poems but some other stuff by other
peeple in thair I don' kare 4. [★ ★ ★]

[To John William Corrington]
May 16, 1964

[★ ★ ★] Listen, baby, not to hurt, I know it is so hard to do – like fighting a bull, and *I* am not even *doing* it; but to say, I liked novel very good
but felt middle section dragged a bit. I've got to say, on the other hand, that
Anatomy of Love is a major work of poetry and/or art and that I am proud
to receive a letter occasionally from you from England, Texas and/or
Louisiana and/or in Hell where u undoubtedly are occasionally. No man
could write that well from a continual heaven. [★ ★ ★]

[To Jon and Louise Webb]
June 12, 1964

[★ ★ ★] I think the oddest thing I have ever heard, I could call it funny
but I have been drinking too much tonight today, was a woman editor-
poetess, they were putting out a special issue or something of convict
poets or what the hell, and she was disturbed because 'these men could not
rise, seemingly, above their circumstances . . . all they seemed to write
about was wanting to get out of jail, and why they should not be there . . .'

my god, her pretty pussy should some night some years sit there not
getting out, not even for the moon, not even for a walk down to the
corner for a dull newspaper, does she know what it means to walk back
and forth a certain space and *only* that space and that no matter what you
say, no matter how you scream, that that space will not widen except
through death or pardon or insanity? and even then? fuck it. Jon, you

know. when I by god get letters from cunts like this I near vomit, I look to the sun to make me well. that it grows these blind children.

[To Jim Roman]
[July 1, 1964]

yes, by god, no one is more pleased than I to be the victim of another magic book of the starving Webbs' gutwork and pure glad madness. I don't know about the poems. I know they could print a cookbook that would bring tears to the ears. (and eyes too!) Rexroth was right (in review) when he said my press was too good. but it's like a beautiful woman asking to go to bed with you – what are you going to do? turn her away? ah no, not even at my age! [★ ★ ★]

I don't hear any more from Willie [Corrington] and I guess he's shipping in from England, all lost and hooded in the pages of his second novel. I just hope he doesn't get too efficient about turning them out, but I'm a crank and a puritan and a nut this way: always carrying what's left of my soul in a little glass jar in my pocket like a fishing worm. [★ ★ ★]

[To Kay Johnson, preceded by note to Jon and Louise Webb]

Dear Jon & Lou:
Letter I wrote to Kaja some time back. Forwarded all over Europe, then came back to me. – B.

[handwritten:]
September 15, 1964

Dear Kaja –
All right, I know it was a drunken letter and you've got to stop stealing my stuff! Anyhow you said Copenhagen, so here I am writing to Copenhagen. [★ ★ ★]

[typewritten:]
you know, u really kant get the ingress into a WORD without the typer, the typer is the carver, the ax, the cleaver, the thing with the mouth that hollers about the bloody dice. it machineguns the mind out of penury.

fuck the pen. anyhow, I am sitting around feeling my arms and legs and balls, trying to figure out if I am real or not. I must be: about 3 a.m. I wiped my ass. the sun is just right today, kind of an icy tired yellow, limp vain vaindog of a sky. bull. listen, do you know what we are trying to do? are we crazy or do we mean something with our poems, or is it children's games, or tricks, or colored water? we gotta have blood! bloody shades in cheap hotels; mortar in the streets, shellholes! hoar-frosted wine! and young girls running wild down the streets chased by hungry dogs! my god my god, everything is so dull. even the bomb will be dull. it won't last. we won't last. this is profound. YOU HAVE NO IDEA HOW *profound* this is. all right, listen, don't mess up too much in Cope. – I remain sitting in the sun, 44 years old, 3 or 4 blocks south of HOLLYWOOD, my god my god, and for it all it is a good day, I am not too sick today although I may hit the first man I meet on the street square in the face.

Veryl Blatt (later Veryl Rosenbaum) is the author of The Way It Was *(Torrance, Calif., Hors Commerce Press, 1964) and other books.*

[To Veryl Blatt]
October 11, 1964

[★ ★ ★] Yes, the world's a cat's ass, a real driveling disgust, and the sweetest thing *is* getting away from them, their sounds, their decayed unlaughing laughter & faces as brutal and ugly and impossible as any matter you can dream up, . . . and the eyes, the eyes, no eyes at all. I can well understand men who run into caves and *stay* there. I don't have the guts or the know-how. I walk through their streets, lighting cigarettes and getting drunk and buying their newspapers. but nothing anywhere really. Going to sleep is getting to be the finest thing, and death itself, aside from physical pain, will not be so hard. Well, this is a lot of loose talk for a Sunday but I have to go into a cement building full of 4,000 people and work tonight when I'd rather suck on beer, smoke a cigar and listen to Stravinsky. When is the world going to be arranged for the people to do as they wish to do? [★ ★ ★]

[To Ann Menebroker]

October 25, 1964

[★ ★ ★] have been reading *Saint Genet* by Sartre who turned down Nobel's 52 grand while waiting on a cheese sandwich. S.G. badly written for most part, but good shafts of light there, involuted, and somewhat fascinating like a little box of rusty razor blades. If you have leisure to mull without tension you can pick up a big fat paper-back copy for a dollar and a quarter. Genet, of course, was preceded as a robber-verse writer by Villon, who if I remember, was banned from Paris. Genet, more-like, has it made. [★ ★ ★]

'Snow Bracero' and 3 other poems appeared in Jacaranda *6, February 1965 (Dorbin C259–261).*

[To Joel Climenhaga]
October 26, 1964

I got your o.k. on the 5 poems and hope you will send me a copy of whichever Transient Press mag or mags these might appear in [★ ★ ★] 'Snow Bracero' I had some fun writing, not fun but flew . . . something . . . I used to write the short story some time back but generally dislike short story on waste of wordage principle but if I can get a story line into what I consider a poem-form I am happy enough, or as happy as I will be? [★ ★ ★]

Douglas Blazek, notes Bukowski, 'was, perhaps, the foremost leader of the Mimeo Revolution with his magazine Ole. *He was also a good writer, quite prolific, and an excellent and interesting correspondent.' Blazek accepted three Bukowski poems for the first issue of* Ole, *initiating one of Bukowski's most extensive and most sustaining correspondences of the 1960s.*

[To Douglas Blazek]
[October 28, 1964]

[★ ★ ★] fine, I got your o.k. on the 3 poems, and while I have a theory that rejection is good for the soul, the theory seems to work best when it applies to others.

bio: born 8-16-20. began writing poetry at age of 35. 5 collections of poetry with a 6th, *Crucifix in a Deathhand* to be issued by Loujon Press and Lyle Stuart, Inc. early, in 1965. That's it.

Rough night in the pit last night, bastard on one side telling me how great he was and bastard on other side telling me how great he was, meanwhile the workwhip flashing like a cobra hung to a wind-mill. [★ ★ ★]

my neck hurts. I seem to be dying of something – maybe life – or maybe no young ass. well. listen: bottom of paper here. slipping out of typer. going. hold and luck.

[To Douglas Blazek]
late October 1964

got your letter, and poems enclosed for your consideration.

luck with your mad venture, but hope you get some hard knockers (eventually) because poetry is dying on the vine like a whore on the end stool on a Monday night.

I am snotted-up today, dismal, flu maybe, or maybe just 44 years, a lot of them drunk, anyhow all bent over and have had 2 shots for neuritis from a doc over Hollywood Blvd. who yachts to Catalina too much, and I straightened up a little. He keeps me waiting an hour each time and all I could do was peek at the cunt walking down on the street below and I got rocks but there was nothing he could give me for that.

the woman wants to put food on this table. I've got to get out.

[To Jon and Louise Webb]
October 31, 1964

well, since no pomes I mite as well untrundle the old bullshit harp, but it's not bullshit when I say I got your tired card and know the job has you by the throat, and worn, and I send a white prayer of luck and love for whatever good it might or might not do, and yes, send a page if you get around to it, there's nothing like being tired and tired and tired so you can't sleep or think of hope, but if this book comes anywhere near what you did with *It Catches* I will know that the good angels are near you even if they refuse to do the slave-rote work of drudgery and guts. I wish I could say something to help you through except that I am so often in muddled state and tired too, but if it helps, and it might not, – a book like this lifts my life up into light whether I deserve it or not. I used to have a theory that if I could just make *one* person's life happy or real that would have been otherwise, then my own life would not have failed. It was a good theory but a few whores ran me through the wringer for it, but I do think that for a while a few of them enjoyed not being spit on for a while, and so this made it o.k. for me. [★ ★ ★]

[To Jon and Louise Webb]
November 1, 1964

[★ ★ ★] Very drunk last night. The landlord and his wife came over and we slugged it down. His wife became rather upset when she saw the kitchen and the bathroom. Frances is not a very good housekeeper. But I calmed her down and got her to insulting me. I had let some gypsies straighten out my car for $30 and she said I shouldn't have done this. What should we do, let these people starve? There were 3 of them, 2 boys and an old man with a huge belly. They saw me typing and drinking beer at the window and came up and talked. We haggled at price a little while and then I told them to go ahead. They didn't do a bad job. When I handed the old man the 30 he bent down over his belly, bowed and said, 'God bless you, son.' I figure that was worth the 30 right there. Nobody ever said 'God bless you, son,' to me before. [★ ★ ★]

[To Douglas Blazek]
November 4, 1964

write a book? a novel? I am too lazy, too sick, and such a waste of words, and they wouldn't print it, so why not break it down into poetic toothaches, all not so cumbersome, and I doubt I could stick to the subject, I am not that interested in any area of life or that disinterested either.

they all go the way of novels and then there's nothing left.

of course, I am a whore, and if you know anybody who can advance me $500 I will do the trick because then I know I will be able to write it the way I want to, but you know and I know that nobody like this is going to come along, and so I won't go into the cleaver, and there's some thanks in this.

what was I doing before the age of 35 when I began writing poetry? dying, sweetheart, dying. kind of like. you see, I started with the short story, starving in little rooms around the country and drinking too much cheap wine, and I'd mail the things out to *The Atlantic Monthly* or *Harpers* and when they came back I tore them up. I used to write 8 or 10 stories a week. All I'd do was write these stories and drink as much as possible. Then I heard of *Story*, Whit Burnett, and at least *he* sent written rejects most of the time, and I finally landed my first story there at age of 24. Then a few other places, and then the drink took over. The writing seemed foolish – a con game, a game of prigs and English teachers, a dullard's game. I worked some of the time, very little of the time, and how I made it I really don't know. Drinking was the god. No matter what city, what year, what time. In Philly I used to knock on this bar door at 5 : 30 a.m. An old bartender used to be mopping up then prior to opening. He'd let me in and I'd sit there listening to the wet flub of the strings behind me. He gave me free drinks and he had some himself. I'd stay in that bar until closing at 2 a.m. That's not much sleep, you've got to admit, but it came in handy when I was totally broke and starving – I'd climb into the sack and sleep for a week. I got kicked out of room after room for being drunk and no rent and for bringing in women late at night. There was no grand plan here, no totality of sense, I wasn't looking for anything. It was just sunlight and rain and snow and nightmares and walking around and the drink in front of me. As I say I worked sometimes and the jobs were all bad and low paying and monotonous and searing and they still are. I am unable to do any kind of work with proficiency and have no trade. Anyhow, at 35 the drink and the women had caught up with me. I ended up in the charity ward of the local hospital spewing blood out of my mouth and ass, completely fallen apart, done. They let me lay there 2 days before somebody came along and decided I needed a transfusion. 9 pints of blood plus the glucose. They'd found out I'd picked up a blood credit somewhere. meanwhile my whore smashed up my old car in the streets.

I came out 900 years older. Found a job as a shipping clerk somewhere and got hold of a typewriter. I started writing poems. One of the first batches I sent to a little magazine in Texas. They went. I finally ended up in Texas with 75 cents in my pocket married to the editoress whose father was a millionaire. After 2 years of marriage she decided I was a bastard and there went the million. I had begun drinking again. And writing more poems. I am still in bad shape physically and don't know how long I can make it.

The job I have now is no better than the rest. I am still alive. a woman just left with an 8 week old baby. they are both mine. they went for a walk. I am writing Balzac. There is a fly on the screen. now he is gone.

this is a kind of kernel of things. a man can get bored with another man's life. I don't want to hang you up. but you asked.

trick or treat? yes, I went to the door too. the woman was in the tub. here were 2 little girls with their big-assed big-titted young and sexy and silly mamas, and I stood there in my blood-stained bathrobe, open at the front, torn shorts, 3 day beard, cigar in one hand, can of beer in the other, and I stood there thinking of raping the 2 mamas, but they didn't seem scared at all, I was just an old man in the doorway, and I turned around, put down beer and cigar, and shot the candy into their paper bags: FLOP FLIP FLAP! and they said thank you thank you and they walked off with their sexy silly mamas who were wiggling wiggling wiggling in the moonlight all on fire FIRE! and I went back in and emptied the beercan.

the fly came back on the window screen. I swung the rolled-up newspaper and missed. you see how it goes around here.

hot damn! I got him this time!

the horns of grief need no honing.

[To Jon and Louise Webb]
November 19, 1964

[★ ★ ★] after dinner – our Frances has picked up and gone into the other room. These broads mash me. table talk. I asked what they would do to a man who said (to the authorities) that he was a coward, that he thought war might possibly kill him and that he didn't want to die. He would not state that it was against his morals or his religion. Just that he didn't want the thing to kill him. Frances said that they would probably consider him an idiot. maybe I resented this because this was the very inference I made to the psychiatrist without saying the words when I faced this situation. And then I told her that if a man were really a coward he would have lied about his reasons anyhow, giving religion or morals as an excuse. Then I added that honest men were not truly cowards. F. then said that that was not so, that we all had fears. I said she was picking at words, distorting what I had meant for the sake of argument. Then F.: 'Well, if Charles Bukowski says it's so, then it's so. Isn't *that* it?' I said, 'You and I have had done with each other for tonight. I don't know whose fault it is, yours or mine, but something's wrong here.' Then she went into the other room.

most of the time I attempt to avoid this type of talk and/or yak because I am not interested. I know that her groups become heated and gabble, DISCUSS, they simply love to DISCUSS, and F. is trained in this ping-pong type of thing. Actually most of these people have just lived on the edge of living and so they are full of a bilious sort of stale and clotted energy which they must expel as a sort of poison. I am too tired to argue. It doesn't matter. Let them win; I just don't want to hear it. I didn't even want to hear it in Junior High school, these little mouths with papers in their palms, saying, DEFINE that! ah well, we go on. but no wonder I layed drunk in the alleys, no wonder I lived with the whores.

'If Charles Bukowski says it's so, then it must be so.'

Maybe she's got something there. But it is the first time she has attacked me through my name – meaning that since I have gotten a lot of poems published that this has distorted my ego or made me a bad judge of any meaning. It is possible, of course, yet I am unhappy with her technique. Also little comments on my playing the horses and drinking but as I see it I was doing this when she met me and if it weren't for the child I would not be with her now. I have lived with many many women and it all ends up the same: they want to shave you down to a wooden dummy to do their bidding, and, after all, I'm CHARLES BUKOWSKI!!!!

so to hell with it. [★ ★ ★]

[To Veryl Blatt]
November 23, 1964

[★ ★ ★] the baby is like a shiny apple, except the eyes, loops of eyes extracting signs from the air, and look, there it sits knitted in all that skin, a child, a girl, and outside – the bucktooth world, ah, myself sucking on a cigar and wonder, wondering.

there are too many ways to drown even if you don't want to drown.

140

it is terrible
staring down at a red and white
checkerboard oilcloth and
wondering.

[To Douglas Blazek]
[November 23, 1964]

everything finally kills us from carrots to the timeclock or no time-clock at all, and it's the faces that kill us too: faces like putty granite with raisin eyes snapped in, and the way they walk and the way they laugh and love and hate and drive their cars and piss into the diminishing areas of our lives. we are the pitiful beggars – we don't even want the coin, we are so sick we don't know why.

the drink kills me and saves me too, my whole insides have fallen apart; hemorrhage Friday, coughed up a half pint of blood, but you've heard all this, and even now the old fingers, once again, rip down on the typer, and I listen to some rotten half-ass classical music for the in-between hammerheads who have not fallen asleep yet . . . don't worry about a botched-up *Ole*, we are not mechanics, we are lazy, fumbling, aching from the shrill pipes and ugly whores, listen, try to get the CONTENT, that's all. the best living poet I know of is A1 Purdy, 185 Wellington St., Belleville, Ontario, Canada. (Belleville? Bensenville?) You might right him write him and tell him of *Ole*, hide nothing, tell him it's only mimeo but talk a little bit about what you think (my suggestion) & ask him if he might send something rejected dejected or otherwise. It will be good. whatever it is. I have read his collection *Poems for All the Annettes* and I turned the pages one by one reading in a state of pisspoorpissgreat-stun within myself at what he was doing he writes like chopping down trees; he writes about those bees that are stinging the inside of his head. he lays the words down as if they were real instead of angelcake. he might not be able to send you anything for one reason or another, but I'd suggest a try??? I don't know if he's still at above address but I think if you try your letter will be forwarded unless he's dead, and he was drinking a lot of homemade wine the last time I heard from him.

I don't expect *Ole* to last too long and I tell you this because I am a donkey-hard old man and it's better you know it straight in case you

141

haven't guessed. The same 50 poets are writing the same crap over and over again in America. You'll get tired of it. I am. you'll get tired of turning the crank and taking abuse from half-talents. your wife will want love, your factory body will want rest; you will to write. the sour cream will spin up in your mouth and you will spit it out, *Ole* will go down the crapper.

I tried turning the crank once at something called *Harlequin*, I sent 3, 4, 5, 6 page rejections to poetry that came in, talking about everything from big-assed women to T. S. Eliot and what came back?: WHO THE HELL ARE YOU? they wrote, I'VE NEVER SEEN YOUR NAME ON ANY OF THE LITTLE MAG-AZINES ANYWHERE? WHAT GIVES YOU A RIGHT TO TELL ME HOW TO WRITE? HORSE-SHIT! etc. I was surprised at the venom. these people reminded me more of traffic-cops, bankers, foremen, factory owners, clerks, teachers, and I guess . . . that is what they were. But I hadn't suggested to them HOW to write, I'd only suggested why I didn't care to print that particular group of poems. I never *claimed* to be a poet. I claimed to be some type of editor who intended to print some type of thing when it came along, but, only once or twice did it come along. I stopped cranking or my wife divorced me, or anyhow, that's past. but it wasn't long before I was drunk again at high noon, fallen down in back alleys with dogs sniffing at my feet to see if I was alive or kids poking sticks in my back to see if I was alive and truck drivers pulling up short and getting out to look and see if I were still alive. What decision, they arrived at I don't know. also, my grammar hasn't improved since then and spelling is harder than fucking when you don't want to while intoxicated. [★ ★ ★]

There is nothing worse than talking about poetry or poets or our-selves, is there? It keeps us from doing the thing. It keeps us from the knife, maybe, or the red hot poem blue flame smashing, through the wall hol-lering blowing bugle & slobbering the real good tears that will bring all the priests and whores and clouds and garage mechanics and Sir Winston Churchill into the same quiet bar to talk about mice and waste and grass and towers and strange things like people with beautiful eyes, fine candy bars, new symphony music or the great color of the bartender's shirt. [★ ★ ★]

Bukowski's review of Layton's Laughing Rooster *appeared in* Evidence *no. 9.*

[To Douglas Blazek]
[December 1, 1964]

[★ ★ ★] all drab, drab. and it's that kind of day, drizzle, damnation, the plants have and puff in air that has no air, the plants sweat and the screens crawl with the one or 2 stupid lost flies of summer, who have somehow failed to find a spider, who have somehow failed to die. my 12 weeks old daughter wails in the other room; her cries cut through all my poems, all my writing, but she is a sweetie, they have not gotten to her yet, she is all eyes and skin, she bends, she bubbles . . . she wails. now the old woman comes in with the kid and she sits in a chair at my elbow, as I type and she has the kid and the radio plays *In the Clock Store*, badly, and I'd like to say, Listen, don't you realize that I AM WRITING TO BLAZEK! WHAT THE HELL IS WRONG WITH YOU TWO BROADS? (do you hear the cuckoo? she asks. do you hear the alarm clock? she asks.) well, kid, there has always been something, some woman screaming for a bottle of wine or the landlord at the door for his rent or the police with a passkey or God's left-handed angel stealing my cigarettes from the dresser. well, this will be a lousy letter. sometimes I stand a better chance. Sometimes she is busy with something important – like reading a *New Yorker* in the other room.

I remember one, this one was a looker, I was drunk all the time and how I made it I'll never know, or I will, the horses were going very well this year and a half, I could do no wrong: I didn't know what I was doing, just one long run of luck (good) and I drank it drank it and kept going to bed with this woman with all that body, and I remember one night I drank so much (I had been hitting it at the track all day) that I fell off the couch and I was down there on the floor and I saw these LEGS smooth cool nylon magic filled down into those spikes, my god, magic, and that placid face looking down at me and she was smoking and I saw the earrings and I could feel the rug on my neck and the whole world swirling around: buildings full of janitors, jails full of quiet men held in a web, alleys of murder, swans asleep on lakes and I looked up at her from the floor and I said: I'M A GENIUS AND I'M THE ONLY ONE IN THE WORLD WHO KNOWS IT!

Blazek, she looked at me for maybe 20 seconds and then she said YOU DAMN FOOL, GET UP FROM THE FLOOR!

and she was right and I did get up, I laughed and walked over and poured myself a glass of whiskey and looked at those legs. electricity yellow and whiskey yellow and nylon colored legs. she's dead now and the legs do not look so good anymore but I can't blame her for that.

[★ ★ ★] On Layton, he's up in Canada, I don't know where. You can probably contact him through Alan Bevan (editor) c/o *evidence*, Box 245, Station [*illegible*], Toronto 5, Ontario, Canada. Bevan sent me his latest book *The Laughing Rooster* to review, which I have done, and am waiting on word whether it's going to run or not. I tore a little meat but also went on in waving wands of glory over some of the poems. Layton's been around a while and maybe the way the teeth of the machine work, too long. he's getting to be a craftsman. I mean in his own way. not theirs. but it's still bad. he's finding it's too easy to lay it down and make it sound good. the words flow off the ribbon good, but not just quite right. this comes from working the bull, from knowing the steps, knowing the crowd, when and how to hook the sword perfectly and bring in the ears and the tail too and bring down that BIG one out of the stands for later over the springs zeep zeeep zeep ZEEP, another sword. But Layton – even with knowing too much what he is doing, is still far ahead of the rest. – how many people will come through for you with work, I do not know. the poets I have met are generally notorious snobs, they are not very good people. what I mean is, some of these Awrtists . . . might think mimeo below their dignity. really, most of them eventually buy the shadows, they buy the stink . . . the *New Yorker* or *The Atlantic* can wave them on in with a dollar bill and get them to stick their heads right up that dirty crotch. I don't understand it, there is very little that I do understand. If *Life* magazine walked in with their cameras they'd smile and smirk and pose and talk like highschool boys with their first drink working toward the first dizzy worthless bitch dressed in taffeta. I mean, you may write these boys, and they may write well but I am not responsible for the rust and bologna that crawls into the soul and makes a snob or a prick or a jackass or a fink out of a man who can, or who once could, lay down a good line.

– the old woman says to give her love to your 3 year old. I give my love to your lucky dog who can't speak English. give your wife a kiss from me too. arrg, we are getting sloppy. some good classical stuff on now. I go the classical & the new experimental & the 12 tone, which of course, is now old. we all get old so fast. I like jazz too when I like it. – I've got to get ready to go in to the pit. my back aches already. I can see now the sheer empty bash of faces, the screaming guggling words; the dumpling of a foreman in his white shirt and eyes of spit . . . the blood is everywhere.

hold to something.

[To Douglas Blazek]
December 8, 1964

Harlequin was a grunion, a brick goblet, a drowning moll, and there was something about a dwarf, a dwarf at the door and I had 75 cents in my pocket and it was early morning in Texas and she stayed in bed and the d. took me out and showed me showed me the old man's lands and lakes and belongings and I was not impressed and I did not say anything only rather yawned but the dwarf thot I was a sharpy he thot I married her for money which wasn't exactly so and I do not want to tell you exactly what it was because it was more personal on her part than mine and more sacrificial on my part than hers & dollars be damned, and it didn't last, of course, she had the millions coming and wrote bad poetry and I had 75 cents and wrote poetry, and there I was and she had the magazine and then she wasn't too interested and left submissions in the closet or under the sofa or mixed in with the kotex and I took to answering these things and became more or less a part of the magazine until she met a Persian with a stickpin and a lisp and that led to divorce and then I heard she was in Alaska and she married a Japanese fisherman or school teacher named Kami and Kami had wonderful manners, a gentleman, and *Harlequin* more or less c e a s e d, I could give my god I cd give you more but it's so dry; I think shots of light are best, nice stores tories stories have slivers and yawns.

[★ ★ ★] I really don't know if there is enough plentitude of talent to deserve even one magazine. and when I say talent I mean JUICE TO MAKE THE EARS JUMP and the hands look like hands, know they are hands and the window screens to look like mother's panties, I mean SOMETHING. I just don't think it's there – maybe a line or 2, and then limp again, making the same old picture. maybe it's the human race, maybe we're just full of shit and no light, maybe we're still full of shit after we shit it out.

There are many things that bother me. I know that I have never passed a man on the street that I liked – most of them giving off a kind of ether of disgust and stumbling and clay-eating, snot-eating grievance. I don't like the human race at all. this is my confessional, father, pass the wine. [★ ★ ★]

[To Douglas Blazek]
December 9, 1964

no murals, noting nothing, the overtime has got me, I am dead, dog-fucked tired and the old woman drops tin cans in the bathtub and walks around complaining that life is hard, the baby is cranky she says and she has a cold and maybe the baby has a cold too. my old woman has had a cold ever since I messed-up with her. well, look. yeah, a cold head too. what I mean. I got *Ole* and the few moments I have left before going into the mill again, maybe I could say something, although I feel my sight is a little twisted today. what's wrong with the foreword, introduction? I agree, we gotta put balls on poetry. this lisping home freak has layed pale in dead libraries long enough, let's bomb on out. [★ ★ ★]

let me say off and on and over as time keeps running that it was a lively number a good number and I can say this easy without lying which I have not learned to do yet and so you wanted to know and so now I've told you, & we look FORWARD to more *Ole*, poetry with balls!!

and I will put this in an envelope and tool through traffic, weaving around the old ladies and grinding toward the death, my foot to the floor, all insurance companies have already dropped me and the police leap out from behind the palm trees of night on their scooters to hunt down the nub of snarling over the wheel, go go go!, down Sunset, to Alpine street, then a left and out of car and leap into fire of death and fire of dead faces and why I still will be able to walk around and move my fingers I'll never know. [★ ★ ★]

The '2 books' are It Catches My Heart in Its Hands *and* Crucifix in a Deathhand, *which would be published in mid-1965. Ed Blair was a New Orleans poet, collector, and patron of the Loujon Press.*

[To Jon and Louise Webb]
December 25, 1964

[★ ★ ★] That the *N.Y. Times* has put us with the big publishers and *The Collected Poems* of D. H. Lawrence etc. for rec. Xmas reading is fine – we 3 small tough beer-drinkers, sidewalk painters, criers in the dark. Hell, we put one over, didn't we? And you're right: the fat head is for the rest; we'll just go about our business.

You two people are almost myths now, almost literary history and you're still alive. The love of my luck was falling into your hands for these 2 books. No other poet of this century or any other has been so blessed.

Blair speaks of the envy of the others. Let them god damn envy! Those Black Mountain School snobs, let them smell their own turds! The Kenyon boys, let them write their celluloid senseless inoffensive poems; the Corringtons – let them write their novels of incest and beetle love and honor and refuse to answer their mail; and all the others: let them go to hell too.

I am for the small man who has not forgotten, for the man who loves his beer and his women and his sunlight but who is not quite wise enough (ever) to know where next month's rent is coming from. [★ ★ ★]

· 1965 ·

[To Jim Roman]
January 11, 1965

Who the hell is U. Grant Roman via 'ML' and signed Jim Roman?

You Rebs oughta forget *that* war awhile. There've been other wars, and I was born in Andernach, Germany, August 16th, 1920. Yet when I bummed through the South, and particularly in Houston, they kept calling me a 'Yankee' in the bars and threatened to beat the shit out of me. I always got so drunk, tho, they never got around to it because it would-n't have been much of a victory. [★ ★ ★]

I was re-reading your 'Outsider' catalogue the other night, and some odd & pliable & weird & strange assortments in there. I keep thinking of the one woman in there (forget name) who said she'd burn all her works and damn near did. I might say it's refreshing compared to the almost stan-dard preciousness of some of our better talents. If I'd saved all my note-books I wouldn't be able to move around in this kitchen – or read them either. Yet you can't tell the possible value of some of that stuff, say even later. (their stuff, I mean.)

Imagine having something, say, some scrawls by Whitman or T. S. Eliot or old Ez? Even these jaded fingers might tremble?

Keep the despair bottled. We'll all out under a handful of cropped and drying blooms –

PHILIP HENRY SHERIDAN BUKOWSKI

The essay Blazek accepted was 'A Rambling Essay on Poetics and the Bleeding Life Written While Drinking a Six-Pack (Tall)'; it was printed in Ole no. 2, March 1965.

[To Douglas Blazek]
[January 13, 1965]

this is still Los Angeles, yes, and it's Jan. 13th. and the rent is due again, and I shove the green into his hands and he drives off in his three cars. Listening to Meyerbeer, an opera, somebody has gone mad and now runs off and sings with her other-self. the bile backs up into a shoal which gets so large ya can never swallow it. I have spoken. Silence in the back rows!

Glad the essay got past you, although I am always ready for the reject, I am a dark alley loser from way back, and I write badly enough when I try and when I don't try, and so all right. Although I drank more than a six pack getting it done. It was 6 writing it in long hand and then 6 or 8 typing it, dropping and adding, translating . . . all right.

No, Purdy didn't tell me he'd send anything. g.d. shame. but we've got to let him live. He's going to the North Pole or something on some crazy kind of grant. He scrapes through the hard way (or the easy way) doing things like this. Maybe he's wiser than we are, we who are walking into those buildings where they scrape the meat and replace the eyes with apple pits and bird droppings.

No, I'm not any good at babies' names, and it's a torturous thing I don't enjoy at all, and always figure it's best to forget the thing and leave it up to the woman since it seems to mean more to them. Except if they come up with something outlandish I can't craw down.

I have nothing, right now, for mimeo press book series although I may try and give you a submission later and glad for invite. Going to New Orleans in March to help Webb wind up *Crucifix* but all I'll prob. do is end up getting him drunk, which isn't very nice, but it's kind of relaxing while it's going on and you're not paying the price until later, ah. If I should submit something it would not be poetry, I think, but rather a wild literary blast rolling zombie easy and graceless headless type of thing, easy on me and perhaps confusing to the reader. I have a title in mind I have been trying to get rid of, *Confessions of a Coward and Man Hater*, and I could encompass a lot under this, like say the time the black in a Dallas hotel came into the room with a poker and wanted to blow me and I opened my blade and sat there and when he got close I lifted it and showed it to him saying, 'Oh, be careful, you might CUT yourself!' and he ran from the room with these pig squeals. This kind of stuff is drab to anybody but me, but look you get away with it by erecting a facade: you tell them while all this was going on you had D. H. Lawrence's collected works in your suitcase. I bullshit too much. But I'd like to try it eventually. I have a lot of loose language inside of me.

O.K. to put address with essay. I can handle writers and callers by breaking their hearts and their arms. I do quick work. cheap.

By the way, nobody has sent me $500 to do a novel yet, which is really one hell of a relief. I might find out I can't write a novel. This way is easier. [★ ★ ★]

[To Douglas Blazek]
January 25, 1965

the alka seltzer's sparkling and down it goes. depressed fit of cut cat running by without a tail where it had a tail before, or my head is strung like beads around a savage day. All that crap. Anyhow, I have been drinking too much, and on top of that – another kind of mess, and the time has gone by and I haven't done anything, I am ashamed, I am lazy, I am stupid, I am King Kong bending over for a button, I am a torn picture postcard of East Bermuda.

yes, if you get to feeling you want to use any excerpts from any of the letters, lay to it. And don't worry about defamation of character. I have nothing to hide and anything I say in a letter goes anywhere anytime, and if they don't like the taste of it, let them suck empty beer bottles. or their bloody thumb's footprint.

I will submit something for your mimeo series of indecent literature (wild-hair mad talk; not poetry) and if you want to use my name on a circular, go ahead. My only hope is that you will like what I do well enough to print it. My tigers sometimes stumble like mice in wine cellars. But I will probably not be able to write you anything until I get back from New Orleans in late March, early April, after helping Webb wind up *Crucifix*. There's a matter of a few more poems, signing pages, drinking beer and pounding nails, walking the streets at night and moving in and out of the taverns looking for the man without a head, asking the question, waiting for the white bull that smiles. I will do you something for you. A welsh fandango that will clean the fingernails of your soul. o o oh. [★ ★ ★]

don't worry about the 'bandwagon'; if I'm riding a bandwagon then I guess this blood on my gut is only ketchup and the stones over the heads are only the aria of a multi-color dream that can be snapped off like a carnation. I get all the bayonets when I walk out of the door; I move through them like fields of wild flowers, saying hello to half-buddies, punching time clocks, snarling at supervisors. The young girls look the other way: I spit through a hole where a tooth has rotted out, let the belt out a notch and move on through, and I come back in dazed, punched-out, fooled again, tricked again, wasted again, and the old woman glares at me as I peel the celluloid from the pint of rye and move between the sheets far from the glory of the lucky soldiers and the green-eyed crapshooter. If I am riding a bandwagon, let me get off. The zone of sharpshooters still surround me and they pick me off little by little while humming patriotic hymns and eating bumblebees.

if the world digs me it is only to bury me.

I resent anybody being published because he has a name and only because he has a name, and this is being done much, and I don't understand it, and it's more fag and fart and drag and death, and *Poetry Chicago* is good at it; almost everybody's good at it – publishing name crap when meanwhile some young artist is on fire all flame flame flame FLAME and they let him burn away to knife or razor across the string of wrist or throat while Mr. X-somebody dulls the screams with flat verse on flat-printed expensive paper.[★ ★ ★]

[To Douglas Blazek]
Early February 1965

Any drawings or fanciness are not going to be worth a Negro's shitola here to you, but what drew me to your mimeo outfit (*Ole*) was that I thot you were a hard-muscled brain of a drunk laboring lost son-of-a-bitch without a chance like I am.

I can't do you a foreword because if I did you a foreword (on these grounds) there would also be other people I should do a foreword for also.

Look, you are not that great and neither am I – and I don't know where next month's rent or tomorrow's poem is coming from.

I've been drunk for several days (am drunk now) trying to figure how to answer you.

Sorry on the heart-attack thing. But most of us who write don't live too long because we eat ourselves up one way or the other.[★ ★ ★]

There are 3 poems here, in this order:

(1) – (great and beautiful) – 'Up a Different Creek'

(2) A sweet last line damning us – 'Plastic Dimestore Life' and

(3)'Testimony Concerning . . .'

But wait before you inter me with the bones of hard-head disbe-lievers –

(a) I still believe that more untalented fake poets are being published than ever before.

(b) – I believe that most poetry stinks like the rot of a garbage can, a game of professors & fakers. And

(c) – that writing a foreword to your poetry would do more to destroy you than any heart attack, than any gift of a new cadillac that wd allow you to drive through the latest town of culture and give a wave.

Certainly, I'm drunk and certainly I'm mad, but, also, most certainly, my word won't make your poetry good or your wife and children love you, and, hell, you know this, you've known it a long time. And I don't have to get drunk to tell you and you shouldn't force me to get drunk to tell you – no matter *what* you think of your poetry or any poetry or anybody else's poetry.

I hate to speak like a knowing prick from a pulpit, yet you've put me up in the pulpit, and shit! I've fallen down drunk from there, and I can't help you, I can't help myself. [★ ★ ★]

The adverse review by A. Frederick Franklyn that upset Cuscaden, publisher of Run With the Hunted, *appeared in* Grande Ronde Review, *Fall 1964.*

[To Douglas Blazek]
[February 10, 1965]

[★ ★ ★] look, just went out to get mail and here's two letters from Cuscaden, the last airmail and about an attack on me (review of *Run with the Hunted* by a. frederic franklyn (his lower case) and Cus quite upset about it, says freddy boy gets 'almost hysterical; every low blow known to man (dig such lines as "the suspiciously effete contemporaries"!)' 'This bastard's harangue amounts to a disgusting, personal sort of thing . . .' says Cuscaden. I've got to write Cuss a letter and buck him up. He tells me that Freddy boy went on for 5 and 1/2 pages. As you know, Franklyn is with *Trace* and May's right hand agent. I don't go well in Los Angeles I guess (at least, that). Once I was over at May's, brought my own liquor and got blasted. I get nasty sometimes this way and May later phoned me and said,

153

'You couldn't have meant those things you said about me; you must have been talking to a face on the couch, just somebody you saw sitting there. And nobody's ever acted *that* way in my house!' Christ, maybe I smashed a few glasses against the wall, I don't know. I know some weeks later when I was sitting in jail on a drunk rap and looking for somebody to bail me out (20$), the money was on my dresser but I had lost my wallet, and since I am a loner I was dialing long shot chances – May was one, and when I got him he told me:'I can't help you. I am entertaining a man from India.' The shits have me wired for destruction. May knows the book reviewer of the *Times* (L.A. newspaper) and when the last issue of *Coastlines* came out the reviewer listed the names of all the writers appearing in there – except one. Sure, Bukowski. accident? maybe. accidents have been happening to me all my life. I never belonged and never will, and in a sense, I am proud of this. the only shit who can destroy me is myself, and that is when I start writing as bad as they think I am writing, or as bad as I think they are writing. I remember when I bought May the fifth he took it into the kitchen and every time I wanted a drink of my own whiskey I had to ask for it, and I was drunk or I wouldn't have been there anyway, and I believe I remember starting on him then:'Why do you use all that fancy vocabulary?' and so forth. Sweetheart, they are always axing me because I don't smile pretty or come to their tea parties. This poet Sherman came by the other week and he said, 'I've got your archenemy out in the car.' I didn't ask him who my archenemy was – it's a kind of nebulous thing with yellow teeth and a swimming pool that I sometimes think of. . . . anyhow, what was I saying about *Ole*?

Please thank Nathan for the drawings. he's got a good touch.

yes I'll submit something for your book series if I don't go mad or crazy or dull, but yes, first N.O, and beer with Webb, and walking the mighty wooden nightstreets full of hammerheaded whores and newsboys and rats and grifters; 5 will get you 30 that I will carry around a basket of torturous legless writhing hangovers with black rotting hearts of apples in their mouths, but this is the game we play, in this we rape little girls in the upper branches of palm trees while reading the life of Richard Wagner. [★ ★ ★]

[To Douglas Blazek]
February 16, 1965

[★ ★ ★] yours was a fine letter, baby. we don't think exactly alike but I never have any trouble understanding you, which is more than I can say for Shakespeare. you, if something doesn't get you first, are going to be a pretty good writer, maybe a great one. well, hell, this doesn't flush the turds away or keep you out of the factory, does it? I don't know: we get slammed and slammed and slammed so much that it almost feels good. I have run through quite a few women but there was never a child to hold it still. But the women are essentially the same. they look into your soul long enough and it's not changing to fit their fingers so they began the chant, the protest bit:

'Why to you always laugh at yourself? Why do you always make fun of yourself?'

(no answer.)

'I can't stand a man who doesn't like himself.'

(no answer.)

'Why don't you quit that god damned job, then?'

(no answer.)

'You think I don't feel trapped too?'

(no answer.)

'You're jealous. There are many people I like better than I like you and you can't understand this.'

(no answer.)

Yes yes, if you have the special interview issue of *Lit. Times* I do wish you'd mail it. why they refuse to mail me one when I send $ I don't know. guilt? they feel, somehow, I guess as if they've ruptured or fucked me. they shouldn't worry – everytime I step out the door 4 thieves and a bloody toothed cocksucker dog chase me around the block. ah. – the circular is sweetfire (*Ole* ad), and it sure as hell creates an interest, and talking about me in the same hairbreath as Whitman and Rimbaud gives lift to this sagging soul so torn by complaining bitch of woman, and I allow myself a small lift, a splash of water in the eye, a cool can of beer as 45 pigeons circle in the lot across the street, and the mountains are dark today dark, and they are dropping lumber ripping lumber tearing holes in the ground, and a man sits on an orange machine lighting a cigarette and where one hour ago I could see a house from this small kitchen window, I now see matches of misery where there were once dark halls to walk down in order to piss at 3 a.m. in the morning, and Bukowski floats dead, upside-down in a pound, pockets full of rejects, head still crackling racket of complaining womanhood or ladies from Mass who think I don't rhyme with reason. Anyhow, it will be an apartment house. everything passes. m.m. had all that leg and ass and killed herself. we are confused. we don't stick together. Hemingway shotgun. Chatterton rat poison. Pascal's last bath. we all of us ache and are incomplete forever. no victory. another night's sleep, if you can sleep. sometimes I don't sleep for 2 or 3 or 4 days or nights, or so it seems. madness? why not? what man is holy enough to last? the stupid are the survivors. they've got good lasting qualities. I must be stupid. I never thought I'd almost live to see 45. god it's gross. I walk around an old man and I still feel the way I felt when I was 11 or 12 or 14 – that is – sick, unpleasant, not knowing; aching from the sight of wooden faces, wooden jaws, wooden arms, wooden eyes, wooden blood, wooden voices. jesus mother am I the only one stuck in this fright of un-wonder?

I watch this guy playing with his machine from the window. I would say he is dead but the woman would object on grounds of my inhumanity. He's young, has too much hair under a dirty felt hat, and no ass at all, the pants fall flat, a straight line down from the neck to the heels, a line like a hard board. He scratches at mud on his machine. He has a little rag and a scraper and he works at the mud. he picks away. inside of his head it is like inside the head of a blackbird skipping over a wet lawn. tick, tick, and that's it. I am supposed to save this man for democracy. I'm supposed to say something, nice about him. I can't.

stomach in bad shape. I should gaze upon more pleasant subjects. then too, I don't look so good either. [* * *]

[To Douglas Blazek]
[February 23, 1965]

[* * *] I now stoke up me cigar and plus with the coffee comes ye steam of bullshit, so gear your readies, pat yr paddy belly, wipe the come off yr nuts, & hearken baby like a white horse in moonlight listening for the last rider slipping up thru the elms. – I don't know much about the phoney-non-phoney theory of lit., but it might be best to keep the ear down to the heart, not like Emily Post, but more like the assassin or the garage mechanic with Saturday night off, but I don't know if talking about the stuff helps too much. think maybe the easy way is best: I mean let it

slip out like a wet fish outa your drunken hands; and, of course, if the fish intends on staying, you got a stink, you don't have much chance. Planning seldom gets it, although the way you lift your coffee cup or brand a steer or dip the thing into the cobwebbed dauber, might. Speaking of writing (aren't we?) I get much more stuff back than I ever get rid of, which keeps me kind of puritan about how much moxie I do or am supposed to have.

yes, I've heard about C. from other sources; evidently he runs up the gall mast of most. I guess he makes too much money for most, and the other things too, yet I can't get flamed-up. I too like to sit around in safety and I drink endless cans and bottles of beer and smoke cigars until I am senseless and ultra senseless and I go on go on within the seeming peace of rented walls, o lifting and drinking rivers of that yellow piss and pissing it out and listening not to jazz like a good human but to the symphony, the large orange flaming red green white fires of curling steam steel leafy hammer sound sound and form, and men centuries old walk around inside of me, and I feel them feeling it, saying it as if they were sitting across the table from me, lifting a beercan and saying, 'Bukowski, it's hot shit. everything's shit shit, yet look maybe — I don't know. I may not make it. have you ever seen a yellow dog pissing in the yellow sun? Bukowski, rip me open another beer!' I can come crashing in from the racetrack where maybe I have nipped away at a half pint or pint of scotch during the action, but this liquor hardly contains anything except maybe a bridge to walk across so I can get over and past the 50,000 faces whirling dead en masse like other things — like flies, like rocks, like turds. it gets me over. — now I used to hang in the bars, peering through the smoke, lipping the bartenders, walking out into the alley (usually for a beating), fumbling at the whores, and often ending rolled or in jail. after some many many years of this, Mozart or Bobby Strauss or Stravinsky does not seem too bad over a familiar tablecloth and a couple of salt and pepper shakers and a calendar of a peaceful cat. yet, I still gang outside now and then, and there's trouble trouble, and the last time I woke up in a jail with piped-in music, and a kid with a broken arm on the floor next to me. When the last I remember was being in a fancy apartment and lifting some girl's dress up to her waist and kissing her legs. Somewhere along the line madness enters and the police enter, and it's the same old thing. or it's getting home, and hemorrhage again, very close to death again. Some blood and then lying still as a rock, listening hoping for the mending of the threads not quite ready to go. someday they won't mend; meanwhile I am writing this letter to you.

I've got to smile. you're a real romantic, looking for me in that index file in the library in Elgin. Let's see? where would I come in? just before Bunin, Ivan, The Gentleman from San Francisco? no? well. or Bulosan, Carlos? America is in the Heart.

America is in the balls. America is in the factories. America is in the streets, hustling shines and newspapers, climbing down through skylights to the mother-blossom of the safes. I am the toilet paper wiped against America.

waiting on birth always wants to make me cry, it's so sad, like the gliders coming across the hill and ripping through the strings of gas-inflated balloons fingering the freak sky. farfetched? yes, that's what I mean. maybe by now it's all over, and over into the good. [★ ★ ★]

Jeffers, of course, laid it down in blocks of cement and he did not lie, and he lived it too. I guess we owe the curse of Carmel's artist colony to him, I just as we owe the curse of Taos to Lawrence. The freaks and the ants and the pretenders always love to swallow the shadows of the great dead, walk their gardens, stare at their ground, but it does not work − it makes them less instead of more. There are no crutches. nothing is free. I will never forget the finks in the Village cafes with their berets and goats and sandals and happy and ugly faces. I got out, fast. − I've got to go out and pay some god damn bills before they shut things off, rip things out. It's a small court in front with highrise apartments rising, rising on either side, walls of swimming pool darkness and $125 apts. with wall to wall fucking, and we linger out in the grass, remembering the sun, and to the north is Sunset Blvd. (the cheaper section) and the observatory on the brownpur-ple mountain, and the radio is off, and the blue Cad. drives off with its dead man, and an old woman with a red coat walks by. the girl-child is asleep on the big bed in the bedroom. Marina Louise Bukowski. what awaits this little wench? poverty? a father of 60, drunk with dim eyes when she is 15? or a photo of a man who died in 1966? no, it's one day at a time, and my life too and her life too and all our lives, Van Gogh hanging from the walls like a necktie, Brahms' skull 5 feet under rattling and rolling to the fucking of 2 gophers.

all right then, I now give you the gift of a little
s i l e n c e

[To Douglas Blazek]
February 28, 1965

[★ ★ ★] in 4 or 5 days I climb on the train to New Orleans so if you do not hear from me I am not necessarily dead, although maybe so. Not having mail forwarded. Going to read it all when I come back and see who wants my sweet balls in the frying pan, or better yet – enshrined in crusted gold. Brought in 5 horses first yesterday and still only made $7, 5 or 6 drinks, and then I loaded on the high-weight even-money favorite in the handicap (#131), one of the worst bets in the the business. There went my profits. well, that's past; let's only hope I have learned something. at 45, they are beginning to walk around and shut out the lights. get going, Buk, the grave diggers are licking their palms in the sunset!

Purdy makes it with the typer and with grants and talking at the universities and by, he tells me, the grace of his wife. so being caught up in these various segments and his homemade wine, you've got to forgive him, he's a little lost out there. Layton I don't know much about, except he must teach somewhere and probably is getting a little comfortable and have heard in *Lit. Times* fashion, that he believes anything written by Layton is automatically good. this is bad. men change. everything changes. you don't have to be much to realize that. we all write very badly at times and sometimes we write good, which doesn't matter too much either, like a good drunk or a day off when the old woman isn't acting haywire like some Bette Davis throwing a pissfit or the kid wailing wailing the blues, scratching your inner guts with barbwire, and you wonder what ever happened to that small room when you were alone and glad to be alone forever. yet, we go on: having lost the left jab, the hook, we backtrack, stalling, clowning, smirking . . . trying to save one round, sneak in the sleeper punch. sure. sure. could I be an evangelist? sure, for myself [★ ★ ★]

[To Douglas Blazek]
[February–March 1965]

[★ ★ ★] Sheri's pissed at me because I stay down in the mud and also because I put her in a poem now and then. But take the *Cantos*. I understand they are good writing because Pound wrote them. I know there's a lot of Chinese in there, Cantonese, whatever. Sheri tells me they put him in a wooden cage once and did all sorts of crude things to him. All right.

he went to the losing side. Many men are tortured every day. they put tarpaper on church roofs. they dig up beets. they pick lettuce. steal cars. slaughter beef. turn the same screw. wait on old ladies. on and on. they cut us all to pieces. well, anyhow, I took the *Cantos* home. Every time I went to the library I took out a copy of the *Cantos* It was always there. 15 times I took the *Cantos* home. 15 times I took the *Cantos* back, unread. I don't say it is not a good book; I say it is not a good book for me, Ezra Pound and Sheri Martinelli be damned, and all the Sitwells too, and H.D. and all that gang.

I told Corrington to stay away from the novel but he had to run off to Oxford or someplace and become a Dr. and then come back and write a Civil War novel – and the next one will follow course: modern & incest & rape & murder, which happens, but not like turning the same screw happens and putting down the newspaper and looking up and seeing the face of the woman across from you as a dead woman. they write about the seeming-loud things and leave out what is happening to us, to people like you and I, me, and so it's published. they only used to write about kings, people of seeming nobility, mostly, and in a sense, this still holds. I remember once sending a very long story, almost a novel, to a magazine, and it was about an alcoholic who ended up strapped down to a hospital bed, and who heaved up his blood and guts and was left to die in the dark charity ward. They wrote back, 'This is a tour-de-force, powerfully done, but we finally decided to reject it because the central character seemed to have no meaning or worth.' The central character was me. But what man has no meaning or worth? Almost all of them, and none of them. Anyway, the story was finally lost in the mails, or really I couldn't get it back and I didn't have carbons and so to hell with it. But nobility? nobility is useless and beautiful. didn't Cervantes tell us that? the toilet is universal. who knows about the boss finger-fucking the secretary in the stock room and then firing the shipping clerk for taking a 15 minute coffee break? who knows how the streets of Bensenville look at 6 : 15 a.m. in early March? who knows about Blazek and Wantling cutting through a golf course?

yet, I doubt any of us have been broken enough to see. I used to mouth how I used to lay around alleys drunk, but this was nothing, merely a time of easy thinking about sunlight and dirt and country and shoes and flies and warts and flowers. have you ever read the novels of Knut Hamsun? he had to live most of it, and smell it, and take the blade. he could write with feeling for the fool. too many writers dismiss the fool. Hemingway had style and Hemingway had clarity, and wrote more badly as he went on because he leaned on the style which he stole partly from Gertrude and partly from Sherwood Anderson and which came partly from his soul. style is a good tool to tell what you have to say but when you no longer have anything to say, style is a limp cock before the wondrous cunt of the universe. Hamsun never ran out of things to say because Hamsun (evidently) never stopped living. Hemingway stopped, or lived in the same way. Sherwood Anderson never stopped living. and then there are always little men in back rooms, like me, talking about their betters, saying what's right and what's wrong with them. there have always been and always be little men in back rooms: ask Malcolm X, ask Kennedy, ask Christ. [★ ★ ★]

Cherkovsky's Hank *(pp. 145–149) reports that Bukowski finally met Corrington during his sojourn in New Orleans with the Webbs in March 1965. The meeting was not a success and left Bukowski with 'disdain' for his former correspondent, who had now turned to the novel as being more important than poetry.*

[To John William Corrington]
March 1, 1965

I wrote 2 some year back and no response so I gave it up thinking that the England thing and the novel and James Joyce had you by the balls. However, I will soon be 45 and don't care to argue about it. I always answer my mail, tho', whether it's a whore from East Kansas City or Dr. Spock. [★ ★ ★]

The girl-child is Marina Louisa Bukowski and I am a sucker for it. Very large mouth and eyes and when that mouth opens and spreads into the big grin laugh, all sunflowers and sun, and I break in half, she has me. [★ ★ ★]

Both sides of the correspondence with Al Purdy, the Canadian poet, have been published their entirety in The Bukowski/Purdy Letters. *The relationship began in 1964 with a favorable review by Purdy of* It Catches My Heart in Its Hands *and with Bukowski's enthusiastic response to Purdy's own work. This next letter was written during Bukowski's visit to the Webbs.*

[To Al Purdy]
New Orleans March 14, 1965

This won't be much of a letter. Sick, sick, sitting here shaking & frightened & cowardly & depressed. I have hurt almost everybody's feelings. I am not a very good drunk. And it's the same when I awaken here as anywhere. I only want sweet peace and kindliness when I awaken – but there's always some finger pointing, telling me some terrible deed I committed during the night. It seems I make a lot of mistakes and it seems that I am not allowed any. The finger used to belong to my father, or to some shack-job, and now it's an editor's finger. But it's the same. For Christ's sake, Al, I don't understand people, never will. It looks like I got to travel pretty much alone.

[To Douglas Blazek]
March 24, 1965

[★ ★ ★] they continue to build highrise apts. all around here, and little men with hammers and steel helmets crawl around fuck around, talk baseball and sex in the smokey sunlight and I stare out the window at them like a demented man, watching their movements, wandering about them as the kid screams behind me and the old woman asks me, 'Have you seen my comb?' 'No, I haven't seen your comb,' I tell her as a man walks by the window and his face contains the monsterism and brutality and sleepiness and false braveness of a million faces of a million million faces and I want to cry too like the kid but all I think is, – I'm outa beer and I'm broke and the world is burning shit and the flowers are ashamed. something like that. not all like that. just mostly the first part, and the rest crawling in my brain like some beetle. [★ ★ ★]

[To Douglas Blazek]
March 25? 26? 1965

[★ ★ ★] I had a few bad days in N.O. but after 2 weeks we had each adjusted to various madnesses and ignored each other enough to be comfortable. I signed 3,000 pages plus, which was painful, yes. *The Outsider* has not expired and will come out with #4 shortly after *Crucifix* which is finished now and has to be collated and so forth, a big job, slow, but you should have your book soon. They are going to another town. where, I don't know. [★ ★ ★]

no, I don't sleep either. I used to shack with a broad who claimed I never slept. she also claimed I jacked-off in the bathroom which I didn't because the explosion of her body across my sight was all I needed to leap and drive home. she drank too much, she drank more than I did, and you know that's too much. [★ ★ ★]

[To Douglas Blazek]

[?early April 1965]

[★ ★ ★] I remember getting ten page letters from my old man while I was starving in cardboard shacks trying to write the GREAT AMERICAN SHORT STORY and when I first got the letter I'd always flip through the pages and riffle them and search them but nothing green nothing green and I'd be freezing my whole soul in a pitch of vomit darkness and he'd write ten fucking vindictive pages about AMERICA and MAKING GOOD, and it was worse than silence because he was rubbing it in – he had a place to shit, beans, turkey, a warm bed, a lawn to mow, names of neighbors, a seeming place to go each morning

and he rubbed it in good. and here I am an old fuck myself, probably on a ten pager telling you how I feel and what I mean to myself. anyhow, a little green, I wish I had put more on that 17 to one shot this afternoon but I didn't, and so a $5 for dogfood and for which I expect a lifetime subscription to *Ole* if it ever manages to continue??

I remember one time I was on a suicide kick and drinking myself sick hoping I wouldn't do it somehow, or however a man thinks at such time. all nerves shot. all everything deepening. the human face and way a horror forever. crouched under my blankets like a worm and wishing I could be. anything but what was attached to me. grisly factotum of high-steeped blues. God damn God's breath and understanding. I wrote a letter with some English prof's name to it and I verily had at one time almost sensed an understanding. he had written me how some kid had hit him over the head with a brick when he was young and how he understood violence and horror. I was staring pretty much at pretty knife blades way up high in a 3rd. floor place, esp. when the stomach got sick and the blood came and I had to lay low for a couple of hours because I wanted to kill myself my own way, or maybe as a voice from the back would say (I hate voices from the back!) maybe I didn't want to die. anyhow, I wrote him the circumstances of my soul and also my penury (which was secondary) and what happened? this reader of all philosophers, this understander, this guy who got hit by a brick, this teacher of children, this man who drove into a place with his car marked out for FACULTY PARKING . . . what happened???

he didn't answer. for 5 months.

you've got to hand it to me, baby, at least I answered, dig it anyway you want, sometimes even sound helps, it would have helped me when sunshine looked like shit and still often does, but you gift me with letters of genius, open and swimming blood real, no writer that I know of has ever written letters such as you do and I am keeping them and if grace and God and luck be kind some other eye and eyes will fall upon them beside mine.

YOU TELL YOUR WIFE AND YOUR CHILDREN AND YOUR DOGS AND YOUR LAND-LORD AND YOUR GROCER AND YOUR ARCH-ANGEL AND YOUR FUCK-ANGEL AND YOUR UNION MAN TO BE VERY KIND TO YOU CONTINUALLY for you have a touch of grace and damnation and beauty that the world should try to preserve.

and yes all I can say is 'hold, hold.' please try to understand what this means.

. . . might amuse you . . . the proof who didn't write. I met him in New Orleans one night at Webb's place. he still wouldn't speak to me. he talked to everybody else. so what? who wants to talk?

. . . McNamara? seems a little standard . . . yet seems lifted by something. I can't ignore his wanting to be real . . . whatever that means. christ, how phoney we sound, I sound! well, I don't know what else to do. I don't have

FACULTY PARKING

ONLY

I hope you remain alive in order to keep sending me the good letters – your letters mean more to me than any poetry I have ever read because your plain and even and screaming and clear voice talking certainly beats T. S. Eliot, Pound, Shakespeare, John Fante, even Jeffers . . . for me. how do you do it? how many poems DO YOU WASTE by wasting letters on me??

god damn you, then.

look, you asked some puzzling and rather melodramatic and taboo really questions on writing and witchcraft of poetry, for each man is some kind of weird nut, brotherly as a hatchet, and he'd rather keep his balls to himself than spread the flesh for hungry chipmunks of whore shit flaking through clouds of radium. all right, eyow, ok, well, I need some teeth pulled anyhow. –

to wit: 'do you ever get the lousy feeling of where the hell the next poem is coming from – that perhaps you can't see anything worth writing about anymore?'

Answer: no.

'What kind of stage or period or interim do you think yr in?'

I don't know. I am afraid of thinking. I have seen what thinking does to men. I watch my girlchild look at an orange in the sunlight and know that she is all right. I look at our President Johnson who tries so hard to think, so hard to be right, a leader, and I know that through trying that he is a madman. I forgive him. but, like you: who feeds the dogs?

yet, like Hon. Johnson I think I am getting better, I think I am doing better . . . I THINK. I THINK.

> I think I can be another Cervantes
> another Warren Spahn
> Jersey Joe
> Braddock
> Laxative Lazarus shit shouting
> lazarus . . .

> but don't make me write a novel now
> or ever
> unless I g.d. truly feel like
> it – and
> not just for a space on the
> shelf.
> so the way I feel now I guess I won't ever write one,
> I am terribly lazy and more terribly tired

> I need rest to gather
> and they keep the sandpaper on me.
> lack of guts?
> of course.

[★ ★ ★]

– please, you don't bother me talking suicide. suicide is a rat running thru my hair continually. in fact, it's the only way I can get out of my present position. these 2 small rooms. no money. all the time I am writing to you I am holding a conversation with a woman scraping a dish, and if only she were washing the dishes, all right, but she's just fucking around and nothing gets done, all is dead, and the girlchild is a foot to my left and every now and then I reach out she reaches out, we make faces, and I love it, she's round flesh of young madness, but really I am stuck in this center, and the very beginning was an act of kindness, something I did not want, and now more kindness kindness and there is a love for both of them, a mad gambling sort of thing, but they are killing me, not the poetry in me, fuck that, but me, and they don't know it

> and this is the worst:
> to be eaten up
> day by day
> piece by piece and you are the only one
> who knows
>
> while they play jokes with
> celery sticks
> and a good night's sleep for
> them.

I don't think I sleep more than one or 2 hours a night. I know that there are many nights that I never sleep at all, many many nights.

> and it is not that I am having profound thots
> I am not having any thots at
> all.
> just looking at the shades
> this wall
> a drape
> a side of a dresser
> the invasion of ants
> the wind like a mother's voice dead
> to a sissy like me,
> covers shaped like
> matzos

the holy ghost of
Pain

I can't sleep

I used to live with an old whore with
a very wisdom sort of
wisdom and she'd always say

'You tell me to shut my mouth
so you can get some sleep;
well, let me tell ya, bastard,
I KNOW YOU:

YOU NEVER SLEEP!!

so don't tell me ta shut up!'
[★ ★ ★]

[To Douglas Blazek]
[April, 1965]

[★ ★ ★] oh yes, well, on slipsheets and all the stuff, I don't care; I rather like
the paper you use. F. likes to act intelligent and knowing, only she's really
all fallen apart, and it's kind of an act and she runs with these poets who
have workshop meetings and read their stuff to each other and chatter, and
they go to things like 'pot-luck' dinners and long church drools on
Sundays and they meet for coffee and cake at Fay's or Marty's and they
may even have a martini and they all STINK, and sometimes they come here
and sit around and I try to be decent but they chat like monkeys fingering their crotches and I find it less and less easy to be graceful because they
eat up my one or 2 hours of peace that each day away from the mill allows
me before I go in again that night or on a day off they might stay for
hours, and so at times I have gotten a little hard, they will be sitting yammering in the small front room and they will see this figure in his shorts,
cock peeking out, pounding in beerswill rhythm on the hall boards
making for the kitchen, saying nothing, ignoring all, not worried about
Selma, not worried about Viet Nam, just trying to shake people and ideas
from the ratskull and suck down another beer and maybe think about

blasting out for a fifth of CUTTY. They may be fucking F. physically as well.
I don't care too much. We are not married. the kid came along and I did
the thing, moved her in. I think the kid is mine. I thought she was too old,
I thought I was too old. the gods fooled me and reamed it home. one
more hotpoker for good old Bukowski! Anyway, don't worry about postcards from F. she's that way.

I would be honored if you pumped out a book of selected B. bullshit
letters. I don't know if the people kept the letters or if they were assholes.
Must rush off to work, so must shorten bullshit and just pump out names,
say in order of the people I have written the most letter to. [★ ★ ★]

Tom McNamara, editor of Down Here, *responding to the* Ole *essay, wrote
to Bukowski from Greenwich Village.*

[To Tom McNamara]
April 9, 1965

yeah, sweetheart, life is a spider, we can only dance in the web so long,
the thing is gonna get us, you know that. I am pretty well hooked-in now,
have fallen into some traps. and speak mostly from the bent bone, the
flogged spirit. I've had some wild and horrible years & electric & lucky
years, and if I sit and stare out the window now at the rain, I allow myself
the final gift of some temporary easiness before they throw the dirt on.
Yet, even being trapped I know I am trapped and that there's a difference
between oranges and rocks. there's a difference between hard retreat and
puling surrender. O, I save what I can; I never give anything away – I mean
to the shits and chopppers & the clock & the buildings and the mad
masters, the cock-sucking bloodsuckers. yet it's like one man fighting an
army without help; yet when they tape me to the wall I will spit in their
eyes; when they cut my balls off I will drip blood on their shoes . . . so
forth, on and on, endlessly. . . .

the small pamphlets and books of my poems are out of print. You
might find a copy of *It Catches My Heart in Its Hands* in the New York
public library. I know there was one in the New Orleans library when I
was down there. And I like an old man watching a kid run through a broke
field I could not help being somewhat proud that the fucking card showed
that the book had been in and out, in and out, continually, almost never
resting on the shelf. Maybe N.Y. doesn't have a copy. I haven't checked

L.A. This book is my selected poems from 1955 to 1963. I began writing poetry at age 35.

I was down in New Orleans last month helping Jon Webb put together 3,000 copies of *Crucifix in a Deathhand*. Yeah, I helped him a lot; I helped him get drunk. Anyhow, the book will be distributed by Lyle-Stuart Inc., New York, I don't know exactly when. Contains all newly written poems, none of which were submitted to the magazines. Why don't you write Jon Webb, 1109 Rue Royal, New Orleans, 16, Louisiana, and ask him how to get holda a *Crucifix*? Book about finished. Large, wild, and beautiful format, cover and paintings by Noel Rockmore.

I lived in the Village some time back. was disgusted. no men burning in agony, dreaming knives. just con-babies. berets, goats, sipping tea by the window, or whatever they were sipping, I never went in. they looked too comfortable, they looked too money, too phoney, sure. sitting there with their cunt pretending they were Picasso. don't ever pretend. be McNamara without the band. there I go, handing advice like God. an old fuck on a rainy day lighting up a Parliament and dreaming about the slow and easy fifth of CUTTY I am going to drink this Sunday while my mind draws designs on the pavements and the butts of all the beautiful women who don't even know that I am alive. yet, there aren't many beautiful women. sows. lots of pavement, tho. look, I've got to go out into the night. hope I've answered some questions.

[To Ann Menebroker]
April 10, 1965

F. and M.L. have been out of town for 2 weeks and must suppose F. will get to your letter with response after she settles down to the sanctified break of living with me, ya.

Crucifix being collated now, but no price set, and this type of thing done by Lyle-Stuart who will distribute. I hope he doesn't get hooked for the 3,000 copies – I can't buy them. art work by Noel Rockmore, vast cover and 4 plates inside. Large book, like children's fairy tale thing, long wide pages, 100, I am lucky again to fall down into the center of this thing.

meanwhile there is toothache, insomnia, hangover; my wildly staring eye thru the slow drowning. Have been reading *That Summer in Paris* which somebody mailed me. waste. unless you wonder what Hemingway did in the bathroom of his soul.

[To Douglas Blazek]
April 12, 1965

[★ ★ ★] anyhow, Sheri M. [★ ★ ★] gets pissed whenever she believes I mention her in a poem. she says I talk out of school or something like that. One of her boys came down from Frisco and knocked on my door and came in and said they were going to sue because I had used his lady in one of my poems. I was in there with my whore and I was laying drunk on the floor, and I said, ok, if you're going to sue that's the way it works, only I don't have any money, I don't even have a jockstrap. then I turned on a tape I had made while drunk and I layed on the floor listening to my quips and madness and singing, and soon he gave up and went away. I even offered to get him drunk but he wouldn't drink. I guess Sheri thot him a pretty boy; she drew pictures of him all over her magazines, adding curls to his head. But act. he only had regular features; satisfied & blank look; no coal burning. dead, really dead, pal. Anyhow, Sheri I think was for a while sending my letters to somebody at a Yale who was sticking them into a tube that was going to be buried – Pearson, I think his name was – and so there go those letters – buried along with a lot of other modern contrivance. Anyhow, Sheri said her Chinaman husband enjoyed my letters. that's something. S. always trying to get me to change my style to the all-embracing, classical style – the only way to be immortal and so forth. She sent books by H.D. and even had me write H.D. while she (H.D.) was dying. Well, that's all right. But there are enough of them writing the way Sheri wants me to write. I've got to go my way. If I can't reach the gods at least I can see the dirt under my toenails and dream of sleeping with 14 year old girls. Jesus, save me. But not right away. [★ ★ ★]

[To Tom McNamara]
April 16, 1965

Typewriter shot thru 20 times and now dead. Must get another: feel like a man without a cock having a spiritual hard-on and nothing to ram it home with. I can't spin anything without the keys, the keys have a way of cutting out the fat and retaining the easiness.

If you want to run the letter fine but forget essay a while. A man can go drunk on essays & handing out advice & being a master critic (T. S. Eliot, so forth). I've got to go easy because I still don't know where I am.

Guy hit me for a 20 less than an hour ago telling me his word was his bond. If I had back all the money I've loaned I could buy 1/2 dozen typewriters (new) today instead of writing with this fig leaf stem & liquid shoe polish.

You speak of certain names, and I guess we all like the lions who cut the way, yet I met a friend (backer) of one of these lions last year, and I'd rather be a dead cat than feed from certain hands. He told dull jokes all night, drank my beer and argued with his wife. then he tried to slip me a ten. 'I'd like you to meet X.' 'No, thanks,' I told him, 'I've read his books.' Then his wife at the door (to me): 'You're so quiet. You never say anything.'

Hell no, they didn't give me a chance.

Reminds me of when I was in New Orleans last month and 2 college profs drove some miles in to see me and then argued with each other into the night about their degrees and how they were going to take over the university magazine. Finally one of them noticed me, turned to me and said, 'My balls hurt!' I told him that was too bad and then they went on with their talk.

Really, tho, I guess the gods let me off easy. My balls didn't hurt once all night.

Then, you speak of my having starved. Of course, you know that starving doesn't create Art. It creates many things but mainly it creates TIME, and I don't mean the paper bit. If you're good and you have time you have a chance, and if you're good and you don't have time you won't be good very long. I think there is kind of an area of distillation you have to go thru and once this settles there isn't much they can do with you, although you can do it to yourself (see Hemingway, S. Anderson and so on . . .). [★ ★ ★]

[To Douglas Blazek]
April 17, 1965

[★ ★ ★] the old typewriter finally fell apart to unrepairable stage. like the death of an old friend, all the fire we went thru, the drunks, the whores, the rejects, and the occasional home run. I have not learned how to handle this typer yet – it is a very cheap second hand and I see why now – you've got to hit the keys just right or it won't work. I hope you can read the enclosed manuscript. [★ ★ ★]

I get these letters on the essay I wrote for *Ole* #2 and they seem to think I said something; I am a fucking oracle (oriol?) for the LOST or something, is what they tell me. that's nice. but I AM THE LOST.

going on to the collection of letters you were talking about; some of them may be thrown away and some of the people might be pissed at me, and some of them may be too possessive, but I think most of them pretty good people and you ought to get some co-operation. sure, edit wherever you wish, edit out dull parts, print partials or what you think entertaining. no, I needn't see what you're going to print beforehand. that's waste. I am not ashamed of anything I have written in letters. you print what you want and how you want. and I look forward to this bit and hope you can work it out. you see, I wonder what I said too. [★ ★ ★]

[To Douglas Blazek]
April 21 or 22, [1965]

have not heard from you on first part of *Confessions of a Man Insane Enough to Live with Beasts*, but here is second part which I wrote tonight. naturally, I hope it goes. please let me know soon.

tired now. got your letter today which I will get to soon; I mean, answer soon. feel slugged now, and am closing.

[To Tom McNamara]
April 24, 1965

Letters? god damn, man, let's be careful. all right at outset, esp. for tightheads who have been working in sonnet form, writing critical articles, so forth; it gives them (letters) the facility and excuse for wallowing in the easiness of their farts and yawns without pressure. really, writing letters are easy: nobody likes form, and I know this – that's why I discard a lot of it in my poetry (or, I think I do) (from is a paycheck for learning to turn the same screw that has held things together). so now we start with the letter as an o.k. thing, and then the next thing you know instead of being an o.k. thing, a natural form, it simply becomes another form for the expulsion of the creative, artistic, fucked-up Ego, like maybe this letter is, I don't deny it, I don't deny being a part of the poison, and soon a lot of the boys end up working as hard or harder on the letters than they do on their poems. wherever the payoff lies, what?

now look, for laughs and for instance, I've heard a certain old-timer who's never quite made it with his work but who has always had a finger up some big boy's crotch or been in some Movement. maybe I'm being unkind. anyhow he has seemed monied and has seemed able to recognize a talent before the big publishers puke over it and kill it with circulation, publicity and $$$. what I mean is, I now hear this man is going to issue a collection of his LETTERS. now, how in the hell are you going to issue a collection of your *own* letters unless you keep carbons? and if you keep carbons, aren't you more or less writing a literary essay type of precious thing, and keeping a hunk of it yourself because it's so good? or if you don't do that then it's: 'Dear Paul: I hope you have kept all the letters I've written you over the past fifteen years as I am now issuing a collection of my collected letters and, of course, would like to include mine to you . . . hope you still have them, and, of course I would o.k. any deletions you would care to make . . .'

I used to think of a letter as something like this: 'Dear Paul: Sure hot today and have drank a lot of beer. Martha had a wisdom tooth pulled yesterday. The Dodgers lost yesterday. they just can't get their pitchers any runs . . .'

yet I find most literary letters duller than this, and this includes the letters of D. H. Lawrence, Thomas Wolfe, or any I can remember, and, if I have missed some good ones somewhere, let me know.

I had to pick up a cheap 2nd hand portable and as you can see I have trouble controlling it but as long as some of it can be made out, all right. and I sure hope it hits through o.k. to this nice fresh carbon I have stuck underneath.

yes, the LSD is the fading rage, stuff written under LSD, about LSD, my god they all do the *same* thing at the same time – THE IMPROPER PROPER THING, if you know what I mean, and always in the concert of the safety of each other . . . sure, if you want to use parts of my letters, go ahead, why the hell do you think I write them?

somebody in the neighborhood here has his stereo turned up as loud as possible and I do believe because he is enjoying it he also presumes everybody else is enjoying it. It is really only a half-hearted masturbation of music and it does make me ill. I'm not saying I'm a sensitive type but I keep thinking of the continous intrusions that keep slapping against us and it is these intrusions: the small and continuous and everyday ones that finally grind us down either into acceptance or insanity. intrusions are many and varied, like say a dead face, urinal murdered face, hanging onto a living body and looking down into a bag of apples the hand fills in a supermarket as you walk past.

there's hardly any way out, even after you've seen enough, and after a number of years you have seen enough, but you can only close a door and pull the blinds for so long before they come get you: the landlord, your wife, the public health inspector, the men from the insane asylum.

now toothache, tooth breaking off in back, I have about 7 stubs of teeth that need yanking but I am a coward and no money and ashamed of the condition I have allowed my jaws to crash to. I think of the dead down there in their caskets or what's left of their caskets. how are the teeth of the dead? think of all those jaws down there! think of Shakespeare gaping open, unable to drink a beer.

maybe it's because it's so hot today I do not feel well or maybe it's because I have to go to WORK and it's Saturday and I'd rather get drunk, but they tell me I've missed too many days already, and my girlchild has these blue eyes and she thinks I can make it, but some day I'm going to lay it down again and see what happens, watch the walls come down like bombardment, watch the landlord snarl, listen to the lady from relief insult me, roll my own cigarettes, put ice in the cheap wine to kill the gaseous taste . . . the defense and demise of myself comes above all – my choice to fall and not do, stare at ceilings, beg for bread, exist like a pigeon, a sack of manure, a flower under the window with 17 days to live.

I see the flies in the green leaves and I think,

it's strange, they've never read Richard Aldington . . .

'Nash,' mentioned in the next letter, was Jay Nash, who, Bukowski notes, 'ran the underground newssheet, The Chicago Literary Times.' *He had published Bukowski's* Run With the Hunted *in his Midwest Poetry Chapbooks series in 1962. Bukowski notes that he was 'obsessed with Hemingway and the twenties.'*

[To Douglas Blazek]
[late April 1965]

[★ ★ ★] I don't see how *Ole* gets around so much. I hear on the phone. 2 guys knocked on the door and brought me beer. all the same thing: 'I read your article in *Ole*.'

on *Confessions*, of course, I'm glad you accept. actually it's going to destroy a lot of IMAGE that has been built up and it's going to make me freer to move around yes, I know that any section could be extended, and there were more acts to add, I think of them now: the gang of fascists who carried guns, screamed heil Hitler!, drank wine; hanging posters in New York subways; coconut man in a cake factory; the colored maid with big legs who fucked me in a St. Louis hotel; a Fort Worth redhead; myself insane in Dallas and more more more, the things that happen to almost everybody while they are waiting for the executioner.

but look, on doing the novel sort of thing something holds me back. maybe it hasn't jelled, maybe it seems like work, maybe dropping poems off the tips of my elbows is easier. technical point – in *Confessions* I have a place in the slaughter house scene – I think I say something like, 'The Negroes rolled up the wheelbarrows, they were painted a white, a kind of chicken-shit white' or some such line. I remember thinking of correcting it but forgot. I mean the people might think the Negroes were painted a chicken-shit white should read something like: 'The Negroes rolled up the wheelbarrows. the barrows were painted a – ' or let it go the original way. who cares? [★ ★ ★]

word from Nash who also sent a flask Hemingway took a slug from, and now it's mine, a nice gift, and it will see use, good use, and Nash also says that he is going to bring out *Cold Dogs* by the end of this month – which to me, means in a couple of months. This is in response to a ten page drunken letter I printed out via hand to him. at least it did appear to rattle buried bones, finally. *Crucifix* now (see Webb and Lyle-Stuart) is being collated and it won't be long at all, and someday too I will get *Confessions*, and hang it up there on the top row of ye old bookcase with the rest. I don't feel so much like a writer as I do like somebody who has slipped one past, and I guess my detractors would agree with this. I feel like Warren Spahn squeezing out just one more for the lousy Mets, or like the dice are hot but it's gotta end of course it will. I'll peel and die like old paint, hurrah, but anyhow I have been gifted with not ever having had any first-class fame, and this has allowed me to go on writing the way I please to write. I've been lucky, no one can have been any luckier look, I'll be 45 in August, think of it. no guns have killed me and I have not been suckered into any beliefs. uh, just think of standing in a kitchen and pulling up a shade with 45 years on you and letting in the sunlight, thinking of the stockpile crashed behind you, thinking, I might even some day be 65, peering from slits of eyes like a grey tank and pulling at a tiny bottle of whiskey and lighting a WINSTON and watching the blue smoke curl curl climb the air, and still feeling bad, and taking it, wearing an old green sweater with moth holes and knowing death is very close as the young girls sing in the streets and literary and political giants have risen and exploded and disappeared.

the vietnam thing is in the papers every night and the govt. keeps sending over more planes, bombs, troops, battleships, and, of course, I don't understand it, I haven't understood any of the wars, I only know that I am always told the enemy is a big bad guy and unless we show him constant muscle and boldness I am told, he'll someday be in the doorway finger-fucking our wives, but all that I do know is that after the clearing of one war we immed. pump up another, and after you see the same picture book again and again you know that it's only a nightmare train always getting ready to run off the tracks, and you neither fight it, accept it or forget it; you ride along hoping the thing holds to the rails a little longer, hoping for one more beer in a peeling kitchen while listening to Haydn, hoping the enemy has sense and forbearance instead of what we're told he has, and the newsboys hawk the crazy news as our wives burn the toast, think of other things like changing diapers and nose drops, of going to a Sunday's church or wanting a drive down the coast to inhale the turd-filled ocean but the car's too old and the spirit's tired: forget it, baby, I want to sit in here and just drink tonight what again? again Blazek's wife brings him beer. why don't you bring me beer? no, I don't want a boiled egg listen, what do you think of this vietnam thing?

Lewis Mumford said long ago that there wouldn't be any atomic war that we would only live under the shadow of fear for some decades, perhaps for the rest of the century.

how in the hell can Lewis Mumford say that? how does *he* know? as long as there isn't an atomic war he sounds right when one happens nobody will care whether he is right or not. [★ ★ ★]

[To Tom McNamara]
May sicks, 1965

writers are a sick-head lot, a gathering of neon-light tasters, spitting out their words, their absurdities, their bile, their orange-juice blood. we are down in submarines; we don't know; a nervous nasty lot . . .

I'd rather sleep for 3 or 4 days than do anything, so what happens? I can't sleep at all. I worry about motor tuneups and the death of sparrows. and all the women walking around and me not fucking them. then, sometimes I think I am too much topsoil, I want to get under, forget the toteboard and gambol with the worms (later, I know), so the other night I am wandering around at 4 in the morning and I pick up something by a Chinaman, 300 or 200 B.C., a couple of centuries after Confucius, and here's this guy running around giving the word to Dukes and State Ministers and Kings, but it doesn't reach me, I don't have any armies or loyal subjects or disloyal subjects, only a matter of keeping myself alive another 15 or 20 years if I feel like it more wasted time now I've got a pain under the collarbone; I've been going a pack and a half but my pecker is hard when I awaken the few times I've slept. I am angry with white Spanish walls and sound of tires on the pavement no, I don't read much anymore – Donleavy, anybody it's a matter of the juices saying no, no, no. no. there's simply no intake if I power it down against the grain I am deader than I am now and that wd. be some horrible thing, ah.

I hear Lyle Stuart is going to charge $7.50 for *Crucifix in a Deathhand*, my new book of poems. It has expensive paper, format, plates of artwork and so on, but I can't see anybody paying $7.50 for a book of poems, and he has 3,000 books of poems, and so I guess he's going to have to stack them wall to wall and forget it most of the people, I think, who might go my poems, most of them don't even have $7.50 and if they did they'd prob. buy something to drink well, I write the stuff and what they do with it is theirs the paper is supposed to last 800 years or 1800 years I forget which and I don't know, except one bomb or bad poetry will take care of all that.

Your New Bohemia sounds a little disturbing, and it might well disturb the shopkeepers of the Village if the tourists get the buzz. I remember when I was in the Village so long long ago, 25 years ago?, I happened to read in the paper that O. Henry hung out in this certain place and did his writing on the table down there so I went on in, down the steps and looked around red tables nobody there. I thought, O. Henry must have been a fool. I walked up to the bar and ordered a drink and the bartender said, 'Sorry, sir, I can't serve you.' I didn't ask him why I was sober but it made me feel filth as if he smelled some inner stink in me, and I had been feeling mad, thinking suicide, maybe I looked too ugly, too vile anyhow, I did not like the place, drink or no drink then down in New Orleans a month or so ago I am walking along with the editor and he takes me through this kind of sidewalk cafe place and he said Hemingway and Faulkner and Tennessee Williams used to hang out here at one time or another a real commercial hole it was, and I thought, these guys must have been crazy jammed with tourists and conceited waiters. I told the editor that those writers must have been nuts and he said, well, they were drunk.

that still didn't help too much.

there's a lot I don't understand but this is standard when I wipe my ass I guess I understand that this is something that should be done and I understand that I should not go out on the streets naked there might be lions out there vietnam, hitler, caesar, the falling of boards from roofs I do not understand.

do you know something? I am getting sleepy maybe I ought to go to sleep?

there are days of too much of the same and in the whole human mass not an eye or a face or a voice or a sound. Only a frog under a bush only a cat crossing a street a street without tits graveyards books on mathematics chalk for lunch. madhouses. farmers. fish. meatballs. manure. sleep. sleep, sleep, sleep.

[To Douglas Blazek]
May 20, 1965

[★ ★ ★] the woman is standing here beating a big spoon around inside of a water jug, now she's ripping cardboard, banging refrigerator, sniffling, snuffling, now she's making coffee, now the kid suddenly screams, more bangs, these walls are so close, refrigerator again, now she lifts a wet rag and carries it across the room like a sleepwalker . . . they are pouring it to me BLAZ!!!

30 minutes to go before work and I am trying to get this letter off to you

DO YOU WANT ANOTHER COOKIE? I hear her voice say.

fuck it. we march on. an angel will give me a hand-job in the year 1986 it doesn't matter. [★ ★ ★]

little incident last night, foreman saw me standing talking to another man. this is against the rules. he rushed up. we have little slips we carry that show the amount of work we have done. he rushed up and I jammed the slips into his belly.

I'm leaving, I told him.

what?

I'm sick.

huh?

I'm sick of working.

what do you mean?

my 8 hours are up.

I saw you standing there talking . . .

my 8 are up.

why didn't you tell me?

add me up.

then the jackass runs to another minor wheel and says, I saw Bukowski standing there and talking to that man . . .

well, says the other guy, his 8 hours are up.

I walked past and out. I mean, it doesn't mean anything except that these babies are all sucked out and I don't like to talk to them or even look at them, especially near the end of the night. [★ ★ ★]

The book of poems announced here was ultimately published not by Mad Virgin Press but by Poetry X/Change, Glendale, California. It did not appear in print until 1968. The book of 'mostly drawings' was never published.

[To Tom McNamara]

May 20, 1965

strike for freedom of time to have a look around. they have caught me. it's a sad and silly story of doing-in but the main thing is they've got me. 8 years on the same job and just as broke as if I were not working. Of course, the first years were the slippery days when they had a hard time finding me; when I could sit and watch the smoke rise from my cigarette while men were killing each other. and men continue to kill each other and themselves and they've cut a lot of woodwork and a pile of soul from me. there are a hell of a lot of ways to die but I still have a finger on the ledge, I think.

something called THE MAD VIRGIN PRESS wants to do a book of my poems and I don't know if it will be mimeo or what and I don't care. they say ten percent, and I can always use a little beer money. I think I have a title – *Poems Written Before Jumping Out of an 8 Story Window.* I will try it on them and see what they say. Then Border Press is going to come out with a book of mine, mostly drawings interspersed with poems, but I haven't done the thing yet, but will. I like to play with india ink and lots of white paper. I tried some oils one time but what a strain – like going for the 3rd piece of ass. so what I mean, here I am sagged and dying but still fumbling with poems and drawings, and it's a way of going on – like the whiskey and the horses and sleep sleep sleep, if I can get it.

this is an indrawn and particularly kind of cotton and waiting time, faucet dripping, something on the radio 200 years old, the teeth falling out of my head, horns honking, children pissing down their legs in a May afternoon, and below us pipes underground passing the shit to the sea, and the morgues stuffed, men in stained neckties selling ass, more books on Kennedy, myself barely feeling it out – the flailing, the words, the trees, the whores, the ways, Time battering like a tough fullback &, Ace, I do not mean the magazine. smoking cigars and dreaming of Mata Hari. ducking under sparrow droppings. I saw a lizard yesterday. also read a quotation by E. E. Cummings in the newspaper yesterday that I didn't like. all in all, you gotta figure a newspaper is a bad buy because it can make you terribly unhappy and you even have to pay a dime to get that way. Berlioz. somebody writes and asks if I want to read somewhere. I have to tell him no. it's true I don't want to. snails don't do much for me. I have these pains in my shoulders, neck, back, and I walk as if I were mortar. topside. only the tigerlegs kid with the moth-soul. when it rains I cry like Mortons' salt.

you keep it going. we all end as turds yet let's make them WORK for it.

the Spanish troops passed down the streets today their bayonets like whitened teeth and I burned the tablecloth, a picture of Herbert Hoover and a crossword puzzle of Asia. [★ ★ ★]

[To Ann Menebroker]
[May 27,] 1965

[★ ★ ★] yes, the phone call time was a good time and an odd time, a very odd time, and I am always very close to leaping but then was a very most close time, and I'll always remember your clear and watercool voice, you voice sheen blue and easy and clean saying 'hello, Buk.' once when I had just gotten out of jail, had just opened the door – the phone rang – 'hello, Buk.' It was very good.

and now I get up like an elephant of a man, I have been drinking beer, I am going to piss, gross, gross.

the life hangs with us. it's not easy. you and I, we work with words but the words are like bricks stones turds clay turtle shells fucked out by sand, what have you? I can't be generous with myself. I've felt better giving a bum 25 cents, I've felt better being a bum sleeping on a park bench with my youth yowling over my angry and demented bones than I ever have felt writing a poem. what is it? nothing can please us. we are in a somewhat fine cage. you know this. christ is not the only bastard who was ever nailed to the wood. or bastardess. I include you in. I think as time goes on, the female more and more is beginning to inherit the reality and knowingness of our state of being – which is sadly almost zero. but please keep writing your poems. I think it is something about our Age – that men no longer speak so very well. they are frightened to show any more than muscle. ugg. muscle, I have. but muscle isn't going to show us through the bomb or through ourselves. I don't mean to intend a religious yammering or fear of fire. I think if D. H. Lawrence were here now he'd sense some of this – what I would call 'unmanliness,' shits, look, it goes up and down but if we want to save it it's going to take all humans to save it, and if it's not worth saving (and maybe that's it?) nothing will save it. [★ ★ ★]

The book Veryl Blatt had written about is Crucifix in a Death Hand, *published by Loujon Press.*

[To Veryl Blatt]
May 27, 1965

my thanks the good letter on the book. now that the book is over it seems a very strange thing, an almost non-happening, except now I am glad I went down there and saw those 2 people put it together out of matchsticks and starvation and (as you said) love. they battled rats, roaches, hurricanes and my drunken presence. I did manage to sign 3100 pages, some of them with message and/or drawing, but outside of that I was in the way. this book was a little harder than *It Catches* in that I had to write directly into a waiting press. that's good and it's not good. I mean, it's like coming up with the bases loaded all the time. yet I imagine any poet in America, in the world, would have been most glad of the chance. my luck all came late and there is only so much they can do to me now with these two books behind me. I'm glad you're keeping the 2 books, your kids, your typer and yourself. it is difficult for people like you and I to live out the day, and I too have been through the bloody divorce thing, and christ I can't figure it all – the breaking up, the looking again, the not-looking again. If I could only sleep for ten years but maybe by then the Chinese will have called our hotshot bluffs. If I do not hold the trend of thought here – been to track all day, worked an hour in pits, said to hell with it and came in. played with Marina [★ ★ ★]

[To Tom McNamara]
Late May [1965]

got the *Journal Unamerican* and enclosed buck for next 5 issues. this pb. just zany enough to bug-gas us all. comic strip best of all – 'Mr. Hurts,' my god!

you didn't let me know you were starting a mag. I will make some attempt to submit but am pretty burned-out after hurling together *Crucifix*. look, if you tell Webb – 1109 Royal St., New Orleans . . . or Lyle Stuart 239 Park Ave South, New York, 3 – you are going to review the book, I'm sure you'll get a copy. Or why don't you walk in on Stuart, wave this letter at him and tell him you are the editor of *The Journal Un/American* and *emanon* and demand a copy of *Crucifix*. this would be much more dramatic! Stuart runs a pretty good liberal paper himself.

this is late may 1965 and I have not yet killed myself although I fell down drunk in the bathroom last night and vomited over myself, I, Charles Bukowski, mad poet, fuck, and asshole. I was once married to this millionairess who had to let me go mainly because she couldn't understand me. 'You're always laughing at yourself, demeaning yourself. I like a man who *likes* himself.' well, that's all right too, only we are all crazy in our different ways.

working into the 2nd 6 pack now and a pint of CUTTY sits on the shelf. I intended to go to work tonight but this woman and child don't seem to be worrying about $ or rent or survival so why in the hell should I? sometimes it's just not the night to go in and if you do go in that night you are dead, you know what I mean. our man Blazek having money trouble now, and how any of us survive – what sweet hell, what a going on! my trouble is that I don't know how to do anything but get drunk and write poems, and often the poems are not what they should be. can I hand the landlord a poem for the rent? I'm fucked, we're all fucked, we don't stand a chance. I might get some green with a novel but I still don't feel like writing a novel, may never write one, and so there goes that. It's terrible just to try to stay alive and not quite know why. just to eat a little and wipe the ass and stare at a lightbulb. the gophers and worms are foxy; – they stand in line with my last rejection.

Steve Richmond says he gets letters from you. what ya trying to do, Mac? – wake us all up?

[To Al Purdy]
Late May, 1965

I do not write too often because I do want to keep it easy and not let it be a drag. I am engaged in writing several young literary fellows right now and my balls are dragging. you know – everything's new to them: life's a drag, life's horror, life's anything but writing a poem; life's more like talking about writing a poem and clutching hands. well, shit, maybe I am a little hard on the boys, and some of their letters are good but it does become a merry-go-round. [★ ★ ★]

some kid in New Orleans tells me you wrote him a personal note and said you'd send your *Horse* on into him. you don't know what this means to the kids, al. it can keep them going a couple of years, it can keep the factories and the whores from killing them. but I guess it'll get them anyway. [★ ★ ★]

[To Douglas Blazek]
Sometime, 1965

oh my god blaz, I write you because I believe you are the only person who'll understand but the agony is almost too much it's standing on all four legs – my god my god, there I go, being literary – I want to kill myself so badly but there is no suitable instrument so I keep drinking and wishing – a gun a gun a god damned sweet GUN – wham! – it's over. I mean, baby, I am sitting here with a toothache that is reaming the life out of me, and it's not just the pain, it's everything, it's this pain on top of all the pains!! – I was writing a poem last night and what happen? I am perfectly content drinking, pounding out my silliness, and then what the shit??? the landlady comes down and she and her husband want to get drunk with me again, they get their kicks that way, I say things that bring them to life, fine, fine, and so I chop the head off the poem and go on down there, and I know what it's going to be, he puts on his recording of *Oklahoma* and we all sing, me with a forged frog in my throat, and I say, look, don't you have *Guys and Dolls*? I am a guys and dolls man, I am a loser from way back, I like to hear them songs. of course, he don't got *Guys and Dolls* he got *Oklahoma* so we sing Oklahoma until the very tired frog dies and swims in my dead brain. so the old lady finally comes down with the kid and I've got an excuse to leave. o.k., so I wake up this morning with this tooth reaming the shit out of me, it still is, sweet baby, but somehow writing you it seems like you can feel my fucking pain and that makes it less. I almost laugh & sometimes I think you are the only living American human being, Blaz I'm nothing, all the poetry I've written is swill, I hurt all over, and it's just not the tooth. now fucking rain dripping down like hemorrhage of my brain and my elbows and knees busted and bloody now from falling down in the streets gaging plunging 2 nights ago, naked albatross of hell, me, falling again and again, until all blood blood, nose blood toes blood, I don't understand anything, anything, look look, now I wake up this morning and I ask the woman, I tell the woman, OH MOTHER OF GOD THIS TOOTH IS FUCKING THE SHIT OUT OF ME!! I NEVER KNEW PAIN COULD BE SO PAINFUL AND SO CONSTANT!! (I should have remembered from other bad days) and I said look, do we have any aspirin or anything around??

and you know what she said Blaz?

in a yawning imbecile voice, she said,

'ah don't know . . .'

'what the fuck do you know?' I asked her quietly. but it was no good she was asleep again, snoring, vacant, vacant, unfeeling, waiting for her next session of the poetry workshop to come her alive and make her jabber her silly shit jabber.

so here I sit now, in the hands of round blue purple pain mashing the beer in, and I'm quite a solitary, I take it mostly alone like this, but for once I wish you were here, I wish a *human* were here, I'd like to hear you say, 'Shit, Buk, I'm sorry you feel bad.' that's all I'd need to hear – then the pain couldn't do anything. [★ ★ ★]

oh my god, and just earlier a terrible happening. I am bitter and yapping a bit about the pain the good God has sent me and the woman goes in to the bathroom she says sleepily

'I think I have some Numz–it in here.'

184

fine. I let her flounder around in there, then many minutes go by and I get nervous, I am kind of on the cross you understand, a kind of bad situation, and I go in there and there she is sitting on the can, so I walk out. I give her more time. then I see her rise and go to the medicine cabinet. she hasn't even bothered to flush she doesn't know where the hell she is. I reach over and flush the toilet for her, then I stand there and watch her staring into the medicine cabinet. I've got patience. I wait 5 minutes, 10. I try to outwait her. she's either too stupid or too shit clever for me. I've told her 3 or 4 times that she is insane but I don't think this is true she is simply dead, dead, dead, dead, and she will always be dead but I don't quite want to let myself believe it because I must live with her because of the child and the child is a very beautiful child, and it's the *musts* that kill us . . . forever.

finally I can't stand her bland vacant stare into the medicine cabinet any longer. 'Jesus, forget it!' I tell her. 'forget the whole god damned thing!'

she walks out into the other room. in 30 seconds she is asleep snoring like a Canadian woodsman yet I understand from her writings and her mouth and her many liberal and educated friends, that she really wants to help the human race, that she is looking toward a better world, that the problem of the Negro should be solved, that, after all, with proper planning and govt. we could *all* have all that we need and being in need I look at her and she snores snores snores . . . and I might as well be dead.

love has got to have another name; the people who use the word shouldn't love begins an inch at a time; in slogans or brandished across a universe, it doesn't work you'll see this is the failure of Communism – the theory is proper; there just aren't enough human beings around to work it. people continue to shit upon themselves and scream for theory, when anywhere anyday anytime the smallest kindest touch falling like a raindrop can start the whole thing going. but it's just not in them and here I might make you angry – for I say it's in me, I feel it running up and down my arms, like cool moonlight, I am ready to begin, but they continue to be nasty, to fall asleep across the body of my pain. so fuck it, finally, and fuck them – they want me on the across and they won't get it. I have the great secret that they do not have: you needn't wait on death; you can call the day and the moment.

I am a loner, Blaz, and it's too bad for you are one of the few men I could ever feel contact with, and it's too bad I'm not in Illinois or you're not in Chicago but poverty out few talents keep us apart otherwise I would slug it out on the front lawn with you after 50 beers and show you that 20 years difference in age is not a begging for a lack of guts. yet guts to go on living or guts to kill yourself — it's the asshole same thing, and if you ever get word that I did it across the kitchen table, I'll know that you knew and that the choice was clean, a clean sweep, a shit goodbye, and an asking for more nothing — just a changing of the same dirty drawers, all right? all right.

I think mostly of continents of men like ants going nowhere not wanting too much not caring, fucking stealing writing bad stuff eating and living bad stuff all the horrible kitchens of unliving women bringing us our badly cooked meals to our badly worked bodies until we go mad or until we go simple and believe that the whole thing makes sense.

the tooth is banging away, it will not give up. wait I know the place of an old cigar like a bragging beautiful white kitten in a toy box in heaven. I found it. reams of blue smoke across this kitchen. a ltter a letter to Blaaesake. blaz.

yes, I am drunk and terrible and the ladies come out of the church and I want to fuck them all it is Sunday and the ladies come out of the church and I want to make them come in their red and green and yellow dresses my tooth is killing me yet the leaves of the plant outside this window say hello hello

> but I want to make all the women come
> and they walk past my window
> big and bold and insane and daring
> in color and wobble
> 30 feet high on spikes
> CLACK CLACK CLACK CLACK CLACK
> asking for it
> and if a man gives it to them he gets 5 years in jail
> for rape. it doesn't make
> sense. [★ ★ ★]

Blazek's Mimeo Press had published William Wantling's Down, off & out.

[To Douglas Blazek]

[June 2, 1965]

[★ ★ ★] this is now the best part – woman and 8 month old child gone
to attend a poetry session weekly one a night somewhere and I sit here
opening more beers and writing to somebody I have never seen and the
kitchen light comes down and my fingers smack like drunk spiders on the
keys and I don't know what is next on the page, except same old alphabet
of scrambled eggs of me trying to wormout, attend, sing, pray, bullshit . . .
meanwhile, thanks for the Wantling, well-done – you give mimeo a live
and foodish red-meat look that others fail to do like me go get the
Wantling and check on the beer. also have a pint of scotch after I run
through these 12 1/2 quarts, so it figures to be a burning and perhaps ugly
night, but maybe easy enough wait my good god, she's put it away somewhere. I could look but it would take hours and by then too drunk to
write. some of the poems went, or almost went for me. but I always got
the feeling as if I were being kidded a bit – like the con with the tray
under his shirt – but didn't mind that too much; writing was clear and
contained little poetic malarkey. on the capital punishment essay, I felt it
began well when he spoke of society in the all-over scope but when he
began to get down to his knitting he got drab, academic and wrote badly.
the all-over book was good reading, tho, except is it nec for poet to place
month and year below each poem? isn't this too precious? sometimes I
think it is better to wonder when you *did* write the things, or, if you did
why pull at threads, tho, when the world is falling cesspool fat into its
glory turds? I shouldn't complain about dates at poem-bottoms; getting
older, cranky fits dreams of Miles Standish fear of somebody smelling my
dirty underwear.

I hope that you are still alive, I hope that I am not now speaking to the
top of a coffin lid there was a bar I once sat in for 5 years. maybe I told
you the early barkeep, Jim, used to let me in 5 a.m., 2 hours early and I'd
watch him mop and clean up and we'd talk quiet and easy and drink free,
and then they'd swing in at 7 a.m. and I'd watch them come and go, the
lesbians, the whores, the dimminds, the canned-heat drinkers, the office-
workers, but nobody to STAY, I was the only one who stayed and it worked
into my mind that if I could just get onto that stool each 5 a.m. somewhere somehow there, I wouldn't be too much touched by the asshole
war of the world, and it was a strange and necessary time: many hours of
not-talking, staring at the barwood, watching the sun come up and go

down, of listening to them laugh and fight, and knowing that I, myself, would never have the strength to go anywhere, do anything want anything, just another beer, and watching somebody's head turn on a neck, watching the wrinkles in the neck, watching the head turn in the collar, maybe thinking, idly, DOESN'T HE FEEL THE HELL OF EVERYTHING? ARE THEY ALL BRAVER THAN I AM? ALL OF THEM??? there was nothing to do but manage to get drunk every night without money. this was due mainly to the fact that I could drink enormous quantities of all types of drinks for hours hours hours without becoming intoxicated – at least not in their sense. I could feel things running up and down inside myself but I needed it so badly, so much more of it, that even all they gave me was sad, it didn't work, and this goaded them on and the drinks came and I slugged them down blank-faced and waved a thanks each time, never forgetting to do this since I never are, I needed the nourishment. I went down from 190 to 131. I was the joke, the discard, the madman the night bartender used to fight me at his leisure when he needed a scarecrow to slap around and wanted to impress the ladies. I took him one night; after 50 beatings I had finally had enough; what happened, I don't know, except I stayed out of the bar that day and drank muscatel and ate boiled potatoes and rye bread, and they pulled me off of him and broads sat round him and said 'o, poor, tommy, poor poor, tommy . . .' and he fucked them all later but then he just sat there holding his head and the broads wiped him with their hankies and I sat there and I hollered out, HEY: WHAT THE FUCK IS THIS: I WANT A DRINK! and the relief bartender came down and leaned close and said, 'I'm sorry, sir, we can't serve you.' and I walked out.

now here I sit in this place with woman and child and I am not any different than I was then, I wonder if they know this? the girl-child simply does not care, they have not gotten to her yet – she is sweet honey on the side of my hot brain but nothing much helps. Mac says, 'write a novel.' 'just for me and Blaz and Richmond and Wantling . . .': well, look, I don't believe much in this groupism, but I do BELIEVE I COULD WRITE A NOVEL FOR 4 people to read??? maybe what kills the novel is that you are writing into a tomb-mouth. think of it, the title and the atrocity: *A Novel Written for 4 People to Read*. I ought to do it.

Stravinsky, Percy Grainger, hell, Mahler, the world was is and remains full of good men who fall dead across the doorsteps, and if they don't kill themselves some son of a bitch will do it with a mail-order $12 rifle, or like with Gandhi, or like with Christ, let's laugh, it is not a game to win, it will never be a candy christmas forever, and sometimes the guy with the

$12 rifle belongs, we no so little we know so little of how it works, and now believe me I do not mourn Kennedy anymore than I do Caesar because it seems that to get to the SO-CALLED TOP, it is most evident to me that you have to kill a lot on the way to get there. but I am speaking more or less of the working sadness of everything – how everything never seems to work. and why should it? we've been given minds and bodies and a love that will not last. how long can a man try before he gives way to death? why does Wantling discourage me when he becomes so drab about capital punish.? shouldn't I expect the drab? now they give me *Madame Butterfly* by Puccini. where are the people? where are the beautiful women? all these women reach up into their asses and wipe away shit. I am discouraged. I can figure it out. it is the education, the lore that this society has yoked me with and the things that I have found out do not fit with what I was told. and, please believe me, it is not just the female race who reaches up into shit, it is EVERYTHING . . . and, I cry too much like a disturbed man, but what do I hold onto?

now that, hell, you've told me this, and, now, that I am so very much here?

well, kid, they'll soon be back from reading their poetry to each other, and so I'd better think of hauling in the string, shit, I am like at the bar in the old days, really gone but my fingers insisting on the keys for the hell of the lonely blues and hacksaw evidence . . . my god, umm. [★ ★ ★]

> wanted to see and I lolled and I saw
>   and I didn't see anything like
>   what Whitman saw

> I only saw the most terrible horror
> that made me a drunk for ten years and
> a half-drunk for the rest of my
> life:
>   not what they *want* to save or what
>   they want to KILL—
> but that they can't see that there isn't anything here

> that they have lied to me for so long
> and expected me to be thankful for
> it.

let them
wait.

[★ ★ ★]

John Logan was editor of Choice: A Magazine of Poetry and Photography. *Two poems by Bukowski appeared in issue no. 5 (Summer? 1967: Dorbin C384–385).*

[To John Logan]
Early June, 1965

christ, have finally gotten around to some letter of telling you I got the o.k. on the two poems and although it is now past the mid-night of sobriety I type on. why do drunks always like to brag upon their deaths? it's getting tiresome and I'm very tired of myself. [★ ★ ★]

2 people have so far told me that Rexroth has written an article for *Harpers* called 'The New American Poets,' and so I guess I can take the ribs being 45 and tough and having only written ten years, it is substantial nevertheless that I was always outcast everywhere I went, schoolyards, whorehouses, jails, I always got the foot in the face, there was always the subnormal whom I only tolerated telling me his troubles, through the factories, through the hells, and there was always ALWAYS somebody *else* making it, which I didn't mind as long as I was lifted. [★ ★ ★]

[To Al Purdy]
Early June, 1965

[★ ★ ★] yes, I fucked up in New Orleans but will always remember your letter 'to hell with remorse'! and this wuz big help, baby, I am such a butcher, I guess the headshrinkers would say I am trying to hide some weakness while drunk or so forth, that I am really a homosexual or once fucked my mother, or burned a snail with a match and that I can't face all this, really the trouble with head-shrinkers is that they have never lived—they take it from the white rats and the hand-job Freuds and then change it a little, but essentially if they saw enough men in jails and factories and wars and riding lime-burning boxcars, they'd know that what bothered us was lack of life, being hounded and poor and pissed-on and marked on down to the grave [★ ★ ★]

[To Douglas Blazek]
early June, 1965

stinking hot, night, just took a good crap and somebody whaling the shrieking guts outa a violin on the radio, dropped 30 or less at track (I am improving) but there's whiskey here and I have been drinking for a good 2 hours but feel very little except empty washtubs and the snoring of lambs, look, Purdy wrote, and part of it:

'had intended to type new poems or ones I wanted to save in case anything happened to me in the north, so use carbons to send along to you so you can pick out any you think Doug Blazek might want. One was published, 'Hunting Season,' but much changed from then . . .'

well, kid, I've read the poems over and can't separate them and so am sending them all on to you for a look-see. Like Norse, Purdy is a pro, and what I mean by a pro is a man who has lived enough and is still alive. you're the editor and I don't want to shove anything on you and it doesn't mean a damn to me whether a man has a rep or not so long as he can lay it down. the trouble is that when they get reps they soon stop laying it down, most of them. [★ ★ ★]

further from Purdy: 'I mean, we're all shits in facets or aspects, our only hope being the sum total of life doesn't amount to being a shit.'

I'll write him that I sent the poems to you and that the little ax is in your hands. all right? [★ ★ ★]

McNamara has somebody who steals his mail. he found one of my letters in a garbage can with words written all over it like 'shit,' 'fuck,' and so forth. a bad situation. the worst sin in the world is when the poor try to rob the poor. the enemy is fairly obvious, why weaken our ranks?

hope I have not pissed you in not going overboard on the Wantling but long ago decided to play it straight (corny, what?) and so I say whatever I say. or like there used to be a cartoon where this guy would say: 'I am Popeye the Sailor Man and I am what I am.' It used to cost him a lot of times until he got hold of a can of spinach; me, I use scotch and/or beer, just much beer. [★ ★ ★]

On Richmond Bukowski notes: 'Reclusive, strange poet, has lived in little house by the beach for decades. Published various magazines and sheets, which included Earth, Earth Rose, *and* Hitler Painted Roses.' *In 1966 Richmond was arrested for distributing an 'obscene publication'; the case was not finally dropped until 1971.*

[To Steven Richmond]

early june, 1965

gagging on too black coffee. bad image. I am supposed to be dunking my head in a vat of beer. fuck it. I don't like images. won't have them. Webb works on the image bit. I enclose a clipping from the *Courier*. he even has me six feet six. I'm 5 11 and 3/4's. I did drink 30 beers at one sitting but this is the only thing to do when people are talking and looking at each other. it's the only thing to do. If I drink whiskey I have a tendency to reach over and rip off somebody's shirt. I don't care for the interview; it's juvenile and standard, written by a rich young man right out of college but this is the type of thing that goes in those papers. [★ ★ ★]

[To Steven Richmond]

June 11, 1965

[★ ★ ★] I don't mix too well with people, I am now so old and have this old woman too and we have gotten this unexpected child, and she's art, I love her every bone, but it's all kind of foolish, I am almost done, tired, and I just don't know what to say to young men, I am not a talker, Webb found that out when I went South, I just sat on a chair, and a couple of profs came down from the University and yammering and I couldn't say anything, shit, I felt foolish dumb and in many ways am, they were so bright, they came up with a lot of jazz and action and life and I liked them but I could contribute nothing, too many factories, too many drunk tanks, too many women, too many years, too many park benches, too much everything, and that is why I do not invite you over, you'd think I was stale or cheese or freezing you. really, hell, there's nothing to say. I guess I'm what is known in the terminology as a 'loner.' even at work I catch it. old man walks up to me on coffee break. I am sitting on a truck in corner, dark corner, while they talk baseball and so forth, and he walks up:

you mind, he says, if I ask you something?

no, I answer.

you're kind of exclusive, aren't you?

yeah.

I mean, you don't mix with people.

I guess not.

you don't like people, do you?

most of them I don't.

you're anti-social then.

I suppose I am.

You're miserable! he screamed at me and his face, as they say, contorted, almost tears and he walked away.

Steve, that I've gotten a couple of books published has nothing to do with it. I could now get broad and easy imagining that I have *scope* or *some damn thing*. it won't work. I've never felt good with the crowd and it started in grammar school, I sensed that they touched each other, understood each other, but that I did not belong. and now, 45 years old, I find I still do not belong, fuck dramatics, but the worst part is that I do not even belong with the *best* ones, the living ones, I seem sliced off forever by some god damn trick, either my imagining or some type of insanity, but even the good ones leave me dangling and I feel like a fool, and I know that I am a fool for I feel what I know, and my ex-wife used to get mad at me because I laughed at my stupidity and my mistakes, and this is not well. laughing when you fall and she quickly got rid of me when the man did not seem as good to her as the poems, and yet she must have read the poems wrong for the man and the poem were the same thing. so she took her million dollars and married an eskimo. god fuck that. [★ ★ ★]

[To Douglas Blazek]

June 12, 1965

well, I gotta figure you aren't dead but I'm drunk mainly . . . listening to Dos Passos on radio, my god, he sounds like an englishman! a fop! umm, ummm. they've gotten to him, he's soft and sly and addled, christ, I mean he's gone back on everything, if you know what I mean. I feel shame for him. his whole speech and thought garbled; here you are an unknown kid in Illinois with more clean and feel and real than a world-famous what????? god, life rakes the shit out of us! now I turn to a little dark Bach organ work, better. Bach was supposed to be a man of God but I always get the idea when listening to his organ works that the devil is talking to me, giving me the straight deal on what is – am I mad? hell yes, maybe so. [★ ★ ★]

so I write you a poem:

DRUNK AGAIN AND WONDER, WONDERING, AND SO SIMPLY DETERRED THAT THE
BUCKLE OF MY BELT SNAPS LIKE A FART IN THIS FROZEN SNOW OF LIFE –

horsefeet down the window's way
is it real? where am I hell,
drunk again? curtain like the
sadness of a Garbo film
or people climbing into lifeboats
in a shitty swine-like
effectual sea. old songs like
bats in the dark
kissing my nose.
the characters in Camus and
Genet (I guess a lot get into
Genet)
are almost
right – they hardly
try.

why?
it seems to me that
man is rising up to meet God
man is disgusted *at last*
disgusted
with his waste and
disgusted with God always being
Right –
it is time for man to be Right and
for Man to be the perfect image of Man.

God's ways may be perfect and good
but for me
I've seen enough hurt

and if I am being tested beyond my reason
then what reason I have
can only resent this.

I remember much:
men in unemployment lines forever
good men
frightened and laughing and real
nothing wrong with them
hardly as much wrong as with those who were
sullenly and righteously
working.
I remember much:
old women living with me
who had once been beautiful
and who resented me because I was never
beautiful. God forgot
me.

in jail the last time there was a
blonde boy on the floor
laughing
holding his arm.
'I think my arm is broken. Christ,
they worked me over
but I know if I tell the judge I will only get more
days. I want to get
out.'

there it was. so much real seems never true
or thought of as true. they have a trick —
they hold us all down to
stone —
we presume that what we want is beyond us always
and that
as men
we must eat turds and smile

yet I feel that someday
God be damned
the turds will fit the mouths of the
killers
and the rose will grow out
saying softly: it will be
so.

crist, rlly blasted out now [★ ★ ★]

[To Tom McNamara]
June 16, 1965

Yes, I am getting the idea Stuart is less than lovable, rather a businessman in spite of his liberal paper, but he did finance *Crucifix* when nobody else would take the $ gamble and that's something no matter how you turn it.

yes, some of our best and worst stuff in the music business, the musicals, and I have an idea *Guys and Dolls*, the good oldie, will hang in as a classic . . . many of the songs have not gone stale which is what so quickly happens to so many of the pieces from the boards.

the job is killing me true and here's this kid running on the floor hollering hollering and the radio is on and the woman plods around in her pajamas and my back and neck and balls hurt and it looks like rain and the men with the shovels will soon be coming for me.

o, the men with the shovels will be coming over the mountain

the men with the shovels will be coming and

I'll be coming

too.

Jon and Louise Webb the pros who did *It Catches* and *Crucifix* swinging onto a train out of New Orleans and looking for a city that doesn't make them sick but I don't know what to recommend having been around the handle many times and coming up with nothing myself.

all I have left is hoping for luck at the racetrack and getting drunk and trying to stay out of the jails. by the way, one line left out of a poem in *It Catches*, in 'Dinner, Rain and Transport,' just before the line 'with the force of a jackhammer' should be the line 'I can prophecy evil,' but little matter, they did a miracle job, these 2 not any longer young people, in a small room with a small press and broke and tired . . .

the baby is screaming so loud I can't think. have got to wait for better times. no sense in getting angry or going the self-pity bit, just work on, somehow now I get off the table so these bums can eat. I've been stand-ing up here screaming.

[To Douglas Blazek]
[Mid-]June, 1965

you asked to look at a nature poem and I have enclosed one for you to look over. you've got to realize that they ran the nature poem boys out a little before 1914, and it's a little late in the day; in fact, it's about 11 : 47 p.m.

yeah, the mother-humping emergence of *Crucifix* has somehow shut off the stream and the typewriter has turned on me like a tiger leaping at his trainer, to hell with whip and chair and just having *had* dinner. it is a curious situation, something like a broken neck, maybe worse. yes, I was hoping Webb would let me illustrate the book myself but guess he didn't want to take the chance – I sent him some early drawings which haven't been returned – and then all of a sudden he whipped in this pro with long line of credits. but maybe Time will prove Webb right. [★ ★ ★]

[To Douglas Blazek]
June 24, 1965

fly on curtain, woman scrubbing pot, child stopped hollering, the air of the world filled with gray and blue and me, and it's Thursday, 2 more days nights at the pits and then a long drunk, the horses, same old bit, but somehow a climb-out, a fulfillment, at least away from machinery and stone-glazed bosses of this democracy of this freedom they tell me I have and that we should fight for.

listen, I'll send you *Notes from Underground* if you want to read the story but send copy back when you get a loose dime as it's my last copy, all right? will send by crawl mail . . . book rate.

I had a grandmother who used to pray for my infidelity, she'd come in while I was asleep and make these big-ass crosses over my body and mumble her incantations, she bugged me sure, but she was mostly senseless, life-drained, and it would not have been any victory to rip her arm off. I mostly had visions of her pissing, the yellow whirling fluid corkscrewing from that ancient blob of warted body. [★ ★ ★]

the lights keep going on and off here, might be a bombing, or the enemy working on the wires, or might be some of these big crosses old grandma made over me fucking each other in the air. . . . body trouble? mostly I get stiff as a board, pains all through, sweet sweet stuff, and mostly during this time the woman is talking some utter drab zero nonsense and goes on and on and I lay there and listen listen and then *I* pray: Jesus, I pray to thee, please make her be QUIET just a little while, I can't breathe, it is like a STEAMROLLER, big daddy God, TAKE IT OFF ME!, but he doesn't and she talks on, spilling it all over me, a neurotic chip chip chip of sound without sense, all twisted up with her poetry-meeting Unitarian Church world-saving complex. then the kid crawls in and: WHHHHAAA!! WHAAAA!!! it's hardly any good for me most of the time, and during all the sound sound, these pains shooting through my body, ah. . . . and I had to be a wise guy and think: this one is too old to get pregnant. [★ ★ ★]

AFTERWORD

It's easy, reading these letters, to see why Bukowski's correspondents saved them. Apart from the sometimes striking idiosyncrasies of format which gave them an unusual impact (and which we mostly can't see in book form), their often searing vividness – a stream of feeling and suffering more than stream of consciousness – gives them an impact which must have been easy to recognize. Besides, during these years all of those addressed in the letters printed here were aware of Bukowski's poetry and already valued it for similar vividness of impact.

Bukowski's letters have an unusual immediacy, compared to those of other noteworthy modern literary correspondents. (Think of Lawrence, Pound, Fante, or Creeley and Olson; all are variously fascinating as letter writers but give infinitely less by way of self-portrayal.) Bukowski seems, with trusted correspondents, to pour himself forth with little forethought or purpose other than to render his immediate experience. Only a small minority of surviving letters have a mainly conventional kind of purpose – answering or posing questions, conducting literary business. More often, even when the letter accompanies submissions of poems or other writing, there is a full outpouring of the self in its present situation, generally incorporating notations of the immediate mundane circumstances: people passing or working outside, activities in the apartment, toothache, hang-over, radio sound, etc.

It is a cliché to lament the decline of the personal letter in our tele-phone age, but Bukowski never doubted its value. 'I think the letter is an important form,' he writes early on.

> You can touch everything as you run around. It lets you out
> of the straightjacket of pure Art, and you've got to get out
> once in a while. Of course, I don't restrict myself as much in
> the poem as most do, but I have made this my business, this
> freedom with the word and idea [★ ★ ★]. (22)

He escapes from the straightjacket of pure Art, we note, not by self-indulgence but by a *discipline* ('my business') of writing designed to earn

199

the freedom with word and idea. Yet even so, the personal letter offers a welcome further relief: no worries about unity, shaping a whole, or revision, for instance. Still, it's a form it would be dangerous to grow self-conscious about. When Tom MacNamara proposed quoting from both past and future Bukowski letters, Bukowski sensed a danger.

> Letters? god damn, man, let's be careful. all right at outset, esp. for tightheads who have been working in sonnet form, writing critical articles, so forth; it gives them (letters) the facility and excuse for wallowing in the easiness of their farts and yawns without pressure. [★ ★ ★] then the next thing you know instead of being an o.k. thing, a natural form, it simply becomes another form for the expulsion of the creative, artistic, fucked-up Ego [★ ★ ★] and soon a lot of the boys end up working as hard or harder on the letters than they do on their poems. wherever the payoff lies, whay? (103)

Self-consciousness and posing are the enemy, in all their guises and whether in writing or personal behaior. It is his suspicion of such posing that makes much traditionally admired literature unpersuasive to Bukowski:

> 'I have just read the immortal poems of the ages and come away dull. I don't know who's at fault; maybe it's the weather, but I sense a lot of pretense and poesy footwork: I am writing a poem, they seem to say, look at me!' (14)

(His recurrent jeering at the coteries and mutual admiration societies of the 'creative writing' crowd provides many amusing passages of invective throughout the decade.) Against such falseness there is unself-conscious 'natural form,' whether of the letter or of the kind of poem Bukowski writes. Bad poetry, false poetry, is the self-important ego on display: 'I am not primarily a poet, I hate god gooey damned people poets messing the smears of their lives against the sniveling world [★ ★ ★].' (47)

The letter form is liberating when unselfconsciously undertaken – and undertaken at the typewriter, essentially. Technology helps, not inhibits, his epistolary self-expression. To Kaye Johnson he explained: 'you know, u really kant get the ingress into a WORD without the typer, the typer is the carver, the ax, the cleaver, the thing with the mouth that hollers about the bloody dice. it machineguns the mind out of penury. fuck the pen.' (75) When his machien broke down, he said he felt 'like a man without a cock

200

having a spiritual hard-on and nothing to ram it home with. I can't spin anything without the keys, the keys have a way of cutting out the fat and retaining the easiness.' (101) Bukowski's handwritten letters are done in large printing and seem laborious; the machine allowed him speed and copiousness with less effort.[1] Spontaneity meant occasional whimsical spellings (and infrequent misspellings), it meant free play with capitalization (almost always the first person pronoun retains its capital, however) and sometimes with layout. But Bukowski is surprisingly fastidious about punctuation, consistently using the semi-colon in the traditional way, for example. Spontaneity also allowed improvision in vocabulary: we find quite a few nonce words and coinages enlivening these letters, with onjly rarely a loss of intelligibility. the improvision co-exists with a certain purity of diction: taboos on obscenity, of course, are not respected, but there is a remarkable absence of clichés, catch phrases, or ephemeral slang.[2] Perhaps most strikingly, spontaneity meant a rich inventiveness of imagery, as in the phrases just quoted.

The Bukowski letter, then, has something in common with the 'spontaneous prose' described by Kerouac in 1957.[3] Or it may be seen as a kind of performance art, an improvisation analogous to that of a jazz soloist. The mood of the moment, whether exhilarated or suicidal, comradely or belligerent, is the essential subject matter. Bukowski kept no carbons of his letters, and writing with self-abandonment meant that he often professed not to remember what he had said in prior letters (as in interviews, phone calls, etc.). Responding to earlier prospects of seeing some of his letters in print, Bukowski agreed enthusiastically: 'I'd like to see what I have written too' (September 30, 1965; to Blazek). But even without knowing what he might have said, he always gave permission to present the authentically embodied self warts and all, with no censorship: 'I've got nothing to hide,' he told the Webbs. 'That I drink or play the ponies or have been in jail is of no shame to me.' (31)

If the letters render and project a self with striking vividness and uninhibited fullness, we can yet remark on how narrow the focus is, how painfully constricted the life. The constriction is the price of the intensity. For Bukowski in the sixties, after periods of omnivorour reading in earlier years and after decades of wandering (see *Factotum*), the *Racing Form* would seem to be the main reading material, the hated job alternating with drinking-and-writing and playing the horses the main activities. For the now settled Bukowski, it was a period of intense physical and mental suffering and intense productivity. Writing poems and letters – he tells us as much – was what kept him from suicide or insanity: that the drink. A man too self-conscious and inarticulate to enjoy most forms of face to face meeting, especially with literary people, he found in his intense exchanges with a few kindred spirits (Jon Webb, Doug Blazek and Carl Weissner most notably) the sense of community that we all need, and the impetus to keep writing. Russell Harrison puts this well:

> the very fact that Bukowski is engaged in an extensive and ongoing correspondence is significant. It bespeaks a social need that we would not at first suspect in a writer who, in his fiction and poetry, has placed an unusual emphasis on his protagonist as an isolated individual, a loner. That the correspondence was important is evidence by his promptness in responding.[4]

Bukowski told Wantling in 1965, 'Sometimes I am corresponding with 15 or more people at once, but finally after I work them over a few rounds they have their way and edge off.'[5] By 1967 he was slacking off a bit: 'it's all right to be a good guy and to send 12 page drunken letters to 40 different people but after a while there just isn't enough Bukowski to go around any more.'[6]

Writing letters fed the impulse to write poems and indeed sometimes (especially to Blazek) the letters themselves modulate into verse as they go. And while Bukowski was never too much interested in literary chitchat, criticism, theory, or analysis, the letter form allows him to throw off a number of passing evaluative remarks about other writers, from Hamsun and Kafka to Ginsburg and Creeley, and about his sense of what literature is for, what makes it good. He never quotes Pound's phrase to name the function of literature: 'nutriment of impulse' (indeed he rarely quotes at all), but he seems to agree with it. Clearly he hates any sense of literature as an accomplishment or of literacy education as what gives polish to a man or woman. The literature that matters is what keeps you from dying. If he seems (to someone like me, of more conventional tastes) narrow in the range of his appreciation, he makes up for it in the passionate existential seriousness of his approach: 'Poetry must be forgotten; we must get down to raw paint, splatter. I think a man should be forced to write in a roomful of skulls [★ ★ ★]' (14) Such an impatience with literature as 'belles lettres' ('this fiddle,' in Marianne Moore's phrase) has a long pedigree. Wordsworth, for one, the revolutionary who wanted to write like 'a man speaking to men,' would have agreed.

A final word should be said on the consistency and integrity of the self so vividly and dramatically presented in this book. The man who cheerfully quotes Popeye's 'I am what I am' reminds me of Lawrence's jaunty citing of 'The Miller of Dee':

> There was a jolly miller once,
> Lived on the River Dee.
> He laughed and sang from morn till night,
> No man more blithe than he.
> And this the burden of his song
> Forever used to be:
> > I care for nobody, no not I,
> > Since nobody cares for me.

It hardly needs saying that the insoucient attitude in both cases is only one element of a more complex stance in the world, balanced by (perhaps protective of) other instances of great sensibility. Bukowski was never without sensitivity to the uniqueness of the preson he was addressing. The letters to Ann Menebroker, among those here present, are particularly revealing in this respect: their delicacy of tone contrasts markedly with the more macho strutting sometimes heard (e.g. in the letter to Marvin Malone of August 1962, a letter which refers crudely to the same Menebroker he could write so self-revealingly to). More painfully amusing, as revealing different 'voices' of Bukowski's letter writing, is the early series sent to the publisher of his first chapbook, E.V. Griffith, progressing from the impersonal to the totally exasperated to the abjectly apologetic. Towards the end of the decade we find an extremely long letter to Carl Weissner provoked by his comic embarrassment at having identified Weissner in a snapshot as a girl. The tenderness of feeling for his baby daughter is another recurrent note that fills in the self-portrayal. So does a remark he made in response to the joy given him by the Webbs' publication of his second large scale book collection. '[A] book like this lifts my life up into whether I deserve it or not,' he writes, adding:

> I used to have a theory that if I could just make one person's life happy or real that would have been otherwise, then my own life would not have failed. It was a good theory but a few whoes ran me through the wringer for it, but I do think that for a while a few of them enjoyed not being spit on for a while, and so this made it o.k. for me. (77)

We come back to the literary vocation which in the long run is what makes these letters valuable to a wider public than their addressees. '[★ ★ ★] it's up to a man to create art if he's able, and not to talk about it, which, it seems, he's always more than able.' (174) Deprecating, as usual, his own public persona, Bukowski writes:

> I say or do nothing brilliant. The most brilliant thing I do is to get drunk – which any fool can do. If there is any dramatics in me, it must wait on the Art Form. If there is any ham in me it must wait on the Art Form. If there is any D. H. Lawrence in me it must wait on the A. F. (25)

It was D. H. Lawrence who said, 'Art speech is the only speech,' and these declarations by Bukowski put the emphasis finally in the same place – on the achieved writing. The ability to be buoyantly stoic, to declare, 'I have nothing to hid and anything I say in a letter goes anywhere anytime, and if they don't like the taste of it, let them suck empty beer bottles' (86), is a liberating and enabling self-sufficiency. The letter writer and the poet are a single, coherent entity. One result is that, while we may find a difference of emphasis and tone in references to the asme person over time, we don't find here the kind of bad faith recently noticed in the letters of Philip Larkin:

> a warm and appreciative letter to X is followed, often on the same day, by a warm and appreciative letter to Y in jeering dispraise of X, and so on. Bad faith was a form of good faith; it meant that Larkin was still keeping his options open.[7]

Bukowski's letters give us a whole self in many moods. His courage and endurance and sheer hard work at his writing are exemplary. He told a correspondent that 'it is good to have your own courage but it is also good to take hope and courage from the ways of others. this I haven't been able to do until lately.' (185) The encouragement he found in his correspondence can be shared by us. 'I wrote letters to many in those days,' he has said, 'it was rather my way of screaming from my cage.' It is gratifying for the reader of these sometimes agonized 'screams' to know that the decade ends with his escape from the Post Office into a successful career of living by his writing alone.

– Seamus Cooney
Western Michigan University
Kalamazoo, Michigan

NOTES TO AFTERWORD

[1] He had to suffer the complaints of his neighbors, though, and was forced to agree not to type after 10 p.m. in his first apartment (see Jan. 28, 1964, p. 102).

[2] Neeli Cherkovski made a similar point about Bukowski's diction: 'In the heart of the sixties he remained untouched by hippie terminology, employing it only sarcastically to prove a point' (*Hank*, p. 189). Curiously, one of the few literary allusions to familiar quotations that I have spotted in these letters is to Spenser's remark that Chaucer is 'a well of English undefiled' (Bukowski calls the Cantos 'a well of Pounding unrecognized' [5]). (Another allusion is to the last lines of Eliot's *Prufrock*.)

[3] See Jack Kerouac, 'Belief and Technique for Modern Prose' and 'Essentials of Spontaneous Prose' (1957), reprinted in *New American Story*, ed. Donald M. Allen and Robert Creeley (New York: Grove Press, 1965), pp. 269–271.

[4] Unpublished paper by Russell Harrison, whose *The Outsider As Insider: Essays on Charles Bukowski* is forthcoming from Black Sparrow Press.

[5] Letter of June 23, 1965, not otherwise excerpted in the present volume.

[6] To Louis Delpino, August 2, 1967.

[7] Jonathan Raban, *The New Republic* (7/19–26/93), p. 35.

INDEX

211